2-79

Buying
Your Own Business

Other titles in
THE ADAMS BUSINESS ADVISOR SERIES

Adams Publishing books are appropriate for professional development seminars, training programs, premiums, and specialized reprint activities. They can be ordered through retail outlets everywhere, or by calling the Special Sales Department at 800-872-5627 (in Massachusetts 617-767-8100).

AN ADAMS BUSINESS ADVISOR

Buying Your Own Business

IDENTIFYING OPPORTUNITIES
ANALYZING TRUE VALUE
NEGOTIATING THE BEST TERMS
CLOSING THE DEAL

Russell Robb

Adams Publishing
Holbrook, Massachusetts

Published by Adams Media Corporation
260 Center Street, Holbrook, MA 02343

ISBN: 1-55850-544-X

Printed in the United States of America.

J   I   H   G   F   E   D   C   B   A

Library of Congress Cataloging-in-Publication Data
Robb, Russell.
Buying your own business / Russell Robb.
p.   cm.   — (An Adams business advisor)
Includes bibliographical references and index.
ISBN 1-55850-544-X (pb.)
1. Business enterprises—Purchasing—Handbooks, manuals, etc.
I. Title. II. Series.
HD1393.25.R63   1995
658.1'6—dc20   95-41505
CIP

This publication is designed to provide accurate and authoritative information with regard to the
subject matter covered. It is sold with the understanding that the publisher is not engaged in
rendering legal, accounting, or other professional advice. If legal advice or other expert assis-
tance is required, the services of a competent professional person should be sought.
— From a *Declaration of Principles* jointly adopted by a Committee of the American Bar
Association and a Committee of Publishers and Associations

This book is available at quantity discounts for bulk purchases.
For information, call 1-800-872-5627.

Cover design by Marshall Henrichs

Contents

Acknowledgments

A number of years ago I was attending a seminar. At the end of the day, the instructor passed out a blank page with just one word at the top— *DREAMS*. We were asked to fill in the blank. I thought for a moment. Then I wrote down several personal dreams, one of which was to write a published book ... someday.

It has been a formidable task in that the writing has been woven around my regular job—nights, weekends, holidays, vacations. Needless to say, the book would not have been completed without my partner in life and my partner in this book: Leslee, my wife of twenty-five years. Her willingness to spend the hours at the computer in order to get this to a publisher made the task easier, and the constant encouragement from my four children, all adults, kept me at my task.

Others to whom I am indebted are Franklin Wyman, Chairman of O'Conor, Wright Wyman, Inc., the mergers and acquisitions firm for which I work, as he contributed enormously in the rewrites. I have also relied heavily on many of my business friends, particularly those who shared with me the personal experiences described in the chapter "Case Studies of Buyers."

Finally, I am indebted to Dick Staron, the editor who took a chance on me as a first-time author and encouraged me to keep writing when I was only halfway through and wondered if there were another 60,000 words left in me.

How to Use This Book

The process of buying a business is usually long and difficult. In compiling this book, I spent more time reading relevant material and thinking about the subject matter than actually writing. Many of the references and quotes are from businesspeople I know in the Boston area. It is my genuine feeling that their knowledge of the mergers and acquisitions business is not just regional but applicable nationwide.

The outline is sequential. Because the mergers and acquisitions (M & A) business may have terminology foreign to many readers, it is advisable that you skip to the Glossary section early on. The jargon of M & A includes such phraseology as "deals crater because of seller's remorse." I believe this language is colorful and depicts the culture of the business.

The book was written to be anecdotal, using numerous experiences. Perhaps the most interesting reading is Chapter 26, "Case Studies of Buyers," because the actual buyers leave us with their personal "lessons learned." This is not an academic book, as it does not rely on theory or textbook-type explanations. The examples are true, although a few are purposely disguised.

In writing the book, I have tried to impress upon you the formidability of the task of successfully acquiring a business. Additionally, on numerous occasions I emphasize the need for professional advisers to assist you in the potential transactions, e.g., in the chapters "Use of Intermediaries" and "Your Acquisition Team."

The book reaches out to discuss the trials and tribulations of acquiring small businesses, family businesses, and troubled companies. Along with pointing out opportunities, I try to point out warning signs and red flags.

Buying Your Own Business can be used as an ongoing reference book. Such chapters as "Valuation Techniques," "Finding the Deal," "Picking Apart the Financials," "Negotiating," and "Letter of Intent" are how-to, nuts and bolts analyses.

From a practical point of view, the chapters on "Letters, Memos, Forms, and Contracts" and "M & A Organizations" inform you of helpful resources.

Whether buying a business at all is really worth the effort is discussed in the chapters "How and Why People Buy a Business," "Should You Buy a Business?," and "Profile of Individual Buyers."

Technical advice is explained in "Representations and Warranties" and "Legal and Tax Issues." And when it comes to advice, there is no lack of opinions, as discussed in "Why Deals Fall Apart" and "Pearls of Wisdom."

Hopefully this book is fairly easy to read, informative, and enjoyable. It should be noted that throughout the book, I have referred to and quoted from many authorities in the mergers and acquisitions business. These additional viewpoints make this book even more comprehensive.

Good luck!

Foreword

This book was written for those individuals who want to buy a business, particularly a business in the middle market, frequently referred to as companies with sales between $2 million and $50 million.

Having sold three small businesses of my own and having been an intermediary for buyers and sellers since 1985, I have firsthand knowledge of this subject. Although I am an intermediary, I rarely try to sell a business to an individual buyer. This book is an attempt to educate individual buyers so that they will have a better chance to successfully buy a business.

Harvard Business School case 9-385-330, *Buying an Existing Business*, clearly summarizes the search process:

> Searching for a small business to buy can be difficult; not only is there no established marketplace for these firms, but you are trying to purchase an entity created and cultivated by another individual, and you are attempting to make it mesh with your own style, character and interests—all at a price which is both fair to the seller and affordable for you. This process can be extremely time-consuming, expensive, and frustrating. Even if you find a likely candidate, "looking under the hood" of a small business will not always reveal the true state of the operation. The most rigorous analysis and background checks will not ensure a sound acquisition. And, unlike a used car, which you would probably turn over in two or three years, the business you acquire will be yours for an indefinite period and may become either a cornerstone of your accumulation of wealth, or a drain on your resources.
>
> While the available research indicates that good acquisition candidates are few and far between, sound search techniques and a realistic

personal assessment can significantly improve your chances of success and remove some of the random elements from the process.

Unlike the real estate market, which is very efficient in bringing buyers and sellers together, the buying and selling of middle-market businesses is somewhat inefficient because of the need to keep most transactions confidential. Strict adherence to confidentiality prevents the information's being easily obtainable or widely known. The secretiveness of selling a business causes buyers to be proactive by cold-calling owners and seeking to buy companies that are originally "not for sale."

I am sure that most readers of this book have never bought a business—which is why I wrote the book. You may be competing for deals against sophisticated buyout groups that have systematized every step in the acquisition process and have a fully experienced acquisition team (e.g.: attorney, accountant, appraiser, investment banker, environmental consultant, etc.). Furthermore, these professional buyout companies have computer programs ready to crank out letters of intent, financial projections, and due diligence checklists; a database on senior and subordinated lenders, etc.

As a potential business buyer, you have a formidable task ahead of you. Despite the odds, however, people successfully buy businesses. In fact, we have documented many of these individual success stories. As a feature article in *Forbes* magazine, November 8, 1993, by Fleming Meeks and Nancy Rotenier stated, "Buying a small business can destroy your ego, ruin your marriage, wipe out your bank account. It can also be the most exhilarating thing that will ever happen to you."

Buying a business makes sense if the process is well thought out beforehand and the business is well managed afterward. Some of the most likely candidates for buying a business are people between forty-five and sixty years old. One organization that focuses on vocations for older people is Eldercorps, a Cambridge, Massachusetts, firm that has coined the word *elderpreneur*. Its founder, Radcliff Romeyn, states that elderpreneurs are seeking new ventures, and assuming some risk, for the sake of personal growth and validation as well as reengagement in the society around them.

Ironically, as this older population expands, more and more businesses and organizations are reducing their workforces and demanding early retirement. A very large number of older adults are facing twenty to thirty years of healthy, productive lives with no work, reduced income levels, and very little guidance or social support for focusing their creativity and energies.

Most of the individuals buying middle-market companies are in this group because such people are more apt to have the financial resources, business experience, and confidence to be successful. Furthermore, a significant number of executives from public companies who lose their jobs as a result of mergers want to buy their own companies.

As stated in the Price Waterhouse publication, *The Buying and Selling a Company Handbook*:

> Buying a company is an enormous undertaking. You will be faced with matters both predictable and unplanned as you approach the market, and your vigilance will make the difference between success and failure. Your commitment, of course, will serve as the foundation on which your success is built. Buying a business is unlike anything you have before encountered.

This book will teach you the process of buying a business. Granted, you should be a self-starter with an entrepreneurial flare. With the purchase of a business you will bear much responsibility, have a lot of uncertainty, and need to rely greatly on your intuition. People buy businesses because they want the independence, they want the challenge, and/or they are bored with their previous job. Not only have most buyers never bought a company, neither have they run one. This book is created so that the task of acquiring a company becomes less onerous, creates more pleasure, and results in more successful acquisitions.

Good luck on your journey.

CHAPTER 1

How and Why People Buy a Business

The middle-market mergers and acquisitions (M & A) business is very fragmented. There are *investment bankers* who reach down to the middle market, and there are *business brokers* that traditionally sell "main street" America businesses who sometimes move up to sell middle-market companies ($2 million to $50 million in sales). Additionally, there are nationwide *intermediaries* like Geneva Business Services Inc. that have multiple offices and fill the gap between the investment banker and the broker.

It will be helpful if you understand the terminology used for the different middlemen who can help you identify a company to buy and/or provide other services in buying a company.

Finder: A finder will identify the seller to the buyer or vice versa, but will not provide other services. For this introduction, the finder will charge roughly 10 percent of the success fee. The finder merely introduces the two parties; he or she does not attempt to determine the sale price or negotiate the transaction.

Broker: Like a real estate broker, a business broker usually represents the seller. He or she identifies buyers, qualifies them, prices the business, negotiates the deal, and assists in the closing. The use of the term "business broker" implies that the businesses for sale have sales of less than $1 million.

Intermediary: An intermediary provides all the services of a broker but addresses the middle market. An intermediary will work for either the buyer or the seller and usually tries to obtain an up-front retainer. When representing a seller, the intermediary will probably write a comprehensive selling memorandum. When representing a buyer, the intermediary will probably be involved with securing the financing for the transaction.

Investment banker: An investment banker is usually a larger firm than an intermediary and is usually involved in larger transactions. While investment bankers are often retained as intermediaries to buy or sell companies or divisions, they also help finance deals by funding bridge loans or by actually putting up some of the capital themselves. They usually provide extensive analysis and deal structuring and receive additional compensation for rendering fairness opinions and underwritings. Also, investment bankers normally are securities brokers and they can legally handle the exchange of securities of public companies.

The middle market is a busy place in which individual and corporate buyers are chasing a relatively few owners who are willing to sell their business. There are probably more opportunities to buy the less sought-after retailers, distributors, and service providers. As an individual, you will be competing with the following acquirers of manufacturers:

- Companies in fragmented industries that want to consolidate to "bulk up" in size

- Corporations that are divesting noncore businesses and using the resulting cash for more synergistic acquisitions

- Businesses in slow-growth industry segments that seek strategic fits

- Venture firms, which are focusing less on startup companies and now are adding more established middle-market companies to their portfolios

- Buyout firms, known as financial buyers, who have been refinanced and continue to have a voracious appetite

As a potential buyer, you should realize that most sellers of privately held middle-market companies do not know how to value their business or set a reasonable price for it. One of the most common mistakes made by these owners is to apply to their small private company a price-earnings multiple similar to that of a public company in the same industry.

A public company could easily be worth 25 to 50 percent more because of its access to capital, its ability to use its own stock for acquisitions, its highly scrutinized financial reporting to the SEC, the probability that the management and directors are not a "one-man band," etc. Unfortunately, there are few, if any, price comparables for privately held companies because when these companies are sold, the price is not public information. The real estate business is different because all transactions are public knowledge.

One of the biggest problems in buying a private company is digging out the true financial numbers and understanding the company's actual earning power. As many as 90 percent of all businesses in this country are family companies. Family companies are run differently from non-family businesses, and you need a keen understanding of the differences so that you can analyze them accordingly. For example, in a family business, the company's senior management is usually selected from the family, including in-laws and cousins. Many family members depend on their income from the business, whether they actually work for the company or not. In many cases, family businesses reinvest only a small portion of the earnings, instead paying out most of the earnings to the family members. Additionally, small businesses are difficult to value because their record keeping is often poor. Financial statements can be inadequate and unaudited.

For a buyer, the acid test of whether the business is financially viable depends on three components:

The salary level of the owner
Sufficient debt coverage from operating income
A return on investment commensurate with the level of risk

Part of the difficulty in buying a business is that the buyer and the seller have different agendas when structuring the transaction. The seller usually wants as much cash as possible at closing and wants to structure the deal so that he or she will pay the least amount of taxes. For reasons to be explained later, selling the stock of the company is the best way to reduce the tax impact. On the other hand, the buyer's goal is usually to pay the least amount of cash up front and to buy the assets of the company; this allows the buyer to write up the value of the assets and also to avoid almost all contingencies of the selling company.

Aside from the obstacles mentioned above, the middle market has these characteristics:

- The resources available to identify selling companies are fragmented.
- It is a busy place, with many individual and corporate buyers.
- It is a difficult environment in which to value private companies.
- Buyers and sellers have different agendas.

To successfully acquire a business, think of the three Ps:

Process: Aside from the buyer who just happens to be at the right place at the right time and perhaps buys a company from a friend or relative, most successful individual buyers diligently adhere to the acquisition process. This book in large part is about the acquisition process: the strategy, the criteria, the search, the evaluation, the financing, the negotiating, the due diligence, etc.

Professionalism: Certain markets are very efficient when it comes to available information, supply and demand characteristics affecting the price, knowledgeable buyers and sellers, etc. The stock market is an example of an efficient market. However, the market for buying and selling midsized companies is inefficient. Frequently the seller is selling a business for the first time (his or her life's work) and the buyer is buying a business for the first time. The seller may not reveal the real reason for selling and does not always submit all the relevant information. For these reasons, a buyer should spend the time and money to assemble an advisory team of professionals—intermediary, lawyer, accountant, appraisers, etc.—to improve the chances of successfully acquiring a company.

Persistence: In case studies of individuals who successfully acquired companies, the predominant characteristic is persistence. Many of these buyers spent eight to ten hours a day for two solid years before they finally closed on an acquisition. Most of them had sufficient capital and were qualified buyers, but the trait that sets them apart from their peers is persistence.

Individuals who fail to buy a middle-market company may be unlucky, or there may be other mitigating circumstances. However, if you are a qualified buyer with a solid business background and a reasonable amount of capital, you should be able to acquire a company if you adhere to the three Ps and follow the advice in this book.

In spite of the difficulties in acquiring a business, it is important to understand the motivation to do so. Part of the answer comes from the quintessential outplacement firm in the Boston area which advises senior executives with salaries over six figures, New Directions. The president of the firm, David Corbett, and his staff help clients find another executive position or, as the name of the firm implies, redirect their vocational life in a "new direction," such as buying a business. In a comprehensive study regarding entrepreneurial people, David Corbett states:

> More than half the working population of the United States think seriously about owning their own business. At least 500,000 managers are being fired every year. For many of them, ownership is an increasingly tempting option. As a practical matter, it is unlikely that someone over 60 years old is going to have much success joining another corporation. Entrepreneurship is an attractive alternative that offers new independence and control, perhaps the ticket to trying something one has always wanted to do. The 55 to 64 year old market is also the single most affluent consumer group today and many of these affluent individuals are candidates for small business ownership. Midlife seems to generate many conflicting choices. The common threads, however, seem to be a need for autonomy, control, independence, and freedom as well as a quest for self-fulfillment and self-actualization and a need to have a career that is meaningful.
>
> The essential ingredient for success is probably the sheer will to win—the total commitment to achieve at any cost. Research shows that 60 percent to 90 percent of new ventures are created as a result of some close connection between the prior work and the new venture.

In the December 26, 1994, issue of *Fortune* magazine, in the article "Why Do We Work?" it is stated, "Robert Weiss, a research professor at the University of Massachusetts asked people in a survey whether they'd work if they had inherited enough money to live comfortably. Roughly eight out of ten people said yes."

Other relevant comments in the article were:

- Today's flat organizations offer less opportunity for bigger, better jobs. Hard work is less a guarantee for success than ever before. As a result, dissatisfaction is on the rise ... 47% now say they either dislike or are ambivalent about the company they work for.

- Work really defines who you are. So much of a person's self-esteem is measured by success at work.

- The corporation is designed to eliminate creativity. Finding the sense of mission in a big business isn't all that easy.

America was built on many fundamental rights, including freedom of speech and freedom of religion. Business freedom is the magic allure of this country for most immigrants, whether it be Cubans in Miami or Orientals in Los Angeles. There are only three ways to obtain business freedom: One either inherits a business, starts a business, or buys a business. This book is about buying a business.

In his book *New Business Opportunities*, Jeffrey Timmons, professor of Babson College and Harvard Business School, states: "Graduates of the Harvard Business School ... long thought of as the West Point for the Fortune 500 ... thrive on this entrepreneurial dream: about one-third end up working for themselves."

Brian Knight, president of Country Business Inc., specializes in selling small and midsized companies. In his book about buying a business, he emphasizes the following reasons why people buy a business:

- Freedom and independence.

- The owner will have broad business experience and will not be confined to a single job activity.

- Rewards will be directly tied to performance.

- Unlimited earning capacity if capable.

- Opportunity for creative talents.

- Can involve other family members.

- Excellent legal tax shelter (private companies).

- A method of building up one's estate.

- Owning your own business is a status symbol.

- Middle-market companies are growing faster than the *Fortune* 500.

One can look back in time and draw various analogies between explorers in the seventeenth century, immigrants in the eighteenth century, pioneers in the nineteenth century, and entrepreneurs in the twentieth century. According to Webster's dictionary, an entrepreneur "organizes, manages, and assumes the risks of a business or enterprise." Historically, the term *entrepreneur* has been used to mean someone who started a company. I believe that an entrepreneur is someone who either starts or buys a company. I also believe that the motivation of both groups is the same, and in that regard I quote Gordon Baty from his book *Entrepreneurship for the Nineties*:

1. To make a lot more money than I could with some other application of my energies during a comparable period of time.

2. To get out of a professional rut—to see ideas through to completion, to gain professional recognition, to accept responsibility for the full consequences of my ideas.

3. To be my own boss, control my own destiny, set my own hours, etc.

4. To prove to myself (my spouse, my father, my ex-boss, etc.) that I can do it.

5. To advance technology, society, etc.

6. To develop and deploy talents I feel that I have outside my area of specialization.

CHAPTER 2

Should You Buy a Business?

To properly set the stage for this book, it is only logical to ask the preliminary question as to whether, in fact, you should buy a business at all!

At a Harvard Business School Association seminar on buying a business, Jim Tonra of McLaughlin & Tonra in Wellesley, Massachusetts, made the following observations:

> If you think buying a business is going to provide you with the opportunity to spend more time with your family, or if you're somebody that's really looking for a better lifestyle, then perhaps you should rethink your decision. Personal considerations are something that's very important. Buying a business and running it the first couple of years is an all-consuming activity. It will eat up time, and it will be a test of your marriage.

In an attempt to answer whether you should buy a business, the following ten points bring the issue into focus:

1. *Self assessment.* In order to successfully buy and run a business, you must have a multitude of skills and talents. It is like being a baseball player who can play all nine positions. Of course you should be a self-starter, a leader who takes charge and is able to execute after a reasonable amount of analyzing. You should work well with people and be totally committed to your mission in spite of setbacks. You should be capable of learning quickly and

working long hours. Your family should be very supportive of your endeavor because of the time and emotional commitment required to run your own business. Are you willing to do menial office jobs that in a large business you would have delegated to one of many subordinates? Is your background too limited to run a company that is totally different from your prior business experiences? I could go on and on, but the point is that this is not a game for the faint of heart, as you will read in the chapter giving examples of buyers.

2. *Your credibility.* Put yourself in the shoes of the seller. The company is often his or her life's work, equivalent, emotionally, to a child. When you offer to buy a company from the founder, a high price may not be enough to persuade him or her to sell. If the owner is considering whether to entrust his or her "baby" to you, then you have to convince the owner that you have the experience, knowledge, and capability to successfully run the company. The seller will want to know your objectives if you acquire the company, and will want to know your background, your skills, your financial capabilities, and whether you have others on your acquisition team. If you are buying a company in the industry to which you have been accustomed, you will obviously impress the owner with your familiarity with this line of work. To the extent that you have credibility in the eyes of the seller, the likelihood that you will be considered a top candidate to take over the company will improve.

3. *Professional help.* Obviously you want to seek advice from your personal friends, but even more importantly, you should align yourself with professional advisers who have done numerous deals before. For example, lawyers are like doctors in that they have numerous specialties. You do not want to hire a lawyer who is a generalist, but rather one who is a transaction lawyer. In other words, if you are going through a divorce, you go to a divorce lawyer. An accountant who specializes in mergers and acquisitions will find innovative ways to raise cash from the target company's balance sheet. And as one experienced buyer, Peter Alcock, said, "A good intermediary is worth his weight in gold."

4. *Do you have a plan?* You may have the credibility and the money to acquire a middle-market company, but you also need a plan.

Forcing yourself to articulate your direction and how you will undertake your search and finance the transaction will cost you some "up-front" time. However, without a plan, the search for a business to buy deteriorates into a haphazard effort whose outcome has to do more with luck than with skill. As the Price Waterhouse publication *The Buying and Selling a Company Handbook* states, "A well designed and articulate acquisition plan demonstrates that you know what you want to do and thus, will make it easier to attract qualified outside advisors to your team."

5. *Your ability to pull the trigger.* In ten years as an intermediary for selling businesses, on numerous occasions I have seen potential buyers lose confidence in themselves and pull back on their attempt to acquire a company. Buying a business is not for the faint of heart. You need to have a lot of confidence. Successful buyers are like competitive athletes: their desire to succeed translates into little hesitation in their actions. One of the biggest mistakes buyers make is that once they become interested in a particular company, they stop pursuing other companies. Unfortunately, only 50 percent of transactions that reach the letter of intent stage close. Conversely, many buyers are reluctant to make an offer by submitting a nonbinding letter of intent on more than one company at a time. It is customary to commence due diligence after the letter of intent, and so the initial objective in buying a business is to agree on price and terms, subject to confirmation through an extensive due diligence checklist. Later in this book, there is a case study on Phil Harris. Phil had all the characteristics of a successful buyer, and in fact acquired a company along with a venture capitalist. However, when asked to reflect on his two-year acquisition search, Phil lamented that he concentrated on one potential seller for over six months, only to have the deal crater. In retrospect, Phil said, he should have pursued other possible acquisitions more vigorously at the same time he was pursuing his primary target.

6. *Do you have enough cash?* To buy a profitable middle-market company requires a meaningful amount of your own cash. As we will discuss later in this book, a profitable manufacturing company with $4 million in sales could require $400,000 to $500,000 of owner's equity. If you have less, then you might

have to buy a smaller company or an unprofitable company, or you might consider buying a company with a partner or raising equity from investors. Until you know what resources you have to invest, you will not know which companies are likely targets.

Cash for buying the business is just part of the requirement. You will need to have money to live on for the year or two in which you will be looking for a company. There will be expenses such as a rented office, secretarial service, travel, entertaining, and of course professional help.

7. *Your tolerance for risk.* Let me be a devil's advocate and pose the question of what happens to you financially if you still haven't bought a company after your search. Can you get a job rather quickly, or do you have alternative financial resources on which you can depend? Many bankers require new owners of middle-market companies to personally guarantee the bank notes. To what extent can you financially withstand the drain if such a note is called? And is your marriage likely to survive the pressure?

8. *Responsibility.* To undertake the purchase of a middle-market company is a huge responsibility if you stop to think of the number of people who will be dependent on you: employees, customers, vendors, stockholders, bankers, etc. You should thrive on responsibility because you will have it thrust upon you. If you have been working for a *Fortune* 1000 company, you undoubtedly have not faced the crisis of meeting a payroll when your company is undercapitalized. The chances are that as a new owner of a relatively small business, you will have personally signed the bank notes, and so you will have a responsibility to your family not to fail. If you have minority stockholders, you have a responsibility to not only protect their investment but give them a decent return on their money. Above all, you will be captain of the ship, and if you hit an iceberg, you will be expected to stay with the sinking ship. In other words, if your company starts to fail, or in fact fails, you as the owner will be the person ultimately in charge.

9. *Patience.* Buying a middle-market company usually takes from one to two years, assuming you devote your full time to the project. I know a number of people who are in their fourth year of pursuing an acquisition; however, their pursuit is not full time.

Many individual buyers lose patience after six months and end up taking another job. One of the messages in this book is that acquiring a business is a matter of the three Ps: *process, professionalism,* and *persistence.* Two of these take patience to achieve. The *process* of buying a business and *persistence* are characteristics that are consistent with patience. While it is important that you have "fire in the belly" to pursue an acquisition with vigor, it is equally important that you understand that the entire process takes patience.

10. *Timing.* Buying a business when the economy is overheated means that you might overpay for the business and/or that interest rates on the bank notes will be at the high end. Buying a business has some similarities to buying real estate and buying stocks. On the other hand, you can't exactly wait around until the next recession to get a great price on a business.

These considerations and questions are strongly stated. The purpose of this book is not to scare you away from buying a middle-market company, but rather to successfully prepare you for such an accomplishment.

A basic matter that needs to be addressed is the cost of an acquisition in addition to the actual purchase price. The following analysis is based on a one-year acquisition search for a normally profitable manufacturing company with sales of $10 million. The figures below are very general, but the largest difference between the minimum and maximum is whether an intermediary's fee is included. (Later in the book there will be a strong recommendation for the use of intermediaries.) The mean total of $190,000 is equivalent to 3.8 percent of the $5 million purchase price.

Acquisition Search
for a Company with Sales of $10 Million

Estimated Costs

Search process (over one year)	Minimum	Maximum
Retainer for intermediary	—	$ 30,000
Telephone, printing, office rental	$ 10,000	20,000
Travel to visit companies	2,000	5,000
Outside valuation advice	—	5,000

Due diligence

Audit and accounting due diligence*	10,000	20,000
Legal†	1,000	5,000
Other—business/management	—	10,000
Equipment appraisal	3,000	6,500
Plant appraisal	2,500	5,000

Financing

Retainer for intermediary	—	10,000

Closing costs

Legal: Purchase and sale agreement	15,000	30,000
M&A intermediary		
(purchase price $5 million)‡	—	120,000
Financing intermediary§		70,000
Raise $2 million of nonbank		
debt at 1.5 percent	—	
Raise $1 million of equity at		
5.0 percent)		
Total	$ 43,500	$336,500
Mean Total		$190,000

---

* The accounting due diligence varies depending on whether the company has compilations or audited statements. If it has compilations, the cost could be between $15,000 and $35,000.

† The legal due diligence varies depending on whether there is litigation that needs to be settled prior to an acquisition.

‡ The M & A intermediary's fee is based on the Lehman formula less the retainer.

§ The financing intermediary's fee is based on the following:

Debt of $2 million × 1.5% =	$30,000
Equity of $1 million × 5% =	50,000
Less financing retainer =	(10,000)
Total financing costs	$ 70,000

CHAPTER 3

Acquiring Small Businesses

Buying Your Own Business focuses on middle-market businesses, but it would be remiss not to devote at least one chapter to small businesses, commonly considered companies with sales of under $1 million.

According to the data from *The State of Small Business: A Report of the President 1993*, "55% of all U.S. businesses have sales volume under $500,000 and 74% have a sales volume of less than $1 million." In terms of employees, the Small Business Administration estimates the breakdown of companies as follows:

Category	Number of Employees	Percent of Businesses
Very small	1–19	89
Small	20–99	9
Medium	100–499	1
Large	500 or more	1

To go one step further, it is estimated that the types of businesses are:

Retail	41%
Services	34%
Wholesale	16%
Manufacturing	9%

The attraction of acquiring a small business is obvious: There is a wider selection of small companies, and the price of a small business is theoretically lower than that of a middle-market company. The selection of small companies is addressed above. The cash necessary to acquire a small company will probably be between $100,000 and $200,000 unless the target company has just a few employees.

The reasons people are very anxious to own their own business are their need for independence, the challenge, and/or the desire to involve their family in the endeavor. For some people, buying a small business is a viable option. Alternatively, the person can start a business from scratch. Historically, the failure rate is twice as high in starting a business as in buying a business. Buying a franchise is another possibility. However, the best franchises, such as McDonald's, take about $500,000 investment per restaurant, and the relatively unknown franchises, while considerably less expensive, may or may not be worth the investment. Of course, McDonald's receives a royalty of between 2 and 8 percent plus an advertising allocation of 1 to 2 percent of gross sales. As the larger franchises saturate the country, territories become crowded and franchisees sue their franchisors for encroaching on their territory. Historically, franchise contracts have been inordinately one-sided. There are some experts who feel that the golden era of franchising might be over.

Twenty or thirty years ago a business with $1 million in sales seemed like a good-sized business. Today it is common for a small wine store or bicycle shop to have $1 million in sales. I am familiar with such a wine store in which the owner works a six-day week, day and night, and the record keeping of a particular bike shop I know is so poor that it is very difficult to determine its actual financials. These two examples illustrate the two major concerns in buying a small business: (1) dependence on one person and (2) lack of proper information. Aside from these concerns, the biggest problem in buying a small company is often the pricing and/or valuation. The reality is that the owner of a small business usually does not know how to value companies. So the owner often does the following:

- Uses a mythical valuation technique that some so-called authority stated, such as "one times sales."

- Receives advice from a local accountant, who may or may not be proficient in valuations.

- Bases a figure on "sweat equity" or "what he has to get out of it" without any correlation to the hard numbers.

- Bases the company's earnings on what the business could earn if the owner did not "skim" (personally take money off the top).

- Compares a New York Stock Exchange company to this Main Street store, e.g., a price-earnings ratio of twenty.

When brokers represent small businesses, many of them use rules of thumb to place a value on the company. While this methodology may seem inept, it is a prudent starting point for many small businesses that have insufficient financial records. For more detailed information, contact Business Brokerage Press, Box 247, Concord, Mass. 01742, (508) 369-5254 for its annual Business Reference Guide. While the guide has examples of each business specialty, such as hardware stores, insurance agencies, print shops, etc., some generalizations are as follows:

Retail businesses	30 percent of 12 months' sales
Service businesses	60 percent of 12 months' sales
Distribution businesses	35 percent of 12 months' sales
Manufacturing businesses	50 percent of 12 months' sales

Naturally, the rules of thumb are merely benchmarks. The real question is, what are you really buying? cash flow? growth potential? assets? liabilities? risks? More specifically, what are the terms and conditions of the lease, the value and life of the inventory, the condition of the furniture and fixtures, the age of the machinery and equipment, the status of the franchise or licenses, the probability of ongoing business, and the likelihood of employee continuity?

A CASE IN POINT

Buying small manufacturing companies involves higher risk than acquiring larger ones. Small manufacturing companies often have the following characteristics:

- The management team consists of one or maybe two principals—the owner and/or his wife or son. When the business is sold, the management disappears.

- Very few financial, inventory, manufacturing, or quality control systems are in place. Analysis of comparative monthly or yearly backlogs is usually nonexistent, and breakeven points and product costing figures are unavailable.

- Accounting figures are either late or not provided on a monthly basis.

- Customer concentration often exceeds the 80/20 rule, which means that often small manufacturers have more than 80 percent of their entire business with only 20 percent of their customers.

A few years ago a lawyer called me to see if, as an intermediary, I would be willing to sell a small custom sheet metal manufacturer. Normally I would have graciously declined the assignment; however, against my better judgment, I accepted for the following reasons:

- On $800,000 of sales, the owner was taking out $200,000.

- The business was growing.

- There was a very motivated seller.

- Including the real estate, which was assessed at $250,000, the owner was willing to sell the business and the plant for $500,000.

Below are a few facts about the business.

- The two largest customers represented 50 percent of total sales, and the top ten customers represented 90 percent of sales.

- The owner was in charge of manufacturing, designing, purchasing, quoting new business, and sales, and he sometimes delivered the orders on the company truck. He arrived at work every day at 6:30 A.M., and he hadn't taken a vacation as long as he could remember.

- The owner's wife came into the office a few hours every day. She was the principal contact for matters concerning the sale of the company.

- There was a full-time secretary who did three things: answer the telephone, type the invoices, and make out the weekly employee payroll.

- There were no computers in the office, and only after I insisted did they install a fax machine.

- The factory was in a residential area; i.e., it was a nonconforming use, and a new owner could not expand the facility.

- Almost all the machinery and equipment was fully depreciated. There were no Computer Numerical Control (CNC) machines. One machine was over 100 years old.

- Neither the machinery and equipment nor the real estate was appraised. The financials were not audited.

When two offers for the business were delivered, the principals were too busy to consider them. The owner was in the middle of a rush job, and his wife's father had just been taken to the hospital.

This description of a small business is a true case. With the help of another intermediary, we were fortunate enough to find the right buyer, and the deal closed successfully.

Let us step back and assess the characteristics of owners of small businesses and/or startups. Rarely are they management, marketing, or financial types; rather, they are creative engineers, scientists, inventors, salespeople, programmers, and so on who are very entrepreneurial. They are often willing to work eighty-hour weeks, and they do not have support systems such as secretaries and assistants. In many cases they are multi-talented, carry much of the corporation information in their head, build close personal relationships with vendors and customers, and do not necessarily build a management team. It is common for their businesses to have heavy customer concentration and/or a few key products dependent on a limited number of suppliers. Of course, there are exceptions to the rule, but generally speaking the owner/operator *is* the business.

Essentially, companies with sales under $1 million are categorized as small businesses. It is one thing to start and build a company from scratch, but it is another to buy a company when the principal asset (the owner) is leaving and what is left is a weak or nonexistent management team with few, if any, systems in place. Unfortunately, it costs a buyer almost as much in professional fees to acquire a company with $1 million in sales as it does one with $3 million in sales. It may be wiser to raise more equity up front by bringing in other investors and/or putting together an acquisition team than to acquire a smaller company by yourself.

THE REBUTTAL

Notwithstanding my concerns about acquiring a small business, the preponderance of the estimated 300,000 businesses that are sold annually are small concerns. In Chapter 26, "Case Studies of Buyers," there are two examples of enormously successful acquisitions of small businesses.

In the case of Bailey's of Boston, Franklin Wyman bought an ice cream parlor restaurant and candy store with only $7,500 of his own money plus his partners' investment. Over twenty-three years the sales grew from $250,000 to $4.6 million, and Wyman sold out with over $1 million profit. In another case, Circuitest Services Inc. was acquired by Ray Cronin and Jim Grasso for $350,000. In seven years, sales grew from $350,000 to $7.5 million.

In his book *New Business Opportunities*, Jeffrey A. Timmons, professor at the Harvard Business School, states: "Since World War II, half of all innovations and 95% of all radical innovations have come from new and smaller firms. Innumerable innovations and industries began this way: the heart pacemaker, the micro-computer, overnight express packages, the quick oil change, fast food, the oral contraceptive, the x-ray machine, and hundreds of others."

In spite of Timmons's rousing statement, there is usually greater risk, albeit less costs, in acquiring small businesses because they are often less established, more dependent on one person, and subject to customer concentration and can be weak on financial controls.

RECOMMENDATIONS

Before you seek out small businesses for sale, I suggest you determine how much cash you are willing to commit not only to the purchase of a business but also to upgrading it. If you have $100,000 to $150,000 for an initial investment in a business, you probably can expect to acquire a company with $500,000 in sales at a purchase price of $200,000 to $250,000. The balance of your equity investment will be covered through seller's financing and/or bank debt. Remember, you will be expected to personally guarantee bank notes.

Your financial capabilities will somewhat determine the size business you can expect to buy. Perhaps you have heard about books that encourage "buy a business with no money down." While anything is possible, the likelihood of achieving such a feat is remote unless there is something terribly wrong with the target company.

Another consideration is your geographic limitations: are you willing to relocate your home or drive an hour to the business's locale? In seeking out small businesses for sale, you can refer to the Business Opportunities section of the city newspaper, contact business brokers, and call on owners directly. Do not be afraid or hesitant to seek professional advice in this process even though the businesses are small. The issues of valuation, negotiation, and due diligence are the same whether the business is large or small.

There is a temptation to consider any and all businesses that are for sale. However, you should analyze the pros and cons of the four categories as they pertain to your background, your skills, and your lifestyle.

Manufacturing

Pros: Since you are producing a product of your own, you are capable of differentiating your company from the competition. There is a strong possibility that your product or process can be proprietary, giving your company a competitive advantage. Most manufacturers are less dependent on relationships and can build the business worldwide from one location, the factory.

Cons: Usually manufacturing companies are more capital-intensive because of the cost of the machinery and equipment. Operating margins tend to be slim for low- to medium-tech manufacturers. By nature, manufacturers are complex organizations, coordinating product design, procurement, production, distribution, marketing, customer service, etc., to meet the just-in-time requirements of demanding customers.

Service

Pros: The U.S. economy continually shows solid growth in special services, from office cleaning to rubbish removal. If consumers' needs are met reliably and the company partially fills a void in the marketplace, the business should be able to grow nicely.

Cons: The owner/manager has to have a lot of "people skills" to work well with the multitude of employees and customers. Since the business is relationship-driven, key employees could steal customers unless there are sound noncompete clauses.

Retail

Pros: These businesses require a fairly moderate investment compared to manufacturing and distribution businesses and are less labor-intensive than service companies. If the company has a unique concept, such as Boston Chicken, one can raise money and do a national rollout, opening a series of stores.

Cons: For small retailers, the long hours and six- to seven-day weeks make the commitment enormous. Many owners find it difficult to work fifty to sixty hours a week. If a retailer picks the wrong location or a significant competitor opens up a store next door, he or she is often locked into a long lease with little recourse.

Distribution

Pros: Most distributors have 85 percent of their assets in accounts receivable and inventory. If both items turn over quickly, then concentrating on these two components of the business can lead to continued success and growth.

Cons: Distribution is a high-volume, low-margin business. It is not uncommon for both the customer and the supplier to squeeze the margins and demand more. Distributors are very vulnerable to a recession, as the balance sheet is often highly leveraged in order to carry the necessary inventory.

CONCLUSION

Acquiring a small business has the one advantage that it usually costs less than buying a middle-market company. By nature, small businesses have less available financial information, less management in place, and a narrower customer base.

CHAPTER 4

Acquiring Family Businesses

The definition of a family business is that there are two or more members of the same family managing/working in a company in which the business is owned and run for the benefit of the family and its individual members. The average life cycle of a family business is under twenty-five years. Less than 30 percent ever go beyond the second generation, with fewer than 15 percent lasting through the third generation. Given the dynamics of family businesses, one could easily assume that this category should be the number one target area for corporate buyers.

Before I discuss the opportunities and pitfalls in trying to buy a family business, it would be helpful for you to understand the perceived reasons why family businesses have such a high mortality rate.

- Taxes on the founder's estate (the top federal rate is 55 percent) without offsetting life insurance policies force sale or liquidation.

- Family members cannot solve the management succession issue.

- There are rivalries between siblings and in-laws.

- Non-working family members who depend on the business for their income.

In spite of the inherent problems with family businesses, their positive attributes are family members' loyalty, their willingness to sacrifice, and their teamwork. During a recession, family members pull together with a unique kind of durability because they know that it is for their own business that they are sacrificing. Rarely do these businesses have to worry about a team member's jumping ship to the competition. Family members' trust in one another inspires a more open and communicative relationship, which in turn gives the business a competitive advantage.

Like most other middle-market companies, family businesses with sales over $1 million are approached by numerous potential buyers. If you too approach a family business to buy, here are a number of insights:

- While buyers should always do their utmost to determine the real reason the owner might sell the company, it is even more important to find out the reason when a family business is concerned. After all, why wouldn't a family member be the logical successor? Is there something wrong with the company? Is there something wrong with the middle management? Or does the owner really want to cash out?

- It is particularly important that on your initial visit to the company, you obtain a breakdown of the ownership of the voting stock. Often, you might find yourself discussing the possible sale of the company with the founder's son, who has a minority position. In spite of what the son might imply, the key person to contact in future discussions is the family member who has control. More than once, I have been misled by not talking with the key player in the possible transaction. One should recognize that the founder of a company is faced with selling his or her life's work and legacy, which is emotionally very difficult to do. Many times when you are near the closing of a transaction, the founder has "seller's remorse" and decides not to sell the company after all.

- Family businesses, partly because they support many family members, some of whom do not work in the business, are usually run to pay out most of the profits. In fact, many family businesses are Subchapter S corporations, which by nature pay out most of the profits to the shareholders. The result is that these family businesses often do not reinvest enough of their earnings in new plant and equipment or let the earnings build up on the balance sheet.

- The more family members there are in the business, the greater the likelihood that there will be disagreement on whether or not to sell the company.

- Family members in the business should be evaluated very carefully to determine whether they should remain employed under the new ownership. Often family members would not have their position in the company if it were not for that relationship.

THE SAGA OF A FAMILY BUSINESS

A third-generation family business produced frozen pasta for supermarkets and restaurants. Annual sales were $10 million, of which $5 million was sold to one customer, a leading restaurant distributor.

The family patriarch was retired and living in Florida. His son was now CEO of the company, and his daughter and son-in-law were, respectively, in charge of sales and production. In addition, there were two cousins working in the office. Business was brisk, the company was growing at 20 percent per year, and annual earnings before interest and taxes (EBIT) was $1.0 million. The company had been using a marketing consultant, who became alarmed when the sales projections showed that in four years, 70 percent of the company's business would be dependent on the restaurant distributor.

Under the CEO's leadership, the company decided to diversify both its product offering and its distribution channels by acquiring another food company. Because the company was a Subchapter S corporation, it paid out most of its profits to the family stockholders, leaving only $400,000 of available equity to invest in another business. After a one-year acquisition search, the company was unable to identify a target company to buy, partly because it did not have the financial or management resources to acquire a profitable company with sales of around $5 million.

Still faced with a heavy customer concentration and the likelihood of this, and the resulting vulnerability increasing, management decided to sell the company for $6 million. The patriarch owned nearly 55 percent of the stock. He was of the old school and insisted on receiving all cash at closing.

Many qualified buyers visited the company. Seven months later, one of the buyers agreed to the patriarch's terms in spite of the problem of depending so heavily on one customer. In the final analysis, however, the patriarch turned down the $6 million offer and pulled the company off the market.

A family business is a way of life, a heritage, and often the soul of the family. In this case. there were five family members working in the business plus three nonworking members receiving compensation through their ownership of stock. If the company were sold, it would be almost impossible to assure every family member a job. And what of the after-tax money—where could it be invested to give the same type of return? The family name was on every package of pasta, the patriarch was an icon in the industry and a legacy for generations to come.

Needless to say, family businesses take special considerations. The most likely prospect to buy a family business is a family member.

CHAPTER 5

Acquiring Troubled Companies

Buyers are often tempted to acquire underperforming companies because the potential sellers are usually motivated and often will sell for a very reasonable price. However, buyer beware! Companies do not find themselves in trouble overnight; it usually develops over several years.

The obvious initial question is why the target company is in trouble. It is possible to have a good company with a bad capital structure caused by too heavy a debt load. Given the alternatives, it is usually better if the target company has financial problems than if it has operating problems because the former are easier to overcome than the latter.

Unless you have previously turned a company around and/or acquired a company, it is not advisable to undertake both events at the same time. Successful acquisitions are difficult enough in the best of circumstances, let alone trying to execute a turnaround at the same time. There are professionals who are capable of executing both endeavors at the same time, but this book is written for inexperienced buyers. For those acquiring a troubled company, however, the following items are usually the critical issues:

- Large fixed debt payments to the secured lender vastly limit available working capital for daily requirements.

- Products or services are poorly marketed.

- The company lacks sufficient critical mass to gain the necessary economies of scale.

- The company is poorly managed.
- Employees are not properly trained or motivated.

In spite of the above warnings about acquiring troubled companies, if you are experienced in the target company's industry and/or experienced in turnarounds, you have a golden opportunity to buy a company at a very favorable price. As you will find mentioned in Chapter 8, "Valuation Techniques," if companies are losing money at the EBIT level, then it is reasonable to acquire them at book value or reconstructed book value because there are no earnings to capitalize. However, there are some troubled companies that are earning a reasonable amount at the EBIT level (5 to 10 percent of sales) but have such a heavy debt load that principal and interest payments result in a deficit profit before tax figure. In such a case, if there is a negative net worth, the seller probably would be willing to sell you the business for only one dollar if you assumed all the debt, including trade and interest-bearing debt (commonly known as accounts receivable and bank debt). However, in some cases, even book value may be too generous. Alternative acquisition structures could include an earnout arrangement or a payout based on a 5 to 10 percent royalty on sales. One would have to read the covenants of the loan agreement before entering into such an acquisition, as the bank may prevent the sale of the company unless the debt is paid off.

Another item to consider when buying troubled companies is whether you want current management to remain. If the company is losing money on an operating basis, chances are you will not want most of them around after the acquisition. It could be important to have a non-compete agreement with the sales manager as well as the owner because, after their jobs are terminated, they may be tempted to work for the competition. One of the key elements in a turnaround is maintaining your core customers. You need the steadiness of repeat business while you rebuild your customer base.

In many cases the owner of the troubled company also owns the plant and/or office in which the company operates. If your intention is to move the business, then the owner not only will be out of a job but will be left with an empty building. The owner may be more agreeable to selling the troubled company at a loss if he or she is able to enter into a favorable lease for three to five years on the building with you.

Paramount in the analysis of whether or not to buy a troubled company is to identify not only the problems but also how to rectify them. You will need to spend significantly more time in due diligence than when buying a healthy company, both before and after the letter of intent. I bought a troubled company when I was both young and naive. I was so caught up in the excitement of the event and the expectations that I convinced myself to go through with the acquisition. In the process of doing the due diligence, I remembered only what I wanted to hear and psychologically discarded what I did not want to hear. Sometimes there are misconceptions as to what is a good deal. For example, conceptually, buying a business with no money down and the assumption of debt sounds fine. In reality, it may be an awful deal. Buying a business is not like buying Treasuries. In the former, there are risks—sometimes considerable risks. Just remember the song "The Gambler" and singer Kenny Rogers: "You've got to know when to hold, and know when to fold ... know when to walk away, and know when to run!"

Often one person's difficulty is another person's opportunity. As a new owner, you may deem it necessary to lay off 30 percent of the workforce so that the company will become more efficient. Many owners of multigenerational family businesses do not have the fortitude to make these cuts and as a result jeopardize the entire existence of the company. Many troubled companies have become complacent and continue to buy from their old-line suppliers without shopping for new, more competitive prices. A seemingly small savings in either cost of goods sold or SG&A will increase operating profits dramatically.

Sales	100	100	100
Cost of goods sold	<u>65</u>	<u>60</u>	<u>65</u>
Gross profit	35	30	35
SG&A	<u>(30)</u>	<u>(30)</u>	<u>(25)</u>
Operating income	5	10	10

To assess the viability of acquiring a company, you may need to hire a turnaround specialist to give you a second opinion. Such basic questions as what areas of the business are making money and what areas are losing money need to be addressed. Is the workforce skilled and competent to compete effectively with the troubled company's competition? How up-to-date is the machinery and equipment, including computers? If the financials are not audited, how reliable are the stated figures for receivables, payables, inventory, etc.? Usually troubled companies have poor and unreliable financial systems, and the statements are seldom timely and up-to-date. Furthermore, troubled companies often have customer or vendor concentration to such an extent that 50 percent of their sales or purchases is with one party, and the company is overly dependent on that customer or vendor.

Naturally, if you are contemplating the purchase of a troubled company, you do not want to encounter unwelcome surprises, such as unintended assumption of seller liabilities. To avoid this situation, do not buy the stock of the company, even if you have to pass up the tax loss carryforward. The amount you can take each year is limited; for example, if there is a $100,000 tax loss and you acquire the company for $500,000, you can take 10 percent of the purchase price or $50,000 as a deduction each year for two years. Also, you do not want to purchase assets burdened with liens. In an asset purchase of a company, it is imperative to check the Uniform Commercial Code (UCC) filings to be sure creditors have not placed liens on the assets you are about to receive. Since the company's bank will undoubtedly have tied up the assets as part of its collateral for the loan agreement, the seller must receive a release from the bank. If there is a lease involved, you will need to have the landlord assign the lease to you. If the company has the right to sublease the premises, find out if the landlord has any outstanding claims against the seller. If not, your attorney should have the landlord sign an *estoppel certificate*, whereby the landlord agrees that there are no claims pending against the seller on the lease. Otherwise, the landlord might have the right to collect these claims from you, the new tenant. As in any asset sale, be sure you are assigned all advantageous contracts, patents, trademarks, etc.

In conclusion, let us assume that you have done your due diligence on the troubled company and, with some tough negotiating, you pick and choose which assets you will buy at what price and which liabilities you will assume. The assets are free of liens with no UCC filings, and so you take title to the assets. Are you home free? Maybe not! If the seller's remaining company is forced into bankruptcy by its creditors, under the Uniform Fraudulent Transfer Act, if it is held that the seller received less than fair value (inadequate consideration), you as the buyer would lose your claim to the assets. Therefore, if you are acquiring these assets, you probably need either an appraiser to verify their market value or a solvency opinion on the selling company.

Another precaution in acquiring the assets is to comply with the Bulk Sales Act. This act was designed to protect the buyer and give some protection to the creditors of a business whose assets are being sold. In most states the Bulk Sales Act applies only if the business has substantial inventory (this excludes most service companies). Buyer and seller comply as follows:

- The seller provides the buyer with a sworn affidavit that lists the names, addresses, and amount of debt for all the seller's creditors.

- The buyer sends each creditor a notice at least ten days prior to the sale stating that the transfer of assets is about to take place and that the buyer will also assume the corresponding payables, to be paid at closing or, more likely, as each debt comes due.

Without compliance with the Bulk Sales Act, the sale can take place, but the seller's creditors will be able to go against the buyer to collect their debts. If the seller's business is not excluded from the Bulk Sales Act (check with your attorney), then the buyer has two choices: either comply with the act and risk certain creditors causing a delay in the closing or proceed with the closing without compliance but have the seller set up an escrow account to satisfy creditors that demand immediate payment.

From the book *The Warren Buffett Way* there is an ominous warning regarding turnarounds: "Buffett learned a valuable lesson about corporate turnarounds: they seldom succeed."

Profile of Individual Buyers

This book is essentially written for individual buyers who are interested in acquiring companies with $2 million to $50 million in sales, commonly known as the middle market. The likely profiles of buyers are the following:

Layoff: Many people in corporate America have been laid off from work because the competition forces businesses to downsize, or, as some executives say, right-size. Almost every day one reads in the newspaper of another massive corporate layoff. These people may have become cynical about their future with *Fortune* 1000 companies, or, if they are over forty, the odds on their getting another job have diminished dramatically. In this case, self-employment is a viable alternative, and so buying a business is like buying a job. In fact, the largest middle-market intermediary in the country, Geneva Business Services from Irvine, California, actually advertises in the newspapers, "Buy a Job!"

Second career: A number of business managers either take early retirement or are jettisoned from corporate America with a golden parachute. Some simply become fed up with corporate bureaucracy. These individuals may want to prove to themselves and to their peers that they can successfully run their own company. They have confidence in themselves and usually have a business or professional background that is credible.

Entrepreneur: Today's entrepreneur is our modern-day explorer, one who is willing to take risks for adventure. A decade or so ago, most entrepreneurs were associated with start-up companies. However, a more prevalent form of entrepreneurship in the 1990s is buying a business. Numerous studies have been conducted that show that it is much safer to buy a business than to start a business. Four out of five small businesses that change hands are still in business five years later, whereas only two out of five start-up businesses survive for that same time period. Many MBA programs, particularly Babson College in Wellesley, Massachusetts, feature courses in entrepreneurship. One only has to visit a bookstore to realize the vast number of books that have been written on this subject. For many people, owning a business is economic freedom, a chance to be their own boss, and part of the American dream.

Former business owner: Inasmuch as the number one reason owners of middle-market companies sell is *burnout,* these individuals often sell one business and later buy another. We all are accustomed to seeing our friends buy and sell commercial real estate. Frequently, people may buy and sell two or three businesses in their lifetime.

Part of a group: While much less prevalent than individual buyers, groups of two or three individuals will sometimes buy a business together. We all know the problems with partnerships, and so if there are multiple owners, a buy-sell agreement plus an owner's life insurance policy is imperative at the outset. A recent phenomenon witnessed by Geneva Business Services is three individuals who have worked together at the same company joining together, particularly if each individual brings different but complementary skills (e.g., manufacturing, marketing, and finance).

Absentee owner: A number of individual business owners prefer to treat a company the way they would buy commercial real estate and take a passive role. In other words, a professional manager runs the business and the owner keeps track of the company on a weekly or monthly basis, but from a distance. It is an investment even though the owner owns 100 percent of the company.

Lifestyle: When Country Business Inc. of Manchester Center, Vermont, started brokering businesses in northern New England in 1978, it targeted clients ranging from executives who wanted a more satisfying career to city dwellers who wanted a quieter, more fulfilling lifestyle. The firm sells businesses ranging from Vermont country inns to middle-market manufacturing companies in northern New England.

Turnaround specialists: There are specialists like Peter Alcock who have the talent and ability to acquire distressed companies, restructure them from losing money to making money, and then eventually sell them at a handsome profit. Alcock engineered the buyout of U.S. Repeating Arms (Winchester Rifles), a $55 million company from New Haven, Connecticut, that was in Chapter 11, and later sold it to a French conglomerate. More recently he acquired a well-known furniture company that was having some financial difficulty.

Well endowed: Separate from the above classifications of individuals are people who are independently wealthy. They may not be under time pressure to buy a business, but they do want to be their own boss, they want a challenge, they want control, and they want to build their own equity instead of that of someone else.

While the above buyer profiles are broad and would encompass a wide spectrum of people, there is, of course, the distinct possibility that even if a person perceives himself or herself as a qualified business buyer, this is perhaps not the case.

A highly regarded Boston outplacement firm, New Directions, serves former executives with a minimum salary of approximately $100,000. Many of its clients have a genuine interest in buying a business. The founder and managing director of New Directions, Dave Corbett, initially screens the feasibility of his clients' buying a business by asking them to answer these five questions:

> Should I buy a business?
> What business should I buy?
> How to fund it?
> How to find it?
> How do I do the deal?

In the context of evaluating a buyer, or perhaps more importantly in the buyer's own personal evaluation, the following factors should be considered:

- Motives
- Ambitions
- Level of commitment
- Personal risk profile

- Financial resources to sustain one through the search process, which could last two years
- Cooperation of family members

Buying a middle-market company is not a game for neophytes. Purchasing a business enterprise is one of the most complex transactions a person can undertake in the field of commerce. The buyer's background or business acumen may not be conducive to the skills necessary to acquire a business. Hopefully, by reading this book, one will significantly increase one's knowledge of the process necessary to be successful in buying a business. Nevertheless, if the buyer's profile might be perceived as undesirable in the eyes of the seller or the financier, it may need to be strengthened by including a strong partner and/or engaging respected advisers, such as a well-known intermediary.

The perceived credibility of the buyer is *very* important, because without it many sellers will be reluctant to even talk to a buyer. Business owners usually have great pride in their company, and often their business represents their life's work. Such owners are often reluctant to sell their company even at a high price unless they have respect for and confidence in the potential buyer.

Several years ago, I inquired why Godfrey Wood was the most successful broker for Land-Vest, a Boston-based real estate firm that sells multimillion-dollar estates. I was told by one of the principals of the firm that one reason Wood was so successful was his ability to quickly qualify the potential buyer. Because real estate brokers work on commission, they can ill afford to spend half a day showing an unqualified buyer a multimillion-dollar estate. Wood had three pointed questions for the prospect. If he was not satisfied with the response, he would refer the person to someone else in the firm. In other words, the buyer's ability to visit prestigious properties depended on the profile.

Since I am an intermediary working almost exclusively for corporate buyers and sellers, I receive telephone calls daily from individuals seeking to buy a business. While I am cordial and respectful, I too cannot afford to give potential buyers an hour of my valuable time unless they pass my short evaluation test. Admittedly, the following questions are curt and project unfriendliness:

- How much equity are you willing to invest?

- Have you been a CEO of a company and/or have you previously been involved with acquiring a company?

- Would you consider paying a retainer to an intermediary for the acquisition search?

The answers to the above questions give me a quick snapshot of the buyer's profile. Just as lawyers do not accept all prospects as clients, business intermediaries also are somewhat selective. The following twelve points would be my checklist for an ideal individual buyer.

- Is capable of investing $250,000 to $500,000 of his or her own cash in the deal.

- Was previously involved with a corporate acquisition, either personally or for an employer.

- Has had CEO experience or has been head of a division of a substantial company.

- Has prepared an acquisition plan for this assignment or printed a condensed version of the plan in brochure form.

- Has narrowed the focus to target industries.

- Has targeted industries similar to his or her business background.

- Is willing to sign a fee agreement with the intermediary.

- Is willing to pay a financial retainer to the intermediary.

- Is likely to have good personal chemistry with a seller.

- Has already spent some time looking for an acquisition.

- Is willing to pay a full price for the target company and does not have the characteristic of being a "bottom fisher," i.e., one who consistently bids low.

- Is willing to accept a company with some warts (problems).

The following overview of the individual buyer profile is placed in context with analysis of all buyers. The source is Geneva Business Services of Irvine, California.

The Buyers of Companies
Revenues

Group	Less than $3 million	$3-10 million	$10+ million
Individuals	44%	26%	4%
Public companies	28%	21%	17%
Private companies	11%	14%	14%
Investment groups	17%	29%	47%
Foreign companies	—	10%	18%
Total	100%	100%	100%

The figures above are self-explanatory in that individuals buy more companies under $3 million in sales than any other group. I believe there are more companies in the United States with sales between $1 and $3 million than there are companies with over $3 million in sales. Since the middle market, on which this book focuses, includes companies with $2 to $50 million in sales, individuals do play an important part in acquiring companies in this category.

The profile of the individual buyer is important to understand. If you are desirous of acquiring a company, you will probably be pursuing companies that are also being sought after by both other individuals and corporate buyers. Regardless of the category in which you classify yourself, you will have formidable competition.

In the years to come, I believe that individuals will play a larger part in the purchase of middle-market companies. This phenomenon is explained, in part, in the first chapter. However, the major emphasis will be on groups of individuals, most commonly two or three. Groups of individuals have more credibility, have a greater breadth of skills, and are better financed.

CHAPTER 7

Assessing Your Acquisition Strategy

Most individual buyers of middle-market companies take one to two years to complete an acquisition. The length of this procedure is usually a result of prior inexperience, lack of focus, and, above all, an acquisition strategy that is not thoroughly conceived.

Many buyers are so anxious to look at companies for sale that they tend to consider almost any opportunity that is presented to them. Since most buyers have difficulty seeing enough companies for sale to begin with, asking them to be more selective sounds like an oxymoron. However, the secret of success is to receive quality deal flow that matches the buyer's criteria and capabilities. Before we map out an acquisition strategy, let's determine the basic *criteria*.

CRITERIA

Type of Business

There are basically four types of business:

Manufacturing: The scope is from job shops, which make one-of-a-kind items, to subcontractors, which make production runs for other manufacturers, to producers of products that are sold to original equipment manufacturers (OEM), to makers of branded products that are sold to consumers. Additionally, there are integrated manufacturers that build items out of raw materials, and there are light manufacturers that do mostly subassembly work.

Distribution: Companies that act as middlemen between the manufacturer and the customer historically work on relatively low gross margins and have high turnover. Buyers have to be particularly concerned about the ability to transfer the business relationships with the seller's vendors and customers to the new owner.

Service: Temporary employment agencies, landscapers, travel agencies, etc., can be solid businesses, especially as service providers continually become a more significant part of the gross national product (GNP). The transferability of the business relationships is again critical for the new owner.

Retail: A single retail store is somewhat limited in its future growth. Multiple-store expansion can be dynamic but is very dependent on selection of the right location and is somewhat vulnerable to extension of leases on favorable terms.

By far the most sought-after type of business for middle-market buyers is manufacturing companies, especially companies that make a consumer or Original Equipment Manufacturer (OEM) product. There are a number of reasons for this: Business relationships are more transferable, the assets are more easily leveraged with the bank, the potential is perceived to be greater, and the labor component is far less than for service businesses and usually less than for retail businesses.

Type of Industry

It is advisable to stay within the industry that matches your background because of your obvious knowledge, your greater credibility with the seller, and the probability of more favorable financing from your banker. For example, if your previous employer was a high-tech company, it probably would be wiser for you to stay in the electronics industry than to pursue a totally unrelated field like the food business.

On the other hand, there are business buyers who seek underperforming companies and are perfectly capable of turning around businesses in almost any industry. Furthermore, some buyers who sold a previous business because of corporate burnout purposely want to buy a business in a different industry.

Size

The size of your target company greatly depends on the amount of liquid cash you are willing and able to invest. For example, a general rule of thumb is that profitable manufacturing companies with operating income of perhaps 10 percent of sales sell for approximately 50 percent of sales.

Most of the deals require 25 to 30 percent owner's equity at closing. Therefore, if you had $500,000 cash, you could expect to buy a profitable manufacturing company with sales of $3 to $5 million. The structure might be as follows for a business with $4 million in sales:

Company sales	$4,000,000	
Purchase price	$2,000,000	
Equity		$ 750,000
Bank notes		$ 750,000
Seller's notes		$ 500,000
Total		$2,000,000

Location

An obvious consideration, which depends on the buyer's lifestyle and willingness to travel, is location. Most individual buyers draw a fifty-mile radius around their hometown. Some buyers are willing to move from their hometown in order to buy their desired business. If the buyer is an absentee owner, then closeness is not so critical.

Underperforming

Most buyers want to acquire only profitable companies because the risks are too great otherwise. Unprofitable companies can also be too difficult for a new buyer to finance. On the other hand, some buyers prefer to buy companies that are losing money because they can negotiate very favorable prices and terms.

BUSINESS ENTITY

As part of your acquisition strategy, it is important to choose your business entity—whether you are representing yourself as an individual, as part of a group, or as a holding company. You may wonder why your choice of entity affects the acquisition strategy. The answer is simply a matter of whether being part of a group of buyers strengthens your ability to successfully buy a company or whether the image of a holding company elevates your status for the seller. For example, one individual buyer has formed a holding company, XYZ Corporation, and has prepared a seventeen-page investment proposal. The abbreviated highlights of this proposal are as follows:

Executive Summary

XYZ intends to acquire a manufacturing company with a purchase price between $5 and $10 million. The search is expected to take between 18 and 24 months. The Company has successfully raised equity to capitalize the Company with $500,000. John Smith will lead the on-site management team. Smith has over ten years' experience in the management and improvement of manufacturing companies as well as significant experience in the identification and evaluation of middle-market acquisition opportunities.

Management

A complete description of John Smith.

Type of Business

The reasons for pursuing manufacturing companies.

Acquisition Criteria

More detailed analysis.

Search Strategy

XYZ will seek out "not for sale" companies and will approach companies directly, with more reliance on brokers and investment bankers than is customary among "buyout funds."

Financial Structure of Acquired Company

Seller financing
Bank debt
Investor debt
Liquidity
Management's carried interest

Exhibits

John Smith's resume
Individual references
Screening criteria

Obviously a professionally documented acquisition plan such as this one gives the buyer credibility and respect. While other buyers may have a similar approach, it is very important that you be able to communicate this message in writing.

In addition to representing yourself as an individual buyer or representing yourself as a holding company, there is another way to position yourself as a buyer. By joining forces with one or two other buyers, you can create the *team approach*. A team of buyers often gives the buying unit more talent, more money, and more credibility. Of course, there is a distinct possible downside if the team is not compatible, especially if the individuals have not previously worked together.

As an intermediary, Geneva Business Services works with upper middle to senior management in order to cluster three of them so that they can effectively buy a business together. Geneva does not matchmake the team, but encourages people who have previously worked together to build a group that has a background in manufacturing, finance, and marketing. According to Geneva, the age spread of this group is often forty-five to sixty years old, and they are able to raise between $500,000 and $750,000 of equity, which will allow them to buy a profitable manufacturing company with $3 to $4 million in sales. The biggest hurdle for a group of senior managers in this situation is the mental switch from being employees of a big corporation to owning and running a small company.

ADVISERS

The third aspect of assessing your acquisition strategy is to determine to what extent you will involve advisers, consultants, and other resources early on in the search process.

I may be cynical, but my experience is that even when an individual has $500,000 to invest in a business, he or she is generally reluctant to spend up-front money for advice, intermediary acquisition searches, and professional valuation opinions. Aside from the above biased observation, the following are my recommendations:

Lawyers

Your regular family lawyer may be terrific regarding wills, trusts, real estate, taxes, etc., but when it comes to corporate acquisitions, it takes a special expertise. Corporate transaction lawyers are experts. Additionally, if you inform such a lawyer of your commitment to him or her for your impending transaction, he or she may be motivated to inform you of some potential companies for sale. Naturally, the lawyer has a vested interest!

Since the acquisition counsel prepares the purchase and sale agreement, it is important to predetermine some ballpark figures as to what the charge will be: $10,000, $15,000, $20,000, etc. Hourly rates generally run between $125 and $300. Don't be swayed by lawyers who charge the lowest fees, as a legal mistake in the contract can have catastrophic ramifications. On the other hand, try to negotiate a cap for the total legal expense—an amount "not to exceed $20,000," for example. This should not be onerous for a transaction lawyer.

Your lawyer should review your letter of intent. Although this instrument usually states that it is not binding, it is also difficult to substantially change the letter of intent after the fact. An experienced lawyer should have standard employment agreements and noncompete clauses. The lawyer should also review leases and loan agreements, and provide a due diligence checklist. It is customary for the buyer's lawyer to prepare the purchase and sale agreement and of course consummate the closing. Additionally, your lawyer may be helpful in referring you to the best accounting firm for your size transaction and suggesting the most accommodating bank for your corporate loans.

Accountants

As with lawyers, there are specialists within the accounting community who are experts in mergers and acquisitions. They can help you analyze the selling company's financials and assist in structuring the deal. You may need to have an independent audit to verify the financial statements as part of the due diligence. All of this could cost $10,000 to $40,000.

Your accountant should be alert for any improprieties that would adversely affect you after the business is purchased. For example, the owner may have aggressively written down the inventory so that the company would pay lower taxes. If you are acquiring the stock of the company instead of the assets, the result would be that under your new ownership the profits on this inventory would be inflated, causing you, the new owner, to pay unnecessary taxes going forward.

If the accounting firm knows that you intend to retain it after the closing, it is more apt to be very cooperative in presenting you with other clients who might be willing to sell their company.

Bankers

The first source of debt capital is of course a bank. In addition to the hard-nosed credit evaluation of the business by examining the company's balance sheet, cash flow statements, and business plan, the banker will be evaluating your character and background. It is quite probable that you will have to sign personal guarantees for the notes.

While most bankers in the commercial loan department usually respond to specific deals, it is preferable that you predetermine your most likely bank resources by meeting them in advance. By getting a jump on the all-important selection of bankers, you will save an enormous amount of time during the critical stage of putting the deal together. Financing is so critical to successfully completing the transaction that its availability has to be very high on the list of important considerations. Therefore, it is advisable you narrow down your list of bankers before you become knee deep in the deal.

Intermediaries

The agent between the seller and the buyer is known by numerous titles, such as broker, investment banker, adviser, consultant, merger and acquisition specialist, deal maker, bird dog, and finder, but for the moment we will categorize all of them as intermediaries.

Obviously, intermediaries are a great potential source of leads on companies willing to sell. Using one or more intermediaries should be part of your strategy. How to work with intermediaries most effectively will be discussed at length in Chapter 9, "Finding the Deal." However, there are some basic issues about intermediaries that you should understand.

- Intermediaries are part of a very fragmented profession. Some work by themselves, and others work for sizable companies. Some intermediaries represent only sellers, and some will represent either a buyer or a seller.

- Many intermediaries will deal only with corporations and will neither represent an individual nor attempt to sell a business to an individual. Right or wrong, many intermediaries have the perception that individuals, by and large, do not have the ability to do a deal, and they do not want to risk the embarrassment of introducing an unqualified buyer to the seller.

- Unlike in the real estate market, the fact that a business is for sale is usually surreptitious information because of the owner's paranoia that employees, vendors, and customers will have an adverse reaction if they know of the owner's intention. Therefore, intermediaries by nature are cautious about whom they show the business to and how often they bring potential buyers to the actual place of business.

- Intermediaries may have only a few companies under contract for sale at a given time. However, they know of other companies that probably can be purchased by a logical buyer with adequate capital. Unless you sign a fee agreement, the intermediary, will not discuss these potential acquisitions.

- Intermediaries prefer to work for you, the buyer, on an exclusive basis, for a monthly retainer of anywhere from $2,000 to $6,000, which may or may not be deducted from the accomplishment fee. Many intermediaries use the Lehman formula as a commission schedule, which is as follows:

  5 percent of the first $1,000,000 of the purchase price
  4 percent of the second $1,000,000
  3 percent of the third $1,000,000
  2 percent of the fourth $1,000,000
  1 percent of the value thereafter (perhaps with a cap)

  Therefore, if you bought a business for $3 million, the commission would be calculated as follows:

  $ 50,000 for the first million
  $ 40,000 for the second million
  $ 30,000 for the third million
  $120,000
  $(15,000) less monthly retainer (5 months @ $3,000/month)
  $105,000 commission due at closing

- If you choose to use a number of intermediaries on a nonexclusive basis, you might do well to create your own compensation agreement for the intermediary to sign. You should have your transaction lawyer draw up a simple one- or two-page agreement. Samples of agreements are shown in Chapter 24.

- According to the Price Waterhouse publication, *The Buying and Selling a Company Handbook*: "Professional intermediaries and advisors have little interest in working with would-be buyers who do not know what they want to buy, do not have access to the necessary financing or are not prepared to proceed professionally."

In assessing your acquisition strategy, I encourage you to use a transaction lawyer, a transaction accountant, and one or more intermediaries to not only help you create deal flow but give you a second opinion and/or be the devil's advocate. However, advisers do not make your business decisions. Ultimately you will be the one to decide whether you should buy a particular business and at what price, on what conditions, and on what terms. The purpose of this book is to help you in the endeavor.

NARROW OR BROAD INDUSTRY FOCUS

Perhaps no other matter gives me more consternation as an intermediary than the inability or reluctance of buyers to focus on what kind of company they want to buy.

Most corporate refugees that I have encountered who want to buy a middle-market company have discarded retail, service, and distribution companies. So we are left with manufacturers as an industry focus. Even with some basic criteria established, such as location, size, profitable/unprofitable, high tech/low tech, there is a vast number of industry choices, from the food industry to the medical industry. While many buyers want to keep their options open, it is better if they select an industry that is somewhat related to their background. The intermediary will find it easier to qualify the buyer's credentials to the seller and to the buyer's banker. If the buyer's focus is too broad, intermediaries will be less likely to be helpful to the buyer.

PACKAGING YOURSELF

The most successful individual buyers tend to do a better job of packaging themselves than their peers. Whether it is preparing an investment proposal; creating a holding company; naming your investors, directors, and/or advisers; or publishing a brochure incorporating these items, professionalism goes a long way toward helping your cause. Some critics might retort that you "can't judge a book by its cover," but to some degree the "smoke and mirrors" approach in gaining credibility is effective.

DIFFERENTIATE YOURSELF

Most individual buyers I have met do not understand why I am not overly excited when they tell me that they are looking for a profitable, low-tech manufacturing company with sales between $2 and $5 million that has a proprietary product.

Such an individual buyer means well and should be encouraged in the courageous mission to buy a small business. From my perspective, I owe this individual the courtesy and respect of listening. What I tell the individual buyer (free advice) is usually to have a sharper focus, package himself or herself better, raise some more equity, and not hesitate to pay an intermediary for professional advice, particularly in the search process. With that, the individual usually thanks me, picks up his or her briefcase, and leaves. This scenario is perhaps the genesis of this book. No matter what I tell individual buyers in a half hour, it always seems like I have only scratched the surface.

The above counsel is all right, but if I have one piece of advice to individual buyers, it is to differentiate yourself from your peers. One of the best known and most successful buyout firms sent me the following announcement. Given the proliferation of buyers and the very few available high-quality companies, Dubin Clark & Company would have been among the first to receive my call when I got a good deal.

1984 – 1994
Dubin Clark & Company
cordially invites you
to our
Tenth Anniversary Celebration

This anniversary event will continue until December 31, 1994, and participants will receive a very special award. Each business broker who brings an acquisition we complete in 1994 can obtain 5% of Dubin Clark's equity in the transaction, plus brokerage fees. We will offer you a board seat to be an owner alongside us. Those wishing to accept this invitation should send all attractive potential acquisitions to Dubin Clark.

R.s.v.p.
289 Greenwich Avenue
Greenwich, Connecticut 06830
(203) 629-2030

WHY COMPANIES ARE FOR SALE

When a profitable and growing company is for sale, your first reaction should be, why? Usually owners are very sensitive as to when the industry and/or company is peaking. If this is not the case, the following reasons for selling are possible.

No Heir Apparent

By looking around your own community to identify companies run by owners in their sixties, you could specifically target companies that fall into this category. As you network at your golf club or the local Rotary

Club, keep an eye out for elder owners of companies and then tactfully approach them on whether they would consider selling their business.

Loss of Interest and Burnout

Obviously it is difficult to ascertain which business owners are burned out, but surveys show that this is the number one reason owners sell. If you can keep your antennae out for business owners with this attitude, you might be on to something.

Business Needs More Capital to Remain Competitive

Many industries are consolidating. One such industry is office copier distributors. With the copier business more competitive than ever, gross margins have eroded, which means that the distributors' profits are dependent on more unit volume, which will create more service contracts. It is the latter that are the primary profit generator. Many copier distributors with sales of $1 to $2 million need more capital to buy competitively, so that they can sell competitively, so that they can get the profitable service business. This is an opportunity for you to acquire a business very reasonably and then infuse the necessary capital to allow it to grow.

Estate Tax and Liquidity Concerns

While I do not suggest that you become an ambulance chaser, a lot of family businesses fall on hard times after the founder dies. Many state business directories list companies' banks, law firms, and accounting firms. Perhaps a discreet telephone call to the company's law firm several months after the death notice would be appropriate.

Financial Offer Too Good to Turn Down

Some owners sell not because of burnout or lack of capital, but simply because the buyer's offer is too good to refuse. I know of a former president of a famous fast-food chain who desperately wanted to own a particular house. When he contacted the owner, he was told that the house was not for sale. He told the owner bluntly that he still wanted to buy the house.

The company president returned a week later. When the owner stated his price, the company president had the audacity to negotiate the price, and bought the house! The point of the story is that the difference between no and yes may be just a matter of how much you are willing to pay.

UNDERSTANDING WHY THE TARGET COMPANY'S OWNER MAY NOT SELL

How many times have you heard about business buyers who spent an inordinate amount of time attempting to acquire a company, only to have the seller back off? Heaven forbid, but you too may go though a similar experience.

My first potential deal as an intermediary, in 1985, fell apart. In retrospect, I was naive in thinking I could be successful. I represented a third-generation Italian bakery with $2 million in sales. The business was marginally profitable; however, I was able to find a buyer willing to buy the business, along with the real estate, for $1 million over a number of years. Absolutely jubilant, I drew up the letter of intent for the seller's signature.

I overlooked two critical items. The Italian family business was owned by five siblings, and to have a family of five agree on anything, no matter what the nationality, is highly unlikely. The fact of the matter is that these five stockholders did not agree on the presented letter of intent. The other consideration that I overlooked was what each stockholder would receive after paying off the remaining portion of the real estate mortgage and paying the capital gains tax. Instead of receiving one-fifth of $1 million, or $200,000, the net amount for each stockholder was more like $100,000 spread over five years, or merely $20,000 per year. What the stockholders expected, I believe, was $200,000 at closing. In addition, I was talking to only two out of the five stockholders. Needless to say, the deal crashed and burned. Several years later I inquired how the company was doing. The answer: It was barely surviving, its fate unclear.

The lesson for me as an intermediary was clear: Only represent those sellers in which there is a majority stockholder and in which I have predetermined to the best of my ability the net after-tax payout to the owner(s).

Perhaps it would be helpful to know some other reasons why sellers ultimately do not sell.

Owners Want an Unreasonable Amount of Money

While many buyers hope to close the gap as the negotiations proceed, many sellers have valued their company based on sweat equity, or compared it to public companies on the New York Stock Exchange, or have a preconceived number in mind, such as $1 million after taxes.

Second Thoughts by Owner—It Is the Only Business the Owner Knows

One family patriarch withdrew the business offering after the family had paid an intermediary a $5,000 retainer to sell the company and after there was a letter of intent on the table. The stated deciding factor was a desire to protect the jobs of two third-generation family members, even though the buyer was anxious to include an employment contract for these two managers. On another occasion, an owner received the letter of intent and then never signed it. To this day he will not take or return phone calls from the buyer. Intermediaries call these situations "seller's remorse."

From 1956 to 1958, I served in the U.S. Marines. Being discharged was a big moment, and most of us would count the days as we neared the date. Invariably there would be a few unexpected Marines who would reenlist the week before they were to be discharged. For two to four years, it had been the only life they had known. To be discharged was to leave the life to which they had become accustomed. As a result, a few of these Marines remained in the Corps.

This is analogous to some business owners. It is difficult to advise people how to detect similar situations. The chances of owners changing their mind about selling increases dramatically when there are multiple owners.

Owner Would Rather Leave Business to Heirs

A family business is defined as one in which there are two or more members of the same family working in the company, in which the business is owned and run for the benefit of the family and its individual members. Certainly family businesses are targets for individual buyers. Many owners sell the family business because they need the liquidity, they secretly feel that their heir is not competent to run the company successfully, or they sense that the industry and/or the company is peaking. Nevertheless, many owners leave their company to their heirs ... wisely or unwisely.

Capital Gains Liability the Overriding Concern

How many times have you heard an owner of a business or an owner of a large block of stock with a near zero cost basis say, "I can't afford to sell"? Of course, these people are referring to the 28 percent federal capital gains tax, not to mention the individual state capital gains taxes. There are numerous ways to prepare the business for sale that will mitigate large tax liabilities, and there are ways to structure the deal that will do the same. Invariably, however, numerous potential sellers do neither, and as a result, the owner ends up not selling the company.

The Security of Owning a Solid Company

Many founders and owners have made their company their life's work. When they reach retirement age without an heir, an alternative to selling is to hire a professional manager. The thought of selling the company and reinvesting the proceeds in the stock market or real estate can be less appealing to owners who have little or no experience in these areas.

Loss of Significant Owner's Salary from Business

The owner's rationale for not selling is often driven by the fact that he or she cannot replace the salary. It is not unusual for small-business owners to take out $200,000 to $300,000 annually. Let's assume that a company with sales of $6 million sells for $3 million. Let's also assume that the capital gains taxes are $700,000, leaving the owner with $2.3 million to reinvest. Use whatever interest rate is prevalent at the time of your reading this book and you will see that the business owner will fall way short of his or her salary.

CHAPTER 8

Valuation Techniques

If you are analyzing a privately owned company, there are often a number of items on the financial statements that have to be adjusted or recast in order to understand the real earning power of the company. Business owners are highly motivated to pay the least amount of corporate taxes possible, and the extent to which they stretch to minimize tax liability runs the gamut from legitimate to marginal to illegitimate. Legitimate deductions include abnormally high salaries for the owners, above-market rent for buildings owned by a related family-owned real estate trust, and company automobiles. Illegitimate deductions include salaries for nonworking family members, pleasure trips charged as business trips, and home maintenance expenses charged to the company.

In valuing the target company, a very basic initial query to the owner is the question: What is for sale? The owner will generally prefer to sell stock, since such a transaction results in a single capital gains tax. A stock sale, on the other hand, may be a disadvantage to a buyer if there are depreciable assets on the balance sheet because he or she cannot "step up" the value of the assets and increase depreciation charges. In addition, the buyer will assume all liabilities resulting from previous infractions or product malfunctions. For these reasons, buyers may well value a company lower when they are required to purchase stock. Conversely, in an asset sale the seller will be taxed twice: once at the corporate level and again when distributing the proceeds of the sale out of the corporation. For the right to buy assets, therefore, the buyer may have to place a higher valuation on the target company.

Whether you buy assets or stock is only part of the answer as to what is for sale. Other considerations could include what assets, particularly real estate assets, are going to be withdrawn prior to the purchase. And, are there any obligations of the seller, particularly debt, to be assumed by the buyer?

VALUATION TECHNIQUE 1: MULTIPLE OF EARNINGS

For middle-market manufacturers, the multiple of earnings approach is the preferred method of valuation. For such businesses, earnings before interest and taxes (EBIT) is the standard earnings component to which multiples are applied in determining business sale prices. If EBIT shows no earnings, a multiple is sometimes applied to cash flow and even to gross margin.

Let me give a flavor of what some M & A experts have said relative to the multiples to apply to EBIT:

"Will pay 4 to 5 times EBIT if there are growth prospects and no requirements for additional capital."

"Will pay over 5 times EBIT if net worth is 60 percent or more of the selling price."

"Will pay 5 to 6 times EBIT for companies with a 15 to 20 percent return on investment."

"Will pay 5 to 6 times EBIT if there are consistent earnings, good management, and market leadership."

Mary Young of the Boston office of BankAmerica Business Credit Inc. reported that at the 1994 Buy-Out Symposium in New York City sponsored by Venture Economics, the following observations were made by various speakers:

1. The most common multiple of EBIT is 5 to 7 times for industrial companies and 7 to 9 times for pricing initial public offerings. Thus there is an enormous difference in pricing between private and public companies.

2. It is acceptable to pay up to 7 times EBIT for a stand-alone company but 4 to 5 times for add-on acquisitions.

3. Consumer product companies are selling for 8 to 10 times cash flow.

4. The less a buyer pays for a business, the more he or she can afford to provide for management incentives.

Is the EBIT multiple an arbitrary number? A rule of thumb is that if you buy a new machine for a factory, you should be able to pay for it in five years from the resulting labor savings. Likewise, a business should be able to pay for itself in three to five years, assuming that the earnings remain exactly the same for that period of time. To go one step further, a prudent person might expect a 20 percent return on an investment in a company with steady earnings. On that basis, the company could be paid for in five years at the same earnings level. Therefore, higher or lower multiples are affected by the corresponding difference in the rate of return. Historically, however, a five-year payback has been a de facto standard.

According to Joseph Myss, an intermediary from Wayzata, Minnesota, "The multiplier you select is market driven based on market conditions, comparables, and value in the eye of the beholder. The value the buyer sees in the company affects the market multiplier: Paying 10 times earnings for a company provides the buyer with a 10 percent return on the invested capital based upon historical financial performance. Paying 5 times earnings results in a 20 percent return on invested capital; 4 times earnings results in a 25 percent return." Myss emphasizes that EBIT is most commonly used as the constant of the multiplier. One needs, however, to separate the acquisition and financing features of the deal. Buyers will use their own capital structure as a model to finance the acquisition of the seller and will look at the company from that perspective."

VALUATION TECHNIQUE 2: BOOK VALUE

Book value, a multiple of book value, or a premium to book value is also a method used to value manufacturing or distribution companies. Book value, of course, is total assets minus total liabilities and is commonly known as net worth.

The book valuation technique is usually used as a method of cross-testing the more common technique of applying multiples to EBIT, cash flow, or net earnings. In the following situations, however, the use of book value as the primary method of valuation is prevalent:

1. When the company is losing money on an operating basis. In such cases, there are no earnings on which to apply the multiples previously discussed. Therefore, the reconstructed or fair market value of total assets less total liabilities is used for the valuation.

2. For small distribution companies with sales of under $20 million. Distributors of this size are usually successful because of the departing owners' many close relationships with the company's suppliers and customers. These relationships are tenuous because they are usually noncontractual and nontransferable. Such companies usually sell at their book value plus a modest premium.

Book value is very common as a method of testing valuations for nonservice businesses for these reasons:

1. If the primary method of valuation is using a multiple of earnings, it is helpful to take the industry average of the book value multiples of other companies recently sold. Book value serves as a reference point. Some buyers will raise or lower their EBIT multiple for valuation purposes based on the relationship to the proposed selling price; some buyers will use only multiples of 4.5 to 5 times EBIT. If book value is higher than half the selling price, some buyers will use a 5 to 6 multiple.

2. By pegging the purchase price to a multiple of book value as of the date a purchase and sale agreement has been signed, the buyer is protected against a decline in the value of the business between the signing of the purchase and sale agreement and the completion date of due diligence.

When the book value technique is used, there is an important variation that a seller will probably want the buyer to consider. The assets may have a far greater value if the values are recast to reflect fair market value for machinery, equipment, buildings, and land. Also, the inventory might be adjusted to reflect current values and to pick up items that have been written off in order to minimize taxes. The buyer must also determine that all the assets are actually earning money for the business. If they are not, he or she should request an adjustment in the purchase price to reflect this condition.

VALUATION TECHNIQUE 3: DISCOUNTED CASH FLOW

Discounted cash flow is what someone is willing to pay today in order to receive the anticipated cash flow in future years. It is the method most often used by large investment banks and consulting and accounting firms. The discount rate is based on the level of risk of the business and the opportunity cost of capital. In other words, it is the return you can earn by investing your money elsewhere.

In his book *Creating Shareholder Value*, Alfred Rappaport states:

> The appropriate rate for discounting the company's cash flow stream is the weighted average of the costs of debt and equity capital. For example, if a company's after tax cost of debt is 6% and its estimated cost of equity is 16% and it plans to raise capital 20% by way of debt and 80% by way of equity, it computes the cost of capital at 14% as follows:

	Weight	Cost	Weighted Cost
Debt	20%	6%	1.2%
Equity	80%	16%	12.8%
Cost of Capital			14.0%

The use of discounted cash flow is a hotly debated subject among those in the mergers and acquisitions business, particularly in the middle market. Its use is widely accepted with larger companies because it provides a rational economic framework for valuing acquisitions in that marketplace.

In the book *Mergers & Acquisitions: A Valuation Handbook*, Joseph H. Marren states,

> One of the complexities with using the net present value method is that a target company's future cash flow depends on the method of acquisition and the purchase price. How? A target company's future cash flows are directly impacted by the taxes it will pay. The taxes it will pay depend on the company's taxable income. And the company's taxable income will depend, in part, on its taxable deductions for depreciation and the amortization of intangible assets. Such deductions depend on the target's tax basis for its assets, which in turn depend directly on the purchase price paid for the business.

Other opponents of the discounted cash flow method do not believe in paying for earnings that are not earned. Furthermore, the projections are speculative, and the selection of the discount rate is somewhat subjective. Nevertheless, it is important to mention this method, as it is one of the most popular methods for analyzing large companies. Its use is more appropriate for determining shareholder value than for valuing acquisitions.

VALUATION TECHNIQUE 4: SERVICE COMPANIES

The most important asset of a service company is its employees, from senior management to the most recent hiree. An equally important asset is its customers. The third major asset is the business system utilized by the company. This section focuses on middle-market service companies with sales of from $2 to $150 million.

Such service companies are very difficult to value, since they are highly dependent on the personal relationships of the management and its customers. In talking to the owner of a very profitable public relations firm who wanted to sell her company, I was stunned to hear that she not only got up for work every morning at 4:30 A.M. but was responsible for securing every new account in the agency. Even though she would stay on for a period after the business was sold, this superwoman was almost irreplaceable!

The company had $3 million of annual billings and reconstructed net before tax of about $300,000. Is this business worth $1.5 million? Possibly, but more important is the payout period and the extent to which the owner will remain in the business to retain the key accounts and teach the new CEO how to run the business. The most critical issue is the retention of the existing accounts, and for this reason the purchase agreement might be constructed as follows:

Payment at closing	$ 500,000
Payment in 1 year	333,000
Payment in 2 years	333,000
Payment in 3 years	333,000
Total	$1,500,000

Conditions:

1. Owner works for two years at base salary or for one year plus two years as a consultant.

2. Any loss of an account existing at the time of closing will reduce payout by 50 percent of one year's billing of that account.

3. A loss in the third year will reduce the payout by 25 percent of one year's billing.

Service businesses are varied, and for this reason it is very difficult to generalize valuation techniques that will cover all situations. Glenn Desmond, in his book *Handbook of Small Business Valuations*, (contact

Business Brokerage Press, P.O. Box 247, Concord, Mass. 01742) lists some of the advantages of using rules of thumb or formulas for small service businesses:

1. They are market derived and provide market comparisons.
2. They provide a uniform guide and a range of values.
3. They are easy to use and can be used for preliminary value estimates.

The disadvantage of using rules of thumb is that they are general in nature and there is no single, all-purpose formula.

In the book *Guide to Business Valuations* by Fishman, Pratt, Griffith, and Wilson, it is stated that "rules of thumb should not be used by themselves. They may, however, be useful in assessing the reasonableness of valuations based on other methods." Some examples of rules of thumb are:

Janitorial service:
4 times monthly gross billings plus equipment and inventory.

Travel agency:
35 percent of annual gross sales plus furniture and fixtures.

VALUATION TECHNIQUE 5: USING BUSINESS APPRAISERS

I have seen numerous buyers spend a large portion of their personal net worth to buy a company without receiving expert opinion from professionals in the M & A field. Needless to say, some of these businesses failed largely because the buyer overpaid when going into the deal. One does not have to hire an appraiser to put together a $5,000 to $10,000 "bulletproof" document that is defensible in court. You can hire an appraiser for $150 to $200 per hour to give you a verbal opinion. You might also want to consult on an hourly basis with specialist appraisers who concentrate in providing values of machinery and equipment, inventories, or real estate and buildings.

One of the saddest stories of a business buyer involved one of my closest and oldest friends. He had come from a broken home and had been unable to afford to continue at Andover Academy. He finished his last two years in high school in Texas but was able to earn a scholarship to Yale. After Yale, my friend had a thirty-year successful career at IBM. Upon reaching age fifty-five, he sought to fulfill his lifelong dream of owning a business. In 1988, he bought a small distributorship in

Pennsylvania that sold lockers, stadium seats, and warehouse storage racks. Like many marketing- and sales-oriented people, he drew a "hockey stick" type of sales projection and had grand designs for growth. But he made the fatal mistake of paying too much for the business. With dreams of success, he mortgaged his home, pooled his life savings, and left his secure job. The rest is history. The economy collapsed, the building business tumbled, and in two years he went under. Chapter 11, Chapter 7, the end of a chapter. The experience was almost life-shattering.

Many years later my friend stopped by my office seeking my advice on his new business. I could not help but ask what lessons he had learned from his failed venture. Obviously he had thought about this question before because he did not hesitate to rattle off the following response:

1. Do not stray from the business field in which you have experience. (In his case, he had gone from a high-tech background to a low-tech business of distributing lockers, stadium seats, and storage racks. He had gone from a white-collar to a blue-collar culture, a difficult transition to make.)

2. Do not acquire a company if you will be undercapitalized at the beginning of your ownership. (In his case, he had felt that the increased revenue he could generate from doubling his sales would cover the high debt load.)

3. Be sure you have highly competent people in the business.

4. Hire a business appraiser to assist you in determining how much you should pay for the business.

There are lessons to be learned by all of us, no matter how old or experienced we are—including, of course, myself. One of my important business colleagues, Jim Tonra of McLaughlin & Tonra in Wellesley, Massachusetts, has some very sage advice for business buyers. "Don't be afraid to consult your friends who have a sound business background in order to obtain their unbiased professional opinion on a deal you might be considering." I am sure that the tragedy described above could have been avoided if my friend had followed Jim Tonra's advice.

VALUATION TECHNIQUE 6: COMMON SENSE IN BUSINESS VALUATION

While I am not a professional business appraiser, I have been retained from time to time to value a company. I remember one episode where a plumbing supply distributor had to be valued because of the family owners' impending divorce. This distributor's sales had deteriorated from $8 million to $4.3 million in just a few years, and profits had gone from positive to negative. The company carried well-known OEM product lines, and at one time had had six branch outlets. It had been one of the leading plumbing supply houses in New England.

The divorce was headed for court, and yours truly was to be one of the key witnesses for placing a value on the couple's business. I was not a member of either the Institute of Business Appraisers or the American Society of Appraisers, and, in fact, my entire educational credentials were suspect. I was, however, a "somewhat seasoned" business intermediary who had sold three of his own businesses. All this hoopla is not about how difficult this valuation assignment had become, but simply about how to approach a valuation when one does not have the appropriate experience as an appraiser.

The method I used in preparing my written valuation was so simple it was just a matter of common sense. My client was well known in the plumbing supply business, having served on the board of the National Plumbing Supply Association. Working in conjunction with him, I called more than twenty owners of other plumbing supply distributors. I asked them if they had bought or sold any similar businesses and to share with me their knowledge as to the basis of their valuation. Inasmuch as plumbing supply distribution is similar to most other distributorships, 85 percent of the assets were in either inventory or receivables. Furthermore, it is a personal relationship business, with both vendors and customers having virtually no long-term exclusives.

Based on the above, I documented every conversation and came to the conclusion that my client's business was worth book value plus a 10 percent goodwill premium on the condition that the inventory and receivables were fairly current. Fortunately, like so many litigation cases, the divorce matter was settled out of court the day before the trial, so I never had to defend my appraisal. Nevertheless, I was prepared to base my valuation on the accepted wisdom of my client's peers.

OTHER VALUATION TECHNIQUES

Edmund Sears, a corporate valuation expert from the Benchmark Consulting Group in Boston, lists the major approaches to valuation as follows:

1. Cost-based approaches
   A. Book value
   B. Adjusted book value
   C. Liquidation value
2. Market approaches using comparables
   A. Price to earnings
   B. Price to pretax earnings
   C. Price to cash flow
   D. Price to book value
3. Income approaches:
   A. Capitalization of earnings
   B. Excess earnings methods
   C. Discounted future earnings
   D. Discounted future cash flow

Sears states that appraisals must be done with full knowledge of the facts, circumstances, and all relevant factors pertaining to the subject company. A particular valuation technique that is appropriate for one company at one point in time may not be appropriate for that company at another point of time or for another company at any time.

VALUATION ADJUSTMENTS

Recasting the financials is a major part of the valuation process. Such adjustments involve add-backs to the income statement and represent expenses that a new buyer would find unnecessary or discretionary, so that the recast EBIT would be higher for a new owner.

Let us assume that a company had $20 million in sales and had a reported EBIT of $1 million. The following adjustments will increase the EBIT:

Excess compensation	$ 200,000
Condominium expense	50,000
Travel and entertainment	50,000
Above-market factory rental	50,000
Excess automobile expense	20,000
Pension plan contributions	80,000
Total	$ 450,000
Adjusted EBIT	$1,450,000

If the appraiser were using a multiple of 5 for income valuation purposes, the above adjustments would increase the value of the company from $5 million (EBIT of $1 million × 5) to $7.25 million (adjusted EBIT of $1.45 million × 5).

Just as adjustments are made to the income statement, one should also make adjustments to the balance sheet by appraising the assets at current market value:

Assets	Book Value	Market Value
Machinery and Equipment	$ 500,000	$2,000,000
Real estate	500,000	1,000,000
Automobiles	50,000	100,000
Goodwill	350,000	—
		3,100,000
Stated book value		(1,400,000)
Increase in book value		$1,700,000

If one were using a multiple of 1.5 times book value for valuation purposes, the above adjustments would increase the value of the company by $2,550,000 ($1.7 million × 1.5).

VALUATION CASE STUDY: DEAL STRUCTURING FOR A SERVICE COMPANY

In February 1988, the two owners of a Massachusetts surveying company decided to sell the business. The previous year had been the height of the real estate boom in New England. The owners had each taken out $500,000 from the company, which was organized as a Subchapter S corporation.

The potential buyers structured their offer as follows:

1. Acquirer to buy all of the issued and outstanding stock of the company for $2 million plus a five-year noncompete agreement.

2. $1.5 million cash at closing, with the balance to be paid in the form of a five-year note with annual principal payments of $100,000 and interest on the balance at the prime rate plus 2 percent.

3. Owners to remain with the business for one year at annual compensation of $100,000 each. The purchase price, therefore, was 2.5 × adjusted EBIT ($1 million − $200,000 = $800,000 × 2.5 = $2 million).

4. After the one-year employment contract, the sellers to agree not to compete with the business for five years. They would be compensated for this assurance with a cash payment, beginning after each of the first five years of the contract, calculated as a percentage of the company's previous year's EBIT as follows:

Increment	EBIT	Percent to Sellers
First	$400,000	0
Second	$400,000	30
Over	$800,000	15

5. During the first five years following the purchase, the sellers would be responsible for the payment of any contingent liability or claim that arose prior to the sale of the business.

The sellers refused this offer in lieu of a competing offer of $2,000,000 cash at closing without notes or contingency payments. Ironically, the Massachusetts real estate market plunged and took this highly profitable surveying business into bankruptcy several years later. The lesson here is that it is important to structure an acquisition to anticipate unexpected events, including competition from former employees and declines in the economy. The potential buyers who missed out on this deal were mighty glad that they did. Their safety net, ultimately, was the deal they structured.

VALUATION CASE STUDY: THE WOODCRAFT COMPANY

The Woodcraft Company Incorporated (WCI) was founded in 1963 by Philip Davis, now sixty years old. Phil and his wife run the business but recently have tapered back to working three days per week. WCI's basic business is library shelving, preschool furniture, lockers, and easels. Its products are priced in the medium-high range. The company offers 125 separate items. Davis believes that there are basically five competitors.

Sales are $3 million annually. Peak sales three years ago were just over $4 million. The company sells mainly through distributors, and sales efforts are mostly by telephone. Operating income, after officers' salaries of $400,000, is just under 5 percent. The company operates in a 40,000-square-foot multistory plant in Virginia. There are forty employees. Following a review of the financials, what price would you place on this company and how would you structure your offer?

Income Statement
(in Thousands)

	1994	1993	1992
Sales	$3,200	$3,000	$4,000
Gross profit	1,000	1,100	1,700
SG&A	(850)	(700)	(800)
Operating income	150	400	900
Officers' salaries	400	350	250
Owner replacements	(150)	(150)	(150)
Adjusted earnings	500	600	1,000

Balance Sheet
(in Thousands)

Assets		Liabilities	
Cash	$ 300	Payables	$ 50
Accounts receivable	540	Notes	10
Prepaid expenses	100		
Inventory	1,060		
Current assets	$2,000	Current liabilities	$ 60
Machinery	600		
Automobiles	50	Long-term debt	10
Real estate	150		
Total fixed assets	800	Stock	130
Depreciation	(500)	Retained earnings	2,100
Total assets	$2,300	Total liabilities and equity	$2,300

The seller will not allow you to scrutinize the financial records until you have made a preliminary offer. A quick observation shows the following:

1. Sales are off 25 percent in the past two years, partly because of the recession in the early 1990s, which affected library spending. Gross profit margins have gone from 42 percent in 1992 to 31 percent in 1994. Phil Davis explains that this is due to more

distributor sales than direct sales to libraries. Also, the Davises are taking out $150,000 more in salaries; all of which result in a 50 percent decline in adjusted earnings.

2. The balance sheet is incredibly strong if you look at the working capital plus impressive retained earnings and very little long-term debt.

3. There is little risk of corporate liability if you buy stock instead of assets, a Phil Davis requirement.

4. You like the company because it has a niche position with a long history of profitable operation and is presently being undermanaged.

What is your initial offer on both price and terms?

Answer: You offer $2.5 million based on a stock sale. You are thereby buying the entire balance sheet, including assets and liabilities. Your offer is a multiple of 5 times reconstructed operating income or one times book value of $2,230,000 plus goodwill of $270,000.

Response: Phil Davis accepts your offer as long as it is all cash at closing. You agree subject to due diligence.

Due diligence: During your detailed examination of the financials of WCI, you find that one major customer accounts for 55 percent of total sales and receives extended ninety-day credit terms. You then revise your offer based on the same purchase price but with half cash at closing. The balance of $1,250,000 payable at $250,000 per year is conditioned on your retaining this customer's account.

Conclusion: Phil Davis turns down your offer, as the five-year payout period is beyond his comfort level. He takes the business off the market and plans to maximize his income from the company for as long as possible. Many negotiations end up this way, with companies becoming "cash cows" for their stockholders.

VALUATIONS: PRIVATE VS. PUBLIC COMPANIES

Edmund Sears states in an article appearing in *M & A Today* that

> usually the stock market pricing of public company equities guides the valuation of private companies: IRS R4 Revenue Ruling 59-60 specifies that the market valuation of comparable public companies be one of

the eight valuation factors specified for consideration. Even in the best of times, private companies are a long term investment and an extremely illiquid one. It takes a long time to make a private company acquisition and often even longer to get out of it. Transaction costs are high and consequently private companies normally sell at substantially lower prices than those in a stock market which is highly liquid, is short-term in outlook, and has low transaction costs.

Most private companies are substantially smaller than even the small capitalization public companies. Frequently, they operate locally or regionally rather than nationally and internationally. Further, they are likely to have fewer products or product lines and less diversified market segments. All these characteristics make private companies a much higher risk investment but risk for which the new owners are compensated for with higher rates of return derived from their owner initial investment. The market for private companies is not an extension of the market for public companies. It is a different market with different characteristics which have to be taken into account when looking at price.

VALUATION TECHNIQUES: AN ASTUTE BUYER

George Berbeco is the owner of the Devon Group in Waltham, Massachusetts, a buyout company. The Devon Group has acquired three companies in the past two years, and I consider George to be a very savvy and astute buyer. He has three questions that he addresses early in the valuation process:

1. Is acquisition of the business worth the effort involved?

2. Are the reported earnings really there? For example, if the target company is a divestment, have all the overhead costs been included?

3. Are the earnings going to continue? Beware of "hockey stick" projections, with current sales representing the blade and projections the start of the stick, as they are almost always overly optimistic. For this reason, buyout companies place more emphasis on potential cost savings than on sales growth.

Numerous books have been written on the subject of valuing companies. It is an incredibly complex subject because there are so many variables involved that affect the buyer's offer and therefore the net after-tax dollars received by the seller. As stated by Joseph E. Myss, "Sellers sell the future and buyers buy the past! Sellers are selling opportunity, whereas buyers are buying a track record." With this fundamental difference in approach on the table, one can see why buyers and sellers have a different perception as to value.

CHAPTER 9

Finding the Deal

There are basically six distinct steps in buying a business:

Assessing your strategy.
Finding the right company.
Pricing the business.
Structuring the transaction.
Financing the purchase.
Closing the deal.

Unless one is lucky or opportunistically falls into the right situation, finding the right company to buy is by far the most difficult of the six steps. Most individual buyers who spend full time seeking a middle-market business to buy take from six months to two years before a deal is completed. Most well-organized corporate buyers take three to six months to find an acquisition and three to six months to close the deal, or a year on the outside. A less experienced and less qualified individual will generally take twice as long.

INTENSITY
In the Harvard Business School case study 9-385-330 copyrighted in 1985, *Buying an Existing Business: The Search Process*, the authors make the distinction between *casual* and *serious* search.

> A serious and realistic search will significantly increase the probability of identifying and negotiating opportunities of interest to you.

Therefore, it is imperative to evaluate your motives, expectations, and risk profile. This self-assessment will probably place you in one of three broad search categories: serious and realistic; casual and realistic; and unrealistic.

The serious and realistic search involves:
- High level of commitment to the search
- Expectations consistent with the degree of effort
- Willingness to:
  - Risk at least some personal wealth/security
  - Deeply research the target industry
  - Be patient and wait for the "right" opportunity
  - Move quickly and decisively as needed
  - Pursue the search full-time if needed

The casual and realistic search involves:
- Expectations consistent with degree of effort, but
- Not a high level of commitment to the search
- Less willingness to move quickly or decisively on opportunities
- No specified time horizon for search
- Not being overly hungry to control one's own firm

The unrealistic search involves:
- Objectives inconsistent with level of commitment
- Waiting for a great deal to fall in place
- Looking for bargains and short-cuts

While there is nothing wrong with being a casual shopper (many have found excellent deals), the number and quality of the deals available often reflect the quality and intensity of the search. For example, almost everyone you meet in your search will size you up at your initial encounter, because intermediaries and sellers are usually reluctant to invest time unless they feel there is a reasonable chance you will follow through with your plans. Thus, the better you have assessed yourself, the easier it will be to convince others of the realism of your intentions and get them to work productively for or with you.

WORK TOOLS

In an article, Franklin Wyman, chairman of O'Conor, Wright Wyman, Inc. a Boston intermediary, cited the following:

Detailed acquisition criteria against which you will screen acquisition possibilities.

Knowledge of the sources of business information, such as state manu-facturing and service directories, trade publications, trade show listings, chamber of commerce membership directories, the Dun & Bradstreet *Million Dollar Directory, Wards Business Directory,* and the *Corporate Technology Directory,* to name just a few.

Contribution to your search efforts by your banker, lawyer, and accountant.

A *professional adviser* such as an intermediary who will assist in the search process as well as act in an advisory role in valuation, structuring, and negotiation.

A *search technique* that will disqualify sellers with unreasonable ask-ing prices or owners merely looking for a free valuation of their company.

Negotiating skills to convince hesitant sellers that they should sell to you.

Creativity to structure the transaction in order to obtain the greatest tax advantage to the seller and to minimize the drain on your personal resources. Professional help is usually necessary in this case.

If you add a persistent attitude to the above seven work tools, you should have a winning combination.

TURNING OVER STONES

In today's fast-moving mergers and acquisitions market, good middle-market manufacturing companies that are officially for sale will probably be presented first to synergistic buyers. Historically, synergistic buyers are usually willing to pay more for a company than competitors, financial buyers, or individuals. Therefore, individual buyers are initially not apt to get a chance at buying these good middle-market manufacturers.

If an individual buyer does get a chance to make an offer on such a company, presumably after the business was shown to synergistic buyers, one has to ask whether the business is overpriced or whether there are inherent problems with the business, such as environmental problems.

By now, you have probably begun to realize how difficult it is to buy a good middle-market company. What is more evident is that you approach this situation realizing that you have to position yourself differ-ently from your competition. Your competition includes both corporate buyers and other individual buyers. The market for buying and selling businesses is *not* an efficient market like the real estate market, where properties are listed, advertised, and priced on full knowledge of previous comparable sales. The market for businesses is an inefficient market. For example, information is difficult to obtain, there are few listings, prices of private sales are not published, emotional circumstances thwart transactions, etc.

The above prologue is a way of setting the stage for *turning over stones*, which refers to seeking companies that are officially "not for sale." It is the category of "not for sale" companies that has the greatest potential for individual buyers.

First, when you uncover these gems, there is a good chance that you will not be competing with other buyers.

Second, if you are lucky enough to approach the buyer at the right time, when he or she is burned out and ready to sell, you just might have the chemistry and offer enough money to do the deal.

Third, you have an excellent chance to arouse the owner's interest if you have a respectable background in a similar industry. A former CEO of Ginn & Company, a $75 million textbook division of Xerox, had no problem visiting smaller regional publishers and/or specialty printers.

Consulting Leads to Prospective Sellers

Numerous corporate refugees from the executive level of *Fortune* 1000 companies become consultants for relatively small firms. Nevertheless, they really want to become owners of their own company.

What better way is there for a prospective business buyer to see deal flow than to work for none other than a mergers and acquisitions firm? Ethically it is imperative that the buyer's intentions are known up-front. If the buyer does buy a company through this exposure, he or she will pay a commission to the firm almost as if he or she were a regular client.

The Johnny Appleseed Approach

Johnny Appleseed, a pioneer who was a legendary figure in American history, spread apple seeds from Massachusetts to Ohio by freely casting them from side to side as he walked the territory.

The Johnny Appleseed approach is a pun. The implication is that an individual buyer who works out of his house sets out to buy a business. He equips himself with business cards, a resume, and a criteria sheet. Initially he has lots of energy. He visits lawyers, bankers, accountants, brokers, intermediaries, investment bankers, and friends. He attends breakfasts and luncheons at the Association for Corporate Growth, the Planning Forum, venture groups, the Turnaround Management Association, etc. He writes letters to friends, companies, and all his contacts—then waits for a response.

If this individual buyer is lucky, he will receive some positive responses after six months of effort, particularly if he diligently follows up all his contacts. My experience, however, is that this approach generally does not work. It is not focused, it is not targeted, and it is too broad. Occasionally the Johnny Appleseed approach is successful, but generally it is considered unprofessional and ineffective.

Family Businesses

Family businesses are a natural target for acquisition, particularly if you have a close relative who owns a desirable company.

According to a comprehensive study by the Gallup Organization for the Massachusetts Mutual Life Insurance Company, family businesses represent nearly 50 percent of the gross domestic product and 85 percent of all business enterprises in North America grossing between $5 million and $180 million. Additionally, this study states that 65 percent of family owners intend to pass their ownership position in the business to a close relative. Over the next decade, many family businesses will face succession and estate planning issues which may lead to a change of ownership.

This analysis clearly indicates that if your parents, in-laws, and/or close relatives own a business, you are probably in a favorable position to buy their company (if, of course, they are receptive to your proposal). Mixing business with family affairs can have its problems. On the other hand, obviously there are an enormous number of successful family businesses that are transferred to the next generation. Beware, however; only one-third of these family businesses successfully survive in the family through the second generation.

Direct Mail

Mainsource Corporation, Berwyn, Pennsylvania, 215-644-6743, is a direct marketing expert for intermediaries. According to Robert Groag of Mainsource, sellers are available in large numbers if properly approached. This means hitting the right strategic, critical buttons that make business owners respond.

According to Groag, in order to properly construct an effective direct mail campaign, it is important to know the most common reasons business owners consider selling, i.e., burnout, boredom, lack of growth capital. Second, it is important to know the most common considerations demanded by sellers for the sale of their business, i.e., full value for their company, cash at closing, future opportunity for key employees, etc.

DEAL FLOW

Developing a strong positive deal flow is the key to finding the deal. The secret is to increase the number and quality of the deals for you to analyze. Just finding the deals is a full-time job. Bear in mind that if you receive a number of leads from an intermediary who is not on retainer with you, he or she will eventually become discouraged and lose interest unless you pursue these leads vigorously.

Two individual buyers in the Boston area each have $2 million to invest in a business. That's a lot of money even in this day and age! Both of them are totally reluctant to pay an intermediary a retainer to speed up the search process; yet they have respectively spent over two and four years looking for a business to buy.

Vanderbilt once commented that if you are concerned about the financial upkeep of a sailboat, which in his day was made of wood, don't buy one. On a similar rationale, my feeling is that if you can't afford to retain an intermediary, you can't afford to buy a business. If you save all your money for a closing, you may not have one!

Deal flow is probably the most commonly discussed subject for a business buyer. The following statistics of two individual buyers, Mike Stevens and Phil Harris, certainly emphasize the importance of having a steady source of deals.

Tabulation of Deal Flow Over Two Years

	Mike Stevens	Phil Harris
Companies looked at	428	250
Companies liked	34	20
Offers	6	10
Negotiated	3	4
Bought	1	1

Somerset Capital Corporation of Waltham, Massachusetts, is a private investment firm that focuses on companies with purchase prices of $7 to $100 million. In its Statement of Mission, it states:

> Although increasingly we are approaching companies directly, intermediaries are still the primary source of our deals. Deal flow from intermediaries is evenly divided between smaller investment banks and business brokers. We have de-emphasized dealing with major Wall Street firms, because we have little interest in participating in auctions. A minor source of deals is professional advisors, such as accountants

and attorneys. As our organization grows, marketing will be emphasized so that our deal flow increases to fill our new level of capacity. Our goals for deal flow and companies acquired are as follows:

	Deal flow	Businesses acquired
1994	250	1
1995	350	2
1996	450	2
1997	600	2
1998	750	3

The point of comparing the figures of the two individuals and Somerset Capital is that while Somerset expects to acquire a company in one year, it usually takes very qualified individuals two years. Part of the reason for the difference is that individuals do not have the resources or the experience in maximizing deal flow of experienced investment firms. The above analysis also implies the importance of deal flow.

CONSOLIDATINGS

One avenue to building a sizable company is to buy up "mom and pop" operations in fragmented businesses and consolidate them into one company.

Here are a few examples: All Seasons Services Inc. in Braintree, Massachusetts, has $75 million in sales, mostly in the vending machine business. Every year All Seasons buys small mom and pop vending companies that are struggling financially and/or whose owner wants to retire. Since the vending machine business is very much relationship-driven, it is often easier to buy accounts through acquisition than to hope that your sales force will eventually win the business.

Mindis International Recycling, a metal recycling company headquartered in Atlanta, has grown to over $100 million in sales mostly by buying local scrap yards.

The *Fortune* 500 companies Blockbuster and General Cinema started their original growth by buying individual video stores and movie theaters and/or small chains. While buying a small single-standing dry cleaning business, for example, may not be to your liking, it could be challenging if your game plan is to buy other dry cleaning businesses in surrounding towns.

Buying and consolidating mom and pop companies is a viable way to grow through acquisition.

VENTURE CAPITAL COMPANIES

Traditionally, venture capital funds have a ten-year life cycle, at which time the venture capital partnership terminates. The goal, therefore, is for these funds to resolve their investments either by having the companies go public, selling out, or liquidating the companies.

More specifically, according to Gordon Baty of Zero Stage Capital of Cambridge, Massachusetts, the disasters usually pop up within two years of the venture capitalists' initial investment. The winning companies are apparent within four years. The balance of most venture capital holdings is the underperforming companies, commonly known as the "living dead." It is these latter companies that require the venture capitalists' money, time, and energy, with their best hope being to just get their original investment back.

Baty goes on to say that these underperforming investments are one of the biggest problems for venture capitalists. By nature, venture capitalists are eternal optimists and reluctant to admit defeat. However, they have limited options with these underperforming investments. They can give their stock back to the company's owners as a total writeoff, sell their shares at a low price, liquidate the company, or convert their general partnership to a limited partnership.

Unlike many family businesses, whose owners often have second thoughts about selling when the negotiations begin, venture capitalists are decisive about selling and usually have placed a realistic valuation on the company. Venture capitalists' portfolio companies will have audited financials, a clean set of books, a limited number of shareholders, and no suspect "side deals" with vendors.

With approximately a hundred venture capital firms in Boston alone, there is an opportunity for individuals to acquire underperforming companies where the company may have turned the corner but the stockholders have lost patience. To do so, the individual should certainly qualify himself or herself as a viable buyer, both financially and operationally.

DIVESTMENTS

For public companies, the annual statistics of the M & A business are readily available. Historically, between 40 and 50 percent of the transactions in this marketplace are divestments. With both public and private companies, there are opportunities to acquire small divisions that do not fit the parent company's core business, that are too small for the parent company, and/or that are appendages from other acquisitions made by the parent company.

If you are capable of raising a significant amount of equity either from your own resources or in partnership with others, then you are in a position to approach directors of corporate development of companies that own numerous divisions. Depending on the target's size, the target's leverageability, and your negotiating skills, anywhere from $500,000 to $2 million of equity will put you in the game.

Corporate spin-offs are desirable candidates because once the directors decide to sell a division, they usually carry through with it. Unlike the owners of many family-owned businesses, they do not have seller's remorse and change their mind. Also, divestments have a fair chance of being valued reasonably because the parent company knows what other comparable companies sell for. If the spin-off is from a public company, you will have the advantage of receiving audited financials instead of the loose and sloppy record keeping and unaudited statements usually provided by family businesses. You will have to recast the financials to adjust for the parent company's overhead allocations to the division. Also, for a spin-off from a public company, you probably will be referred to the company's investment banker, who will determine whether you are a qualified buyer. Since the selling process is in the hands of professionals, you will be presented with a thorough selling memorandum, machinery, equipment, and real estate appraisals; a list of assets that will be sold or retained; and maybe a predocumentation of warranties and representations. You will be required to submit your offer quickly, and so if you are inexperienced in the M & A process, be sure the others on your acquisition team are not rookies too.

Spin-offs are almost always put out to bid, and so you will be competing with other potential buyers. The parent company will rarely accept buyer's notes unless the buyer is a formidable company, so be prepared to offer all cash. You are more likely to get the director of corporate development's attention if you present yourself as a buyout group rather than as an individual. Another possibility is to collaborate with the existing management team of the divesting company. The existing management team usually has credibility because of their specific experience and knowledge of that particular business. However, they are often risk-averse and lack sufficient capital to complete a transaction. If you teamed up with the existing management team such that they invested some money and you gave up some ownership, then you could approach an asset-based lender with a plan that would be very attractive.

There are numerous ways to determine which companies have divisions. If you join the Association for Corporate Growth (see Chapter 25), you will receive a directory of the 3000 members in 25 chapters around the country. The group focuses on mergers and acquisitions, and the directory specifies each member's position. In the Boston chapter, for example, there are approximately twenty directors of corporate development.

Another way to track down companies with divisions is to ask your local library if it carries annual reports of various local companies. If it does not, then you can refer to the manufacturers directory for your particular state. If you skim through the directory, it will usually indicate if a listed company is a subsidiary of some parent company.

In the Boston area there are a number of large holding companies like Standex International, Dynatech, and EG&G that have sales from $600 million to $3 billion, yet own a few subsidiaries with sales in the $5 to $10 million range. In 1993, Dynatech reassessed its corporate strategy and put four companies on the block at the same time.

One small medical device manufacturer in Massachusetts was running out of capital. It had two product lines; one had FDA approval and FDA approval on the other line was pending. Since the company had spent most of its capital on developing its products, it had virtually no money left to properly market and promote the FDA-approved product.

Since the product with the biggest potential was the one with FDA approval pending, the company was forced to sell the product line that was already generating sales. The most interesting aspect of this deal was its structure. The medical device company decided to sell the product line for $3 million but retain the right to manufacture the product at cost plus 15 percent for a period of time. The buyer was able to acquire an excellent line of medical products with very high gross margins. With an additional investment for marketing, the buyer could concentrate on selling, since the manufacturing was to remain with the seller for a period of time. The seller received the cash it desperately needed for its potentially greater product, but it also received a profitable manufacturing contract until its new product was up and running.

TURNAROUNDS

Turnarounds have been called a growth industry for investors. The best targets are companies that have not yet filed for Chapter 11 bankruptcy. According to John Whitney, professor at the Columbia University School of Business, "the heart of the matter is fixing problems and understanding operations."

Paul Hunn, senior vice president of Manufacturers Hanover Trust, uses the following four questions as his initial screen before advancing additional debt to a troubled company:

Is the company intrinsically viable?
Is good management now in place?
Can the company return to positive cash flow in six months?
Can it return to solid, honest profitability within two years?

Among the assets to look for in a turnaround, according to John Whitney, are the following:

Excellent product line or service
Sound distribution network and customer base
Proprietary technology
Manufacturing know-how
Skilled workforce
Licenses, patents, or distribution agreements

Whitney goes on to say: "Buyers should not delude themselves into buying a 'bargain' when the only hope is for short-term improvement through balance sheet management. On-the-job training for new owners is risky and expensive, especially for an enterprise as fragile as a turnaround." Relationships with bankers, vendors, customers, and employees are tenuous at best. The balance sheet should be restructured before the deal is consummated in such ways as

Swapping some of the debt for equity.
Lowering interest rates for a period of time and extending maturities.
Negotiating accounts payable downward.

Even though the turnaround company is troubled, it should have a core activity generating positive cash flow from operations. Many troubled companies find themselves in a precarious position because their noncore businesses have substantially diverted their resources, such as their management, sales force, plant, and, of course, cash. According to Carl Youngman, senior partner at Conway & Youngman, a turnaround specialization firm in Wilmington, Massachusetts:

Unless the business has a reason to exist and is worth perpetuating, even to start the turnaround effort is a futile exercise. Once identified, the viable core business must be protected from the rest of the activities in the turnaround company. This protection often means a different set of rules (i.e., financing policies, capital budgets, and human resource issues) than for all other parts of the business.

Unless you are experienced in turnarounds, I certainly do not recommend that you buy a company in this position. You may have identified a few problem areas, such as an inadequate sales organization or inferior financial controls; however, there may be many other problems on the factory floor or with quality control that you have overlooked.

GENERAL OBSERVATIONS FROM BRIAN KNIGHT

Brian Knight is the president of Country Business Inc., a ten-office business brokerage firm that specializes in the purchase and sale of small and midsize companies. While Country Business sells more businesses with sales of less than $1 million than middle-market companies ($1 million to $100 million in sales), it is recognized as selling more businesses in Maine, New Hampshire, and Vermont than any other intermediary.

Knight wrote the book *Buy the Right Business—At the Right Price*; however, the following information was delivered to the New York Venture Group during Knight's speech in September 1984 on "How to Find a Business to Buy."

The demand for small businesses far exceeds the supply. Screening telephone calls from Knight's Manchester Center, Vermont office, most inquirers are looking for small medium-tech manufacturers with a proprietary product and a proven record of increasing revenues and profits. The buyers would like to move to the Stratton, Vermont area and have a relatively short commute to the target manufacturing company. The only problem is that there are very few manufacturers in Vermont, particularly in the Stratton area. What is available as businesses to buy in Vermont are hospitality and retail companies. The first lesson to be learned as a buyer is not to have *unrealistic expectations*.

Concurrent with the first lesson is deciding whether you should buy a company at all! Buying a company, much less finding a company to buy, does not suit everyone, nor does it assure financial success. Buyers can and will succeed if they buy an excellent book on this subject, seek professional advice, and take their time (maybe two years).

Knight emphasizes that buyers should:

- Be self-analytical of their capabilities.
- Write down their acquisition criteria.
- Carefully interview and select a buying intermediary.
- Work on interpersonal skills with the potential seller.

For Country Business, the mission is to find good and profitable businesses, not to represent unprofitable businesses. Knight believes that the key to success in finding the right business to buy is the buyer's ability to commit to the above four items. If he or she can do so, success in finding the deal will be more likely.

SEEKING THE COMPANY THAT ISN'T FOR SALE

The following section was written by Stephen B. Blum, managing partner of KPMG Peat Marwick's Corporate Finance Group in New York, and reproduced by permission.

Finding desirable and profitable privately held companies whose owners will sell for reasonable prices constitutes a tough middle-market M & A hurdle.

Either owners fail to adjust to today's more modest selling prices, and therefore don't sell the company, or a controlled auction escalates the price beyond reason for many suitors. Most attractive businesses aren't on the block for precisely the same reasons that they're attractive; the trick is finding, contacting, and wooing the private business owners who haven't previously thought of selling.

Properly orchestrated, acquisition searches allow purchasers to sidestep auctions, so that the courtship can develop at a pace that both sides can live with. Finding the right seller almost always demands the same patience and ingenuity as finding the right purchaser.

Once you have narrowed the criteria for the acquisition and identified various target companies, the time comes to contact these companies directly and to measure the owners' willingness to talk. Remember, most owners haven't decided to sell their businesses. They may, in fact, have a powerful emotional attachment to their businesses.

Contact Tactics

Use an intermediary to perform an acquisition search.

1. Look at the manufacturers directory or the industry directory in which each target is listed. Often there is a list of officers,

bankers, accountants, law firms, and directors. In some cases, you may have a connection. For example, you may personally know the corporate lawyer or a director. If so, that person may be your starting point.

2. Carefully compose a letter to your contact, or to the apparent controlling shareholder. This letter can, for example, explain that the intermediary has been retained by XYZ Company, and that XYZ has reason to believe that a joint venture between the two companies could make sense. The intermediary might even enclose his or her client's brochure—if your client is ready to reveal its identity to the target. Using the words "joint venture" (or "strategic alliance") instead of "merger" or "acquisition" can put the target more at ease—but shouldn't be used if it is misleading.

3. Follow up by telephone within a few days at most. We all know that most companies have well-trained secretaries who often are your initial roadblock in reaching the CEO. Naturally, the secretary will immediately ask the nature of the call, "Does the president know you?" etc. The response might be, "I'm calling Mr._____ in connection with my letter dated _____." If you do not get through or get a return call, then perhaps one more call will help—preferably prior to 9:00 A.M., before the controlling shareholder's secretary arrives and before his or her day gets plugged with meetings. If you are unable to make progress by telephone, then you may have to attack differently—either by fax or by Federal Express. The more specific you can be in the communication, the better, but be aware that the more you find it necessary to refer to M & A, the more intimidating this may be to the owner.

4. Once you have established a dialogue with the target's owner, you should supplement telephone information with a direct meeting involving the owner and the potential buyer. You should push for this early, while there is momentum. Generally speaking, the immediate goal is to build chemistry between the two parties and agree on the best next step (an exchange of financial data, a lunchtime chat, a visit to the target's headquarters, etc.).

The best acquisition opportunities can be the least predictable, especially if the owners viewed them initially as "not for sale."

Gathering Information on Company for Sale

Assuming that you are visiting the owner and president of a manufacturing company for the first time and you have allocated two to three hours to ask questions and to tour the plant, gathering the following information is desirable.

Business

To break the ice, it is easiest for the owner to give you a quick historical overview of the company—when it was started, major changes and developments, etc. Ask the owner to track a typical order from point of entry—checking credit, entry into the system, schedule for manufacturing or stock item, etc.—in order to get a sense of how efficiently and thoroughly the company executes. Also, ask what the core business is, whether it is a niche business, what makes the business unique, and whether the business is seasonal or cyclical. Is the company a C or an S corporation?

Products

Ask for a description of the products, their price points, their market share, the rate at which new products are developed, the number of SKUs in the product line, and whether 20 percent of the products equal 80 percent of the sales and, conversely, whether 80 percent of the sales are to 20 percent of the customers. How are the products priced, i.e., mostly to market prices, to costs plus profit, or both?

Market

How big is the market? Is this a commodity business (price-driven)? Is it fragmented among lots of small companies, or is it affected by large *Fortune* 500 companies or by foreign competition? How fast is the market growing? What affects growth, e.g., the economy, the weather, military spending, etc.?

Sales

What are the sales for the past few years, and what are projected sales? Describe the average sales cycle from original sales call to receipt of order. What is the channel of distribution—direct sales, sales reps, distributors, catalog, telemarketing, direct mail, trade shows, etc.? What are the sales costs? Do you export or import, or have you considered strategic alliances or joint ventures? Tell me about the sales manager and the sales team. What is your return policy, and how large a factor are product returns on total sales?

Competition

Identify and describe the major competitors, i.e., their size, location, breadth of product line, and pricing. Do they have a competitive advantage, and if so, what is it (financial resources, automation, sales coverage, dealer network, longevity)? Is the competition national, international, regional, or all of the above? To what extent is this a relationship business, or will customers exhibit little loyalty? Are the customers apt to single-source, double-source, or more?

Plant/Manufacturing

How large is the plant? Is it leased or owned? What is the plant capacity? Could production be increased 50 percent in the same facility? How many production people and how many people altogether are there in the company? What are the sales per employee and how does that compare to the industry average (Robert Morris Associates industry analysis)? Is the manufacturing fully integrated, or is it subassembly? Who are the largest vendors, and what terms do you receive on their invoicing? Do you use "just in time" (JIT) inventory, and how much of your inventory is work in process (WIP)? What are the bottlenecks? Describe the quality control (QC). What is the reject rate? What are the labor rate, bonuses, benefits, and average age of the workforce (if it is fifty-five, this could be a problem)? What are the capital equipment needs in the next few years?

Management

Describe the management team's roles, i.e., CEO, CFO, COO, etc. As CEO, how do you allocate your time? What are your major problems and concerns? Who do you use for advisers, i.e., consultants, lawyers, accountants, etc.? As CEO, what are your strengths and shortcomings? What contractual arrangements or incentive plans do you have with the management team? Do you have a management chart?

R&D

How much time, effort, and money do you devote to new product development or new manufacturing process innovations? Does the company have any patents or licenses?

Financials

Are the financials certified? Does the company provide monthly financials? What *key benchmarks* do you use to monitor the company's progress, e.g., gross margin, inventory, inventory turnover, working capital, sales per employee? What percentage of your receivables are over ninety days? How do you handle collections? Do you take 2 percent net ten days on your payables? When and how do you implement price changes? Are all your major accounting functions computerized—purchases, sales, inventory, etc.? What sort of insurance liability does the company carry for potential customer claims? What are your financial projections, and how do you figure them out?

Selling the Business

Why is the company for sale? How long has the business been for sale? Are there other stockholders, and if so, what is the ownership breakdown? Does the owner have the authority to sell, or is it the decision of the board of directors? Are there other offers for the business? Who will be doing the negotiating? What is the rationale or methodology for determining the price of the business? Are there any add-backs or reconstructed earnings? What is the owner's total compensation? Is there any pending litigation or prior litigation? Are there any contractual obligations—to employees, vendors, customers, landlords, intermediaries; noncompete agreements; buy/sell agreements, etc.? Are there any "soft assets" like uncollectible receivables? Would the owner stay on for a transition period? Would the seller take a note as partial payment, subordinated to the bank or unsecured? Is there anything in the offer that is not negotiable, such as an asset versus a stock sale? Are there any violations with OSHA, EPA, unions (if any), etc.? Go over the financials line by line to be sure you understand each item and also to see if there is some possible restructuring of the balance sheet that will help you make a more realistic offer.

Consider removing the real estate if included.

Remove shareholders' receivables or payables.

Remove owners' assets, e.g., automobiles.

Disclose owners' perks.

Review reserves and accruals.

Final Questions

If you miraculously received $500,000 in the company, how would you use it?

How do you grow the business?

What differentiates this company from its competitors?

What is the culture of the company?

What is the company's most important resource?

What haven't we talked about that I should know or what have I overlooked?

Obtain Another Buyer's Target List

Boston is one of the major cities in the United States, and yet in many ways it is a closely knit community. As a result, if you are networking to buy a business, invariably you will meet others trying to do the same thing at one of the various business group meetings.

One unnamed person spent two years canvassing the area, identifying potential companies for sale, and building a database of 300 active accounts. This acquirer personally visited a majority of these companies and kept an ongoing history of his findings. When this person finally acquired a company, a small two-man buyout firm was so impressed with the work he had done over the two years that they bought the search list. The deal was structured with a certain amount of money up front for the list, plus more money if the buyout group closed on a company included on the list. Additionally, the buyout group agreed to give the seller of the list 5 percent of the stock of the acquired company.

The above scenario will work, but obviously the two parties have to have a high level of confidence and faith in each other. It becomes a "win-win" situation for both parties. This situation is just another example of what can be achieved by using innovative ideas.

CHAPTER 10

Use of Intermediaries

Executing an intelligent acquisition at a reasonable price is very difficult even for the experts. For an individual buyer, successfully acquiring a middle-market company can be extremely difficult, principally because of the buyer's lack of experience. Far and away, the biggest hurdle for the individual buyer is finding the deal.

Stephen Blum, managing partner of KPMG Peat Marwick's Corporate Finance Group in New York, states: "If you've decided to purchase a company, you face the question of whether and how to deal with intermediaries. Many buyers go it alone. Some mistrust intermediaries, some don't want to pay a transaction fee, and others assume that no intermediary would want to work with them ... but deciding to do without intermediaries can be risky."

The intermediary can help you in numerous areas, such as ascertaining the criteria, assembling the information, determining the price, structuring the deal, and negotiating the transaction, but many buyers need intermediaries most of all to help them find the deal.

The intermediary community is highly fragmented. As Stephen Blum wrote in his article "Dealing with Intermediaries,"

> The quality of intermediaries varies. The key issue in deciding whom to retain as an intermediary is which people will actually work with you. People matter most. One frequent problem is lack of experience. All too often, senior M & A advisers vanish after Day One, replaced by first- or second-year staffers. Another problem is lack of focus. Many so-called M & A advisers really spend most of their time in other activities such as real estate brokerage or business valuation.

One way to avoid problems with experience and lack of focus is to request a list of recent deals closed by the intermediary along with references to call. Just as in exploring any business relationship, past customers can tell you a great deal. By asking for a listing of recent deals, you will also find out whether the intermediary knows your industry. At a minimum, someone on the team should know the industry issues. Getting deals "closed" takes time. The person who will work with you day to day shouldn't be juggling more than one or two other major projects, or yours won't get enough attention.

Selling or purchasing a business is a personal process. The final test of your prospective M & A adviser should be how you get along. Someone who does not understand your needs will not be able to put the right deal together. Therefore it's essential that you meet and get to know your adviser before committing to the firm. Again: it's important that the person you meet be the person you'll actually work with.

In addition to Blum's comments, the following observations are noteworthy. There is a different skill set for buying than for selling companies. The principal functions of an intermediary *selling* a company are as follows:

- Valuing and placing a price range on the company.

- Writing a thorough selling memorandum to be shared with potential buyers.

- Being very careful about confidentiality with the buyers and carefully screening buyers before releasing information to be sure that they are sincerely interested, they have the financial capability to do the deal, and they have the authority to make the decision to buy the company.

- Identifying logical buyers, which are usually synergistic.

- Presenting the company to the buyer favorably.

- Receiving and analyzing offers, orchestrating the negotiations, and driving the deal to a successful closing.

The basic difference for an intermediary *buying* a company is that a more offensive mind-set is required. The intermediary should be aggressive, imaginative, tenacious, and charming. Bear in mind that unlike real estate, most companies that are bought are originally not for sale. Therefore, the buyer and his or her intermediary must be very proactive in approaching companies. Of course, there are many obstacles to overcome, such as the very simple one of just getting to talk to the target's owner. With barriers such as secretaries and voice mail, there is no assurance that you will be successful. There is even less assurance that the owner will be interested in even talking about selling the company, much less meeting personally with you.

An intermediary who represents buyers must be aggressive, imaginative, tenacious, and charming to be able to uncover "not for sale" companies whose owners will consider selling after all. Additionally, the intermediary has to be skillful and experienced. There are letter-writing and telephone techniques that are critical for bringing buyer and seller together successfully. One of the critical issues for an intermediary is how effectively he "packages" his buying client. A good intermediary will influence the client to create a company with specific acquisition criteria that match the buyer's background. One example is Arnie Kovall, the former chief economist for Beatrice Foods. Whoever heard of an economist as an acquirer of companies? It is not very likely. With the help of an intermediary, however, Kovall formed a company called Wellington Foods that specialized in buying snack food operations, initially in New England. Kovall brought together a board of directors that included the former chairman of Beatrice, a $13 billion conglomerate, and a well-known Harvard Business School professor. The only missing ingredient was sufficient capital, and so Kovall went to the Boston office of Drexel Burnham in 1986. Kovall's concept was to replicate the early years of rapid growth by acquiring relatively small regional food companies. Drexel Burnham was anxious to back him.

Kovall had established a company with distinguished directors, focused on a specific industry that matched his background, involved an intermediary, and lined up a financial backer. Kovall's intermediary would telephone numerous food companies and state: "I represent some former Beatrice executives who would like to talk to you about your company."

Invariably Kovall was able to visit these companies because he had a believable story, he had credibility in the marketplace, and he knew the industry.

Basically you have three choices when it comes to intermediaries:

- Work with them only if they represent the *seller*. With the exception of Geneva Business Services, some large accounting firms, and the investment bankers, most intermediaries do not have a large inventory of selling companies from which to choose. In the case of investment bankers, they tend not to show selling companies to individual buyers.

• Work with them on a nonexclusive basis, but sign an agreement stating that if a deal closes, you are obligated to pay the intermediary an accomplishment fee. You have two options: The intermediary can use its standard agreement, or you can have a transaction lawyer draft your own agreement for the intermediary to sign.

• Work with one on an exclusive basis. This arrangement usually is reinforced with a monetary retainer in order to solidify the relationship and motivate the intermediary on a daily basis. It is important to have a reasonable cancellation clause so that you are not locked in if you are not satisfied. The reason why many intermediaries require retainers is discussed below.

RETAINERS

Perhaps no other item causes as much consternation among intermediaries and their potential clients as retainers.

For clarification, a retainer is a fee paid to a professional adviser for advice or services rendered. Commonly, retainers are paid monthly over the length of the assignment. Retainers could be for a period of from six months to a year and could range from $2,000 to $10,000 per month. Additionally, retainers might be entirely or partly deducted from the Lehman-scale accomplishment fee. Another variation is a one-time retainer of approximately $25,000 paid all at once at the beginning of the assignment, which might include a valuation of the selling client and a selling document.

There are five basic reasons why retainers are usually required by intermediaries:

1. *Intermediaries are not brokers.* Unlike the selling of real estate, in selling a business more time is often required to understand the business, to identify synergistic buyers, to maintain confidentiality, and to address the complexities regarding structuring, taxes, financing, security laws, etc.

2. *Commitment.* With many business buyers and sellers, it is necessary to separate "the men from the boys"—i.e., those who are very serious from those who are not. Many intermediaries believe that being selective is critical to their success. A retainer

is a way to cement the relationship by committing the intermediary and the client so that the two parties are accountable to each other. A "best efforts" basis, where there is no retainer involved, often results in failure even though a large accomplishment fee is involved.

3. *Risk/Reward Ratio.* Many intermediaries deduct part or all of the retainer from the accomplishment fee. The principal should select an intermediary in whom he or she has confidence that the intermediary will be able to complete the deal. Unlike Wall Street investment bankers, middle-market intermediaries do not make millions. In a $5 million transaction, the sliding scale of the Lehman formula works out to a 3 percent commission, which is minuscule compared to commercial real estate, where the commission is often 10 percent. For many clients, paying an up-front retainer with a reasonable accomplishment fee leads to better results than no retainer and a much higher accomplishment fee.

4. *Incentive.* It is important that the intermediary's confidence be constantly reinforced because in the M & A business, "it is a long time between drinks." If an intermediary receives periodic monetary payments from one client and not from another client, the probability is that the intermediary will spend more effort on the former than on the latter. In many situations, the deal falls apart several times before closing. "When the going gets tough, the tough get going" is a well-known expression. If the principal is not paying the intermediary, the principal may not be really interested or may not give the intermediary the attention and resources needed to complete the assignment.

5. *Useful information.* Executive search firms customarily charge their client one-third of one year's total compensation in three incremental payments during the search process, beginning, middle, and completion. The search firm's role is in many ways similar to the M & A intermediary's role in an acquisition search. In both instances, considerable consultation and input regarding the criteria, process, and evaluation techniques are most helpful to the client and should be compensated for accordingly.

An intermediary becomes part of the M & A process and performs the role of a consultant, while a broker is more like a finder, bringing buyers and sellers together. It is no secret in the M & A business that intermediaries who traditionally receive retainers are infinitely more successful than those who do not.

RETAINING AN INDUSTRY SPECIALIST

There are numerous industry specialists in the middle market. If you are able to retain a competent specialist in the field that matches your background, I urge you to seriously consider doing so.

There are a number of intermediaries who specialize in one particular industry. In separate interviews, the following were some of their comments:

"The enormous deal flow means that Broadview is on a 'first name' basis with all the important players in the industry."

"Canon's specialization through his knowledge of the nuances, trends, and personalities enables him to better serve his clients."

"Trent knows the players, can respond to their needs, and can buy, sell, merge, or refinance their business regardless of the size of the company."

"Keep a Rolodex of key industry players."

"Specializing in the medical/life sciences gives a clear message to the market, creates credibility with potential clients, and facilitates ongoing industry relationships, which provides for faster consummation of transactions."

MENTOR/PROTÉGÉ RELATIONSHIP

A new concept for an individual buyer is to become a protégé of an expert intermediary, who will be his or her mentor.

Terry King of Copley-Browne Company in Boston, to the best of my knowledge, originated the following approach. Let me first explain Mr. King's background. He was a leading producer for Geneva Business Services in California before making a lifestyle transfer to Boston. For a year he worked for an investment banking firm, where he completed a large transaction. Flush with significant success, he established his own small boutique investment banking firm concentrating on the "buy side" of transactions.

Mr. King was an experienced professional with a successful record of completing transactions for clients. However, since he was somewhat new to Boston, he could benefit from tapping into the network of a former high-level corporate executive who was seeking to buy a business.

This executive had excellent contacts, and was very credible and capable of managing a business. However, this executive did not have the necessary knowledge concerning finding, assessing, negotiating, and closing the purchase of the business.

The arrangement was for Mr. King, the mentor, to invite the executive, the protégé, to take space in Copley-Browne for $1000 per month. The office was equipped with business directories and databases, and Mr. King had the "know-how" to teach the executive the process of completing a deal. Assuming that the executive bought a company through the guidance of Mr. King, then the former would pay the latter a 2 percent commission.

Although many individual buyers want recommendations, most of them, in my opinion, are reluctant to pay for counsel up front. I believe that this is one of the paramount reasons why individual buyers either fail or take one or two years longer than they might to buy a business. Buyers should take some of the money they have reserved for their acquisition and spend it wisely to receive better deal flow and worthwhile advice.

As a Buyer, What to Expect from the Intermediary

Provide viable financing sources for the deal.

Act as a mature sounding board and second opinion.

Help negotiate the deal.

Not pressure you into closing.

Introduce you to companies that are not being heavily shopped, and have not been on the block for some time.

Screen out companies that do not meet your criteria.

Provide an unbiased opinion on the deal—price, terms, etc.

Bring value to the entire acquisition process and offer alternatives as to how the deal can be structured.

Give you a chance to respond to the potential acquisition before shopping it elsewhere.

Leverage off his or her reputation.

Act as buffer between you and the seller.

Get the deal back on track if it is derailed.

Know the seller's pricing expectations.

Be reasonably sure that the target company is really a seller.

Follow up on all pending matters.

Not juggling one or two other major projects, or yours won't get enough attention.

Have no conflict of interest, or personal relationship with the seller.

AS A BUYER, WHAT TO EXPECT FROM THE INTERMEDIARY WHO REPRESENTS THE SELLER

An in-depth relationship developed over several months.
On retainer with the seller, indicating commitment by the seller.
An indication of the seller's range of valuations early on.
Awareness of whether buyer and seller have good chemistry in case the differences should be addressed.
Understanding of the issues so that he or she can help bridge the gap between the buyer and the seller.
Absolute candor in presenting the company, the industry, the management, and the financials so that any skeletons in the closet are flushed out. All representations should be absolutely true.
Up-to-date financials for the seller.

THE GENEVA BUYER PROGRAM FOR INDIVIDUAL INVESTORS

The following information was provided by Geneva Business Research Corporation with authorization to use it in this book. The Geneva Buyer Program allows individual buyers access to Geneva's inventory of sellers. In this program, Geneva represents the seller and there is no charge to the buyer.

Introduction

Geneva is the largest mergers and acquisitions organization in the U.S., specializing in middle market privately held businesses with enterprise values to $100 million. Since 1986 Geneva has consummated more transactions than any other firm. In addition, Geneva provides in-depth evaluations and M & A analyses of hundreds of companies per year and provides value-building consulting services. As a result, Geneva is a premier source of middle market businesses available for acquisition.

Geneva's experience is invaluable to both its sellers as well as buyers who purchase companies through the Geneva system. The sale or purchase of a business is complex. Geneva's breadth and depth of experience in every facet of the M & A process—the marketplace, sellers, buyers, and financing sources—provides the necessary background to manage each stage of the transaction to a successful close for all parties.

Geneva represents, on an exclusive basis, a large number of middle market companies valued up to $100 million. The Geneva deal flow is extensive and ongoing, with nearly 100 companies reviewed monthly. As a result, the Geneva system provides buyers a wide array of acquisition opportunities. Furthermore, Geneva is retained by the seller. Therefore, there is no fee to the buyer.

Defining the Acquisitions Criteria

The first step of the Geneva buyer program involves an extensive communication process whereby Geneva and the buyer work together to define the buyer's acquisition criteria. A Buyer Manager works with each buyer to present the various options and help the buyer narrow in on specific acquisition criteria. This is often a valuable learning process for the individual, first-time buyer who may not be familiar with the full range of possibilities in buying a business. For most individual investors this is the first and only business they will buy. The professionals at Geneva, who have been through the process many times, provide a valuable resource and ally for the amateur buyer.

In defining the buyer's acquisition goals, four fundamental questions must be answered:

1. What is the buyer's objective in purchasing a business? Will the acquired business serve as a job, a passive investment, or an add-on complementary business opportunity for the buyer?

2. What, if any, funds is the buyer willing to use to find a business?

3. How much does the buyer want to spend on the acquisition? This includes purchase price and deal structure, as well as accounting, legal, and other advisor fees. Each buyer must provide a personal balance sheet, identify available investment equity, and provide financial references.

4. What is the buyer's desired business? This is the most important question and must be answered from the standpoint of the type of business desired, location of the business, and size of the company. Geneva finds that, in general, individual buyers are most successful in industries that they are already experienced in, and in the same geographic location that they are currently in. With familiar industries and surroundings, they are able to focus their attentions on the newly acquired business.

The Acquisition Search

The search for a business to purchase is not a one time event, it is an on-going process. Sometimes an appropriate candidate is found right away, but often the process takes 6–9 months to identify the right business for the buyer.

Once Geneva thoroughly understands the buyer's goals and objectives in buying a business, Geneva begins the acquisition search process.

First, Geneva reviews its current inventory of sellers for companies that fit the buyer's acquisition criteria. This review is conducted electronically, whereby the computer matches the needs of the buyer with the characteristics of the sellers. As noted, Geneva reviews a great number of companies every month, and retains many of them for sale. The Geneva inventory offers a broad array of companies in every business sector: manufacturing, wholesaling, retailing and services. These companies operate in every type of business, from high-tech to low-tech, represent a wide variety of business sizes, and are located throughout the U.S.

At the same time, Geneva adds the buyer to Geneva's Buyer Database. This alerts Geneva's 250 professionals working in offices and with sellers throughout the United States of the buyer's interests. As new Geneva clients are added to the marketing process, the company's dealmaking professionals search the buyer database for appropriate matches.

As a member of the Geneva Buyer Program, the buyer gains constant and up-to-date access to Geneva's deal flow. Geneva's Priority Preview, a monthly newsletter of new sellers that have just entered the Geneva process, is mailed to the buyers in the Geneva system. The Preview spotlights each new Geneva client and allows the Geneva buyers a first opportunity at the business.

In addition, Geneva buyers have access to the company's 24-hour Acquisition Hotline. The 800-number is an interactive communication system that allows buyers to review Geneva's deals telephonically. The system allows the user to specify the desired industry, location, and size.

Another benefit of the Geneva system is buyer access to the Geneva Network, local M & A specialists nationwide that operate independently, but are affiliated with Geneva on certain transactions. These specialists are sometimes called upon to help with a buyer's acquisition search. In addition, the Geneva Network Affiliates have their own collection of businesses for sale, and the buyer's acquisition candidate may originate from this group.

The Purchase

Once the Buyer Manager and the buyer have identified an interesting target, the Geneva Deal Manager or Geneva Network Affiliate representing the seller manages the process.

The buyer must sign a confidentiality agreement before information on the target is released to him. Once the agreement is signed, the buyer is mailed a Confidential Business Review (CBR) on the company. The CBR describes the business in detail, outlining the company's history, products and product mix, customers, sales and marketing programs, suppliers, competition, organization, and facilities. The CBR also provides a complete financial analysis of the company over the past three years, and includes pro forma balance sheets and income statements for five future years. The pro forma projections are supported by market research findings with regards to the company's industry, markets, geographic market territory, and competition.

The CBR is of great help to the buyer and its depth is one of the details that makes Geneva unique in the area of small business sales. The CBR is comprehensive and detailed and, although the buyer is still required to complete his own due diligence of the target, the CBR provides him with an advanced starting point.

Based on the CBR and further review of the target, including a visit to the seller's business, the buyer submits an offer on the business in the form of a Letter of Intent. From this a purchase price and deal structure is negotiated, and Geneva manages the process for the seller through the completion of the transaction.

If at any time throughout the purchasing process the buyer decides not to acquire the company, the buyer is referred back to the Buyer Manager, and the process of identifying an acquisition target is repeated.

TEN MISTAKES BUYERS MAKE WITH INTERMEDIARIES

It almost goes without saying that intermediaries, whether investment bankers or brokers, play a very important part in the mergers and acquisitions business. Whether it is a public company like Bausch & Lomb seeking strategic acquisitions, or a private company like Bain Capital that is a financial buyer, intermediaries are involved in approximately half the transactions.

The relationship between the intermediary and the client is obviously a two-way street. The following are observations that can improve a buyer's relationship with intermediaries:

1. *Retainer.* Most intermediaries want to have a two-way commitment between the buyer and themselves in which each party is accountable for its role in the relationship. Remember, a retainer is a fee paid to the intermediary for advice or services rendered. Commonly, retainers are paid monthly over the length of the assignment and often are deductible in part or in their entirety from the accomplishment fee.

Let's assume for a minute that you, the person reading this, are an intermediary. You know that on average it takes between six and twelve months to complete a deal. You know that deals fall apart for reasons that are often out of your control. And you know that some acquirers are mercurial in their buying habits. Additionally, if you do come across a great company for sale, you are duty bound to show it first to one of your existing retainer clients. After that, you are likely to show it to a buyer who is a close friend, and/or to a buyer who is willing to pay absolutely top dollar for an acquisition.

Now let's assume you are a buyer. If you are not seeing a lot of deal flow, why aren't you? Are you just a name at the bottom of every intermediary's list? Are you just seeing deals that everyone else has turned down? Is an intermediary going to take valuable time and uncover "not for sale" companies on your behalf when in reality he or she already has too much other work to do?

Almost all executive search firms require a retainer partly because the entire assignment is a process. Very few of the most successful intermediaries do an acquisition search out of pure speculation. Just as the buyer wants a hard-working, committed intermediary, the intermediary wants the client to demonstrate the same commitment.

Several months ago an intermediary was trying to persuade the owner of a buyout group to retain me for an acquisition search. He turned to me and said, "I tried a retainer search once before, and it didn't work."

With that statement, I responded rather sarcastically, "If you had a bad meal at a restaurant, you probably wouldn't go back to that restaurant, but I doubt whether you would avoid all restaurants forever."

Needless to say, my analogy was not accepted by the buyout executive, but then again, he has not bought a company for several years either.

2. *Patience.* Acquisitions are not easy. The process can take a year—in some cases longer. The acquirer may not understand that if you rush the process, you may make some hasty decisions that you might later regret. Additionally, many deals "crater" once or twice before closing, and it takes time to get back on track. At the same time, while buyers should be patient with the acquisition process, an intermediary's key responsibility is to

maintain the momentum once it is apparent that there is serious interest by both parties.

3. *Direction.* The buyer often does not provide the precise focus to the intermediary, feeling that it is up to the intermediary to decide. Certainly a good intermediary should be helpful in recommending certain strategic directions the buyer might pursue, but the ultimate leadership must come from the buyer. It is very important that both the buyer and the intermediary spend sufficient time up front in the search to decide what types of target companies should be pursued. Such issues as desirable industries, products, size, geographic location, etc., should be fully analyzed.

4. *Financing in place.* Some buyers have high aspirations for a successful acquisition, only to realize that they haven't the affirmative cooperation from their board of directors and/or major stockholders. Is the necessary financing for such an acquisition really available? One of my former clients was an executive from a *Fortune* 500 company who assembled an impressive board of directors. As an intermediary, perhaps I was naive to believe that there was sufficient equity to do the deal, but the buyer too was wrong. The buyer was missing one of the most important components of a transaction—equity.

5. *Provide buyer's documentation.* An intermediary needs to present the client as a reputable, credible, and financially capable buyer. Writing a mini–buyer's business plan that can be presented to the target potential sellers demonstrates professionalism, thoroughness, and commitment to the acquisition process.

6. *Discern the buyer's competitive advantage.* The intermediary should know the buyer's strong suit, just as a bridge player must know his or her partner's strength. The Brittany Company in Cleveland is a buyout group that appeals to family business owners who do not want their company bought and sold repeatedly for the benefit of the short-term investors. The procedure of buying and holding the acquisition indefinitely is most unusual for buyout groups. This philosophy appeals to some sellers and definitely is Brittany's competitive advantage.

7. *Define the intermediary's role.* There is no right or wrong way for an intermediary and a buyer to work with each other, but there definitely should be a crystal-clear understanding of what the

buyer expects from the intermediary. For example, does the buyer want the intermediary to communicate often or seldom? Will the buyer treat the acquisition search as a priority and take all telephone calls, even if they interrupt something else? Does the buyer want the intermediary to make the first visit to the target company? Does the buyer want the intermediary to do the negotiating and/or some of the due diligence?

8. *Along with the intermediary, listen.* One of the keys to understanding the workings of the target company is to ask the right questions and to listen very carefully. If you are talking most of the time, you obviously cannot do much listening. Therefore, in conjunction with the intermediary, listen to the seller—what the seller is saying, what he or she is not saying, and what is in between the lines.

9. *Recognize the need for hand holding with the seller.* A good intermediary is aware that many sellers have an emotional attachment to their business, and so listen to the intermediary when he or she advises the buyer to be sensitive to the seller's concerns about employees, customers, and the business in general.

10. *Quickness.* In conjunction with the intermediary, you often have to react quickly to a situation to sustain the momentum, to prevent the buyer from going to the auction process, and to be a step or two ahead of other potential buyers. Quickness means that you might have to drop everything and jump on a plane the next day to visit the target company. Here is an example of a buyer who moved quickly on a significantly large company. Three days after receiving the selling memorandum, the buyer visited the target company. A week later the buyer had visited the operation twice more, bringing along an offer. The deal closed in less than two months from the original contact. The quicker a buyer can get to a closing, the less chance there is for the seller to change his or her mind.

SUMMARY OF INTERMEDIARY RELATIONSHIPS

As a buyer, you want to maximize your effort to acquire another company so that the process will be expeditious, thorough, and successful. Even a good intermediary is not necessarily a panacea for an acquisition search, but if a buyer knows how to work with an intermediary and treats him or her with respect, the relationship is sure to be more fruitful.

THE QUESTION OF FEES FOR INTERMEDIARIES

While the Lehman formula is the standard compensation methodology for the middle-market M & A business, there are numerous variations on it and interpretations of its use.

The intermediary's commission from the Lehman formula is a sliding scale of 5-4-3-2-1 percent—5 percent of the first $1 million, 4 percent of the second $1 million, etc. Either the buyer or the seller pays the commission, depending on which intermediary initiated the transaction (the one representing the buyer or the one representing the seller). In some cases, *both* the buyer and the seller are represented by intermediaries, which can result in a double commission. While some people might feel that two commissions are exorbitant, a principal in the transaction should primarily focus on the big picture, i.e., the viability of the deal, the overall price, the terms, and the credibility of the other party. If both intermediaries contribute significant value to the transaction, then two commissions may not be onerous. Alternatively, the two intermediaries may agree to split their fees, either on a 50/50 basis or on a 60/40 basis. In the latter case, 60 percent would be paid to the intermediary who has the fee agreement under contract with the principal.

Modified Lehman Formulas

In talking with an intermediary, it is important to clarify whether he or she uses the "standard" or "modified" Lehman formula. The two most common variations are the double Lehman, 10-8-6-4-2 percent, and the stuttering Lehman, 5-5-4-4-3-3 percent. Based on a $5 million transaction, the following example shows the difference.

Type	Commission	Overall Percentage
Double	$300,000	6.0
Stuttering	$210,000	4.2
Standard	$150,000	3.0

One of the major intermediaries in the country uses the double Lehman formula. Part of its financial success has been its ability to receive this level of compensation from its clients. Additionally, this major intermediary has subagents across the country. If the agent completes the deal, then the two entities split the commission, which means that each one ends up with compensation equal to a standard Lehman.

Calculation of Fee

The commission is based on the value of the transaction. Let us assume that the target company is losing money, has a negative net worth, and has $2 million of interest-bearing debt. You negotiate to acquire the company for one dollar plus the assumption of the debt. Your fee agreement with the intermediary states that the intermediary will receive a minimum commission, no matter what the sales price, of $50,000. What does the intermediary receive as an accomplishment fee? The answer is $90,000. Assumption of interest-bearing debt, usually bank debt, is part of the company's capitalization. In this case, you acquire the company's "stock," which includes all the assets and all the liabilities.

A second case is an "asset" transaction in which you acquire certain assets and assume some liabilities of the following balance sheet.

Cash	$ 10,000	Accounts payable	$100,000
Accounts receivable	100,000	Notes payable	200,000
Inventory	50,000	Long-term debt	300,000
Machinery and equipment	240,000	Book value	400,000
Real estate	600,000		
Total Assets	$1,000,000	Liabilities/Equity	$1,000,000

Let us assume that you buy the company for $300,000 and you take over the receivables, the inventory, and the payables. The seller keeps all the other items and leases you machinery and equipment and rents you the real estate. What is the intermediary's fee? Would it be the $50,000 minimum as stated in the intermediary's fee agreement? The answer is no, not if the intermediary has properly included a commission, like a broker, for equipment leased and/or real estate rented instead of acquired. If the seller rented the real estate for five years at $50,000 per year, the commission would be based on the $250,000 value, normally paid at closing and not spaced out over the entire period. Commercial Realtors utilize the following commission schedule.

Rate	Year
5.0%	1
4.0%	2
4.0%	3
3.0%	4
2.0%	5
1.5%	Over 5 years

If the corporate M & A intermediary does not have a real estate license, he or she should work with a friend who does have the proper license.

In a third example of fee calculation, the buyer has identified the target company and is ready to make an offer. However, the buyer lacks the knowledge, expertise, and confidence to value, negotiate, and close the deal. Therefore, the buyer hires an experienced intermediary and pays a nonrefundable retainer (let's say $10,000 plus a 1 percent commission on the transaction price as an incentive). If the target company is acquired for $5 million, then the intermediary would receive another $50,000. The intermediary could be well worth this expense!

Ancillary Conditions of Fee Agreement

- If there is a retainer, whether it is deducted in part or entirely from the accomplishment fee
- Whether the agreement is cancelable after thirty days' notice, or perhaps after a three-month grace period
- Whether the agreement is an exclusive with the intermediary
- Whether there is a minimum commission to the intermediary (like $50,000) and a possible "cap" on the upside (like $500,000)
- That there is a time period (such as three years), in which the intermediary is protected for identifying a particular target
- That should the buyer, as an individual, take a job with the target company, the intermediary is compensated as if it were an executive search firm, i.e., one-third of the annual salary

A true war story is the time I introduced a buyer to a $14 million company that was nearly insolvent. The buyer convinced the target company to pay him $250,000 as a temporary CEO, with the stipulation that if he saved the company from bankruptcy (which he did), he would be awarded 50 percent ownership of the company. Needless to say, my agreement did not cover this transaction.

Value Received

The real question is not whether the intermediary receives a 3.0 percent commission, a 4.2 percent commission, or even a 6.0 percent commission for a $5 million transaction. Will the intermediary spend a considerable amount of time on your behalf, either writing a selling memorandum or analyzing potential buyers? Is the intermediary experienced in valuations and negotiations? Is the intermediary capable of getting a deal back on track after it is derailed?

Conclusion

As an intermediary, it strikes me that few principals know how to properly manage or work with intermediaries. While the remuneration and fee agreements are very important, managing the relationship between the principal and the intermediary is equally important.

CHAPTER 11

Your Acquisition Team

Acquiring companies in the middle market can be very competitive. While the selling company may be too small to attract an auction sale, invariably the owner of the selling company talks to several potential buyers. Often the most experienced and best prepared acquirers succeed in acquiring the target companies.

Why are some buyers vastly more successful than others? Do these buyers pay significantly more than their counterparts? The answer is, not necessarily. However, many successful buyers, whether they be manufacturers, buyout groups, or individuals, often have preassembled an acquisition team. The team members are usually consultants, advisers, professionals, etc., who usually work outside the buyer's entity and occasionally have a vested interest in the project. Some team members may receive reduced compensation until the transaction closes or until the buyer becomes a regular client of their firm. Successful acquisition teams have a high degree of commitment. They could have the following members:

Intermediary
Transaction lawyer
Transaction CPA
Financiers
Corporate valuation expert
Machinery and equipment appraiser
Real estate appraiser
Due diligence firm(s)

BUSINESS INTERMEDIARY

Much has already been written about the importance of an experienced intermediary, who will often serve as your team quarterback through the entire process and will involve other team members as required and necessary.

Joseph E. Myss, president of the Institute of Merger & Acquisition Professionals and an investment banker from Wayzata, Minnesota, says, "You should consider a team of qualified professional advisers from the beginning. The team provides experience and insight in completing a sale. Your team members are all-important, but not all members are required all the time. Team involvement must be coordinated. A team quarterback promotes efficiency and enhances communication."

Myss goes on to state that a good intermediary will do the following:

- Help you define and understand your criteria and goals.

- Search out and identify qualified sellers.

- Solicit and evaluate selling prices.

- Negotiate the purchase agreement.

- Help close the transaction.

TRANSACTION LAWYERS

In an interview with Dave Broadwin of the Boston law firm of Foley, Hoag & Eliot, he had the following suggestions for those seeking a transaction lawyer:

- Always seek recommendations from reliable sources about lawyers who specialize in mergers and acquisitions. It is extremely important that the particular lawyer have extensive experience in this field of expertise.

- Your lawyer should not just focus on the deal, but should be cognizant of your personal affairs, your tolerance for risk, and your financial limitations. By being sensitive to these issues, your lawyer will know how stringently to negotiate the representation and warranties or whether it is advisable for you to personally guarantee the notes to the seller. If the debt load in the acquisition is heavy for you as an individual, then your lawyer should help you negotiate alternative structures to mitigate that problem. For example, if there is real estate included in the conveyance of assets, then there might be a possibility of renting instead of buying the real estate. Also, the seller might be willing to lease the machinery and equipment instead of including these assets in the purchase price.

- Evaluate the size and complexity of the transaction to determine whether you need the extra services and resources of a large law firm. If the target company has some lingering unresolved issues such as environmental problems, litigation, the employee benefits plan, foreign subsidiaries, etc., a small law firm may not be equipped to handle these matters successfully. Such shortcomings could ultimately cause a breakdown of communications and result in a failure to close the transaction, or the purchase and sale agreement could be unfavorably written from your standpoint. Generally speaking, the larger, well-known, long-established law firms charge more for their services. For larger transactions, sometimes it is psychologically better to use a law firm with a better image.

- Your lawyer should tell you up front not only what the hourly rate is for the ensuing work to be done but also an estimate for the entire transaction. It is better to receive monthly invoices from the law firm and to let the lawyer know that keeping legal fees within the estimate is important. Otherwise, you may end up with a legal bill twice what you originally expected.

- Obviously, the selection of your lawyer will be in large part a result of the personal chemistry between the two of you.

Another transaction lawyer, Dennis White of Sullivan & Worcester in Boston, emphasized the importance of having extensive knowledge about the number and generic nature of the law firm's transactions. For example, if you want to buy a software company, there are so many intricacies in that particular industry that you probably would be best served by a firm that either specializes in that business or has done numerous transactions in it. The lawyer should be practical and pragmatic and certainly a "deal maker" who will not be adversarial with the other side, winning the battle but losing the war.

Lou Katz of Shapiro Israel & Weiner of Boston urges buyers to be sure that the law firm chosen has excellent documentation on its computer for easy access to such items as letters of intent, purchase and sale agreements (asset or stock), noncompete agreements, employment contracts, etc. You certainly do not want your lawyer to reinvent the wheel by writing an original document for each legal process in the transaction. Katz also emphasizes the ability of some excellent transaction lawyers to identify additional sources of debt or equity to help finance the acquisition.

Dana Coggins of the Boston firm Nutter, MacLellan & Fish states the case most succinctly: "Select a lawyer who is most likely to understand both parties, anticipate the problems, and above all, one who has been a successful deal-maker."

TRANSACTION CPA

In selecting a transaction CPA, you might start by receiving recommendations from your banker or lawyer or from your business peers.

The size of the firm may be indicative of the attention you will receive and/or the range of services provided. For example, if you select one of the "Big Six" accounting firms, your account might be relegated to junior members of the firm. On the other hand, if you select a small accounting firm, its resources may be limited and its reputation may not be established. It is customary for the firm that is engaged for the acquisition to be retained after the transaction is completed. During the acquisition process, it would be customary for the accounting firm to provide the following services:

- Analyze the target company's financial statements.
- Value the company.
- Conduct due diligence.
- Structure the deal, with attention to the tax consequences.
- Review the letter of intent.
- Audit the seller's financial status to verify such items as accrued employee vacation time, valuation of inventory, and that the company is current on all federal, state, and local taxes, including payroll taxes.

The firm's fees are important, but not as important as the quality of work or services rendered. Obviously, you have to use your best judgment in this regard. In most cases, you will be charged a blended rate of anywhere between $100 and $250 per hour, depending on whether the person doing the work is a junior accountant or a senior project manager. If you are anticipating a stock purchase rather than an asset purchase, you should expect to pay more in accounting, legal, and overall due diligence fees. For example, an audit could cost from $10,000 to $40,000. These higher fees are usually acceptable because the purchase price of a stock is normally less expensive. The reason is that an asset sale for a C corporation is taxed twice, once to the corporation and again when the assets are distributed to the stockholders.

Industry Specialist

Accounting firms often find themselves with a reputation for having numerous clients in a particular industry. Each industry has idiosyncrasies and knowledge that are only gained from experience. So if you are buying a software or biotech company, do not expect that all accounting firms will be equally up to speed on these industries. If you are acquiring a publishing company, will your accountant know how to place a value on its "back list"? Or if you are acquiring a distributor that services copiers, your accountant should have enough experience in that industry to book the unexpired service contracts as a liability. Recommendations from the chief financial officer in a certain industry could be helpful

Services Offered

Not all firms are set up to offer their clients a broad range of services. Let us assume you want to install an inventory control system adhering to the "just-in-time" (JIT) method. Can your accounting firm provide this service? If you are a small retail chain, you should have a point-of-sale cash register inventory system. Will your accounting firm be able to orchestrate the implementation of this computerized system? If you intend to take your new acquisition public in five years, you probably would do better to start with a "Big Six" firm, which has the necessary experience and credibility in that regard. Does the firm have the capacity and inclination to achieve tax savings not only for your company but for you as the CEO and owner of that company?

Response Time

It is very possible to have the partner of the firm who is soliciting your account be very responsive, but to have the account manager who is assigned to your company be very slow. To properly evaluate the firm's response time, you need to have an understanding of its culture, whether the account manager is overly committed, and how important your business is to the firm.

Reputation

Almost every company has three or four good references, so beware of the names that are volunteered by the firm. There are other ways to check a firm's reputation. Your banker would be a good place to start. Another way is to review the manufacturer's directory for the particular state in which the company is located. Most, but not all, directories list the companies' accounting firms. If you do receive references, especially from clients in the same or similar industry, also ask for names of a few of the firm's former clients.

Chemistry

As important as this ingredient is in the selection process, chemistry is the only one that is determined exclusively by subjective reasoning. Nevertheless, you must rely on your intuitive feelings to confirm your positive reactions or to "red flag" your dubious reactions. Are the principals of the accounting firm overinflating their capabilities and interest in helping your company? After you have done your own due diligence on the firm, it boils down to whether you personally like the people in the firm and, of course, whether you implicitly trust them.

Direction of the Firm

Service companies like accounting firms have their problems, just like other businesses. Hopefully, you will select a firm that does not have internal problems of its own, with constant turnover or layoffs. The large accounting firm Laventhol & Horwath went out of business a few years ago. There were two midsize firms in the Boston area that merged and then a year later split apart again. Is there a positive corporate culture in the firm of your choice? Are the senior partners in accord on how to operate and grow their business? In any event, the internal viability of the firm is an important consideration.

Relationships

Above and beyond the normal ways in which an accounting firm helps its clients, a final factor in your consideration should be whether the firm has strong influential relationships with third parties. For example, would the accounting firm's reputation greatly enhance your ability to obtain your bank loan? If you need to raise equity for your company, does the firm have sources with which to connect you? And if you plan to acquire other companies, certain accounting firms can be more helpful than others in introducing you to the right situations.

FINANCIERS

Many individuals do not line up their financial sources before identifying their target acquisition. This is a big mistake. Your banker can be the heartbeat of the business. Selecting the right banker can be crucial not only to providing the acquisition financing but to the future success of the company. Recommendations from your business peers, your lawyer, and/or your accountant are one of the preferred ways of identifying your banker. Not only do your advisers have specific knowledge of the individual loan officers, but they should be more comfortable in working on your behalf with a banker they already know.

Just as you will be analyzing various loan officers and their banks, they will be analyzing you. In fact, according to most bankers, the borrower's character accounts for half of the six criteria of analyzing a loan, known as the 6 Cs:

Character
Cash flow
Capacity to earn
Conditions in marketplace
Capital
Collateral

For the banker to evaluate you takes some time. One way for each of you to get to know the other is to show the banker a few potential acquisitions to determine how he or she might finance the deal. Naturally, until you have a letter of intent, the banker will not conduct any due diligence on the target company.

If you are involved in a transaction requiring several millions of dollars of debt financing, you may also need to know asset-based lenders, mezzanine lenders, and bridge lenders. When a deal is hot, you have to work very quickly to keep the momentum going. Furthermore, you may be competing on the same deal with another party that already has financing in place. In addition to debt financing, you may need more equity to do the deal, in which case there are individuals and institutions that will take minority positions.

Some banks have a reputation for specializing in certain industries, such as Silicon Valley Bank in technology. Small banks have limitations on the size of individual loans, and large banks may not be interested in small loans. It is important that you take the time to match the characteristics of your loan with the most appropriate bank and banker.

While you may have the ability to obtain a loan when necessary, most borrowers are unprepared for loan negotiations. Of course, before you sign the loan documents, you should have your legal counsel not only review these papers, but perhaps assist you in the negotiations. Again, this is an example of your acquisition group working as a team.

CORPORATE VALUATION EXPERT

While your intermediary and your accountant should be well versed in valuing target companies, valuations can be extremely complex and difficult. Before I spent several millions of dollars in purchasing a company, I would certainly want a second or third opinion, especially from an expert in that discipline. There are so many ways to structure a transaction that could be to your advantage that it is essential that you know your alternatives.

Your corporate appraiser should have the capability to help you in the negotiating process. Appraisers can charge you by the hour, and if they do not have to submit "bulletproof" testimony in court, they can spend a lot less time in preparing their conclusions. Appraisers can be enormously helpful, especially if they are willing to be "on call" on short notice.

MACHINERY AND EQUIPMENT APPRAISERS AND REAL ESTATE APPRAISERS

After the letter of intent and during the bank negotiations, you will need appraisals to help verify the purchase price and to secure the bank note. Having these experts "on tap" will help you round out your acquisition team.

DUE DILIGENCE CONSULTANTS

Many acquisitions fail principally because due diligence was inept. The majority of the work takes place after the letter of intent is signed. One professional, Olivia Robinson of Competitive Intelligence Inc. of Seattle, Washington, provides hard-to-get details on target companies, usually prior to the letter of intent stage. The results of this firm's findings are used by its clients in a variety of ways.

- To negotiate from a more favorable position
- To screen possible acquisition targets more effectively
- To verify suspicions

- To obtain unbiased perceptions and impressions about the target company and its managers

The due diligence after the letter of intent is to determine whether you are going forward with the deal. You want to be sure that you will be receiving the assets you expect and that there will not be any unexpected liabilities postacquisition. Your accounting firm should be able to handle most if not all of your due diligence post–letter of intent.

In Conclusion

As Joseph Myss states: "The purchase of a business is a time consuming and very detailed process. In order to maximize your efforts, it requires an experienced professional team from several disciplines resolving a variety of transaction-related issues."

CHAPTER 12

Raising Cash

The amount of cash you are willing to invest or capable of investing in an acquisition will in large part determine the size of the companies you should target. The following is a very simplistic rule of thumb for ascertaining the size manufacturing company you can afford to acquire. Most manufacturing companies with "average" profits sell for 50 percent of sales. Furthermore, most acquisitions require one-third of the purchase price to be cash at closing. Therefore, let us assume that you want to acquire a company with at least $3 million in sales. While the formula below is very general, you will need the following amount of cash:

Sales of company	$3,000,000
Probable purchase price	$1,500,000
Cash at closing	$ 500,000

I know someone who acquired 51 percent of a printing company with sales of $3 million that had been unprofitable and was just then breaking even for $25,000. This is an anomaly. However, companies that are losing money or breaking even can be acquired with very little cash, especially if the buyer is willing to assume the seller's debt.

Many individuals who seek a company to buy underestimate the importance of raising sufficient cash early on. Let us assume that our buyer has only $200,000 in cash but still wants to acquire a profitable company with $3 million in sales. One alternative is to elicit other stockholders and raise another $300,000. You would not have to lose ownership control even though your investment is only 40 percent of the invested capital ($200,000 divided by $500,000 = 40 percent) because you consummated the transaction from beginning to end. Let us assume that you want to capitalize your acquisition company with $500,000, of which $200,000 will be your own capital. The ownership allocation could be as follows:

Nonmonetary:		
Consideration for putting the deal together		40%
Monetary:		
Your investment	$200,000	
Other investors	$300,000	
	$500,000	60%
TOTAL		100%

Therefore, the ownership of the acquisition team would be as follows based on the above scenario:

Your nonmonetary portion	40%	
Your monetary contribution	24%	
Your ownership ($200,000 invested)		64%
Other investors ($300,000 invested)		36%
		100%

THE SEARCH FUND CONCEPT

The search fund concept is not very common, but it has been executed successfully in the various cases of which I have knowledge. One such acquirer is Andrew Cousins of Amersham Corporation of Santa Monica, California. In his investment proposal, Cousins states,

> The financing for the acquisition will be accomplished through a two-step process. Amersham will first raise the funds to meet search expenses. The Company is seeking equity investors to capitalize the Company with $200,000. The "search fund" will be raised in 10 units of $20,000. For each unit purchased, investors will receive: (1) an equity position in the acquired company equal to 200% of the dollar value of their search fund investment and (2) the right of first refusal, but not the obligation, to invest additional equity in the acquisition.

Andrew Cousins's investment proposal goes on to say:

> Search fund proceeds will finance the expenses incurred in the identification of an acquisition on behalf of the Company and its investors. The fund enables Cousins to conduct a full-time search for a period of up to 24 months. The search fund also establishes an investor group capable of making a significant equity investment. Such a group provides Amersham with greater financial credibility in approaching prospective sellers and lenders, and may facilitate the closing of a time sensitive transaction. Operating expenses are estimated to be approximately $100,000 annually.

Category of Expense	Annual Expense
Salary	$ 50,000
Travel	15,000
Office rent	8,400
Legal & accounting	7,000
Administrative	6,600
Telephone	6,000
Pre-funding expense	5,000
Office equipment	2,000
Total Expense	$100,000

The search fund concept has been utilized by others and in fact is extensively described in Harvard Business School Case 9-387-009 regarding Jim Southern, which is available at cost by calling the institution at (617) 495-6117.

OBTAINING A BANK LOAN

Let us assume that you are in the process of buying a company. Along with presenting an essential business plan, in your meeting with the bank, you include the following items:

1. *Describe how you run the business.* It is important for the banker to fully understand the financial nature of the business, such as whether sales are seasonal, special customer or vendor payment terms, how you check your customers' credit, whether you allow production overruns, how you treat overdue accounts, whether you take 2%/10 net terms, whether you require deposits for special orders, and what financial controls you incorporate in the business.

2. *Describe how you market your product/service.* What is the customer base, by industry and key accounts, as well as by product/service. Also, how do you market your business and what are your competitive advantages? Specifically, who are your competitors and how does your product/service compare?

3. *Describe your company's management.* As well as providing the individual backgrounds of important management personnel, it is important to relate how their background pertains to this particular company. Perhaps no other factor is as important as the ability of management in achieving the company's objectives, both strategically and financially.

4. *Financial considerations.* The bank is particularly interested in managing its risk and seeing that your company has the resources to match planned growth. The banker will want to know how you intend to spend its money and how and when you will pay it back.

5. *Preparation for financing presentation.* A professional presentation showing the following critical considerations is considered essential by most debtors:

- Estimated sales and expenses by month for at least a year's period of time—showing how the bank debt is to be paid down and what is the proper debt covered.

- A balance sheet showing leverage not to exceed a debt to equity ratio of approximately 3 to 1, along with the borrowing power based on 75 percent of receivables and 30 percent inventory.

- A clear-cut analysis of how the company expects to make money.

And, finally depending on the size of the company and previous relationships, most owners of small businesses must submit their personal financial statements and be prepared to personally sign for the company notes.

Returning briefly to critiquing the business plan, here are a few suggestions as credited to Joseph R. Mancuso, author of *How to Get a Business Loan (Without Signing Your Life Away)*:

- Besides stating the company's *overall objective*, be sure to have a *specific strategy* that is rational and appears achievable.

- Elaborate in detail on the company's ability to *sustain profitability and growth*.

- Specify the characteristics of the *company's competitors*.

- Substantiate the *marketing plan* with market research.

Personal Guarantees

Personal guarantees are usually a sticky wicket for owners of middle-market companies. For some, the personal guarantee defeats the purpose of incorporating. While some loan officers might say that a personal guarantee for small companies is standard procedure, the fact is that every item on the loan agreement is negotiable.

In asking Warren Morrison, senior vice president of U.S. Trust in Boston, what the rule of thumb is for obtaining personal guarantees, he responded: "The rule of thumb is, always get them." Naturally, the banker's objective is different from the borrower's. Basically, the borrower has the following alternatives in this regard:

1. Shop around in the hopes of finding a bank that will not require a personal guarantee because of the company's strong financial position and your personal reputation. While this may be unlikely at the outset, the bank may waive your guarantee and counter by reducing the borrowing base from 75 percent on receivables to 50 percent.

2. Establish at the outset that the personal guarantee will be a pivotal issue. If you sign the loan agreement with the guarantee, then it will be your objective to eventually have the bank release you from that obligation.

3. Sign the personal guarantee but place restrictions on the extent and limits to which the bank can collect from the personal guarantor, such as $200,000. One does not want to sign a "joint and several guarantee," which allows the bank to simultaneously collect the bank note from both the business and the individual signer. An "indemnification guarantee" restricts the bank from suing the individual guarantor until the business fails to pay its obligations.

4. Arrange a scenario that will trigger when the guarantee will go into effect, i.e. the personal guarantee will go into effect if you are late on more than three consecutive loan payments or if working capital falls below a specified amount.

5. Alter the loan provision so that the grace period to cure the issue in default is extended from, let's say, a week to fifteen days.

6. Share the personal guarantee liability with other major stockholders, i.e., a 20 percent owner of the company would be responsible for 20 percent of the guarantee liability.

7. Write an agreement stating that the bank will let you off the personal guarantee when the note is, let's say, 70 percent paid off. The banker will use certain benchmarks which must be obtained based on either the income statement or the balance sheet.

In spite of the above recommendations, let us assume that you flatly will not sign a personal guarantee. If your company is financially strong, you can always threaten to take your business to another bank. Or, in lieu of a personal guarantee that might be open-ended, you could counter with another piece of collateral such as your summer house. A real power play is to ask your board, early on in its development, to vote on a resolution that officers and shareholders will not be allowed to sign personally for any debt. Another suggestion by Joseph Mancuso is not to fill out the bank's preprinted financial statement, which implies that you will sign such a form! Instead, substitute a signed and notarized financial form of your own that in essence provides the same information. Also, remember that the days of automatic signing of personal loan guarantees by the spouse are over!

Your Banker

Pick a banker rather than selecting a bank. In this case, a referral from a respected business friend and/or entrepreneur is recommended. An excellent banker can be invaluable to your company and tremendously important to the success of your business.

I discussed the potential relationships between the corporate borrower and the banker with Leslie Wilson and Richard Secher, vice presidents of U.S. Trust in Boston. They measure and evaluate the desirability of a new loan based on a number of key factors:

- The reputation and character of the principal is paramount. If that potential borrower is referred to them by a credible third party like a lawyer, accountant, or other businessperson, that carries a lot of influence. In a relatively small community like Boston, you can usually track down the applicant's background by the third telephone call. The banker either does or does not feel intuitively comfortable with the person. Furthermore, it is extremely important that the acquirer of the business be very experienced in the industry of the company he or she is acquiring.

- The business plan defining the purpose, need, and repayment schedule will be carefully critiqued. If the business is reasonable or cyclical, "the numbers have to work," Dick Secher stated.

- Lenders feel more comfortable if the creditor has carved out a niche in its industry and is not just producing a commodity product that wins or fails on price alone.

- Lenders become more motivated when the potential loan is within a certain size range. For example, U.S. Trust generally makes corporate loans between $750,000 and $10 million; however, its bread-and-butter loan is between $2 and $5 million. If a potential corporate borrower is seeking a $200,000 loan, he or she is less likely to get the loan officer's full attention at U.S. Trust because it takes the same amount of effort, if not more, to process this as to process a $2 million loan.

- Lenders are concerned about the leverage of the balance sheet. If the company is highly leveraged, then Wilson and Secher would like the principal to be personally fully committed also by investing a significant sum of his or her own equity, like $500,000 to $750,000. The purpose of the guarantee is as much psychological as collateral. One of the banker's worst fears is that the owner will throw the factory keys on the table and walk away from a business that has had a downturn.

- Lenders' concerns are numerous, but since the bank is borrowing principally against accounts receivable, inventory, and machinery and equipment rather than real estate in the 1990s, it will want to closely monitor accounts receivable and inventory either by computer systems and/or by having certified statements for verifications. If the borrower has more than 50 percent of its business with one customer, the bank may want the borrower to carry accounts receivable insurance. Bankers often hedge themselves by structuring the loan so that they will lend at 80 percent of receivables and 50 percent of inventory or, more conservatively, 70 percent of receivables and 40 percent of inventory.

Your banker wants to know the following items regarding the loan:

- How much money do you need? The answer to this question places a frame around your discussion.

- For how long? The longer the loan, the more the unknown and the greater the risk for the bank.

- For what use? Fundamentally, is the loan for working capital, a marketing program, to buy out a partner, or what?

- How will you repay it? Your repayment schedule is essential in this regard.

Inasmuch as the banker relies on two items for repayment, collateral and cash flow, your strategy should be as follows:

- When your banker talks about inadequate collateral, you should talk about cash flow.

- Conversely, when your banker talks about inadequate cash flow, you should talk about collateral.

- How will additional money from the bank improve your business? You should be able to show that you can lower your costs, improve sales, or expand your capabilities.

As Mancuso states: "It is imperative that you know what your credit history looks like before your banker runs a credit check on the company. It's very simple—sometimes credit agencies make mistakes, and it's your responsibility to correct those mistakes before your banker sees them."

In interviewing your potential banker, find out what are the secured and unsecured lending limits. Also, determine the size of the loan the banker can execute without going before the loan committee and/or receiving a second signature.

Your accountant can be the critical link between you and the banker by properly presenting the financial posture of the company. In some cases, it is advisable to seek advice from the banker of your choice concerning recommendations of preferred accountants. Additionally, you need a lawyer who specializes in banking to scrutinize the loan agreement, preferably one who represents clients who have negotiated loans from competing banks. It is important that you know the extent to which you can negotiate with your banker based on the knowledge of your advisers who are in the marketplace on a routine basis.

Conclusion

In summary, the critical issues in obtaining a bank loan are the following:

- Prepare a formal written business plan within which you propose to operate. Additionally, make a verbal presentation that is crisp and makes sense.

- State exactly how much money you need, why you need it, and how you will repay the loan.

- The key factor for the banker is to be convinced that your company has the ability to service the debt and repay it. A detailed cash flow analysis month by month is critical.

- In bankers' jargon, the 6 Cs of credit are:

Character:	The key to a long-term relationship
Cash flow:	Ensures repayment
Capital:	Necessary to run the business
Collateral:	To cover any shortfall in the debt to equity
Condition:	Lender's tolerance of risk
Capacity:	Ability to earn more money

- Do your research up front by knowing what bank is most apt to be interested in your industry and/or your company. For example, the Silicon Valley Bank, with six branches in California and one each in Massachusetts and Oregon, specializes in emerging and rapidly growing technology companies. Unlike most conventional banks, which shy away from black-box products or software companies, this billion-dollar bank embraces these companies.

CAPITAL STRUCTURE

There is no better way to understand the corporate capital structure than to refer to the accompanying diagram.

As you can see, the sources of capital are either *creditors, lenders,* or *owners.* Specifically, the *creditors* are the suppliers and/or vendors. Some creditors who are anxious for your business, particularly those who sell a commodity product, can often be persuaded to accept anywhere from 60- to 120-day payment terms. Obviously, the extra 30- to 90-day credit availability is a source of cash.

Second, the *lenders* are the banks and/or equivalents like asset-based lenders, mezzanine lenders, and/or factors. They provide either short- or long-term debt or both, and they have varying requirements for collateral—secured or unsecured. Debt allows your company to leverage itself to quickly take advantage of market conditions. Provided that your operating income can comfortably cover the debt service, i.e., interest and principal payments, and your long-term debt does not exceed your shareholders' equity, then you should utilize this source of financing.

Third, shareholders' equity is a combination of money invested in the company through stock ownership and retained earnings. The latter are profits produced by the company that remain in the business rather than being paid out in dividends. The sources of capital for financing an acquisition are lenders, new owners, and previous owners. Another way of understanding the sources of capital is shown in the following exhibit.

CORPORATE BALANCE SHEET

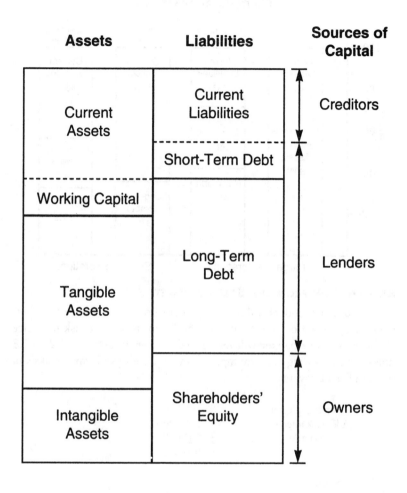

Assets	Liabilities	Sources of Capital
Current Assets	Current Liabilities	Creditors
	Short-Term Debt	
Working Capital		
Tangible Assets	Long-Term Debt	Lenders
Intangible Assets	Shareholders' Equity	Owners

HISTORICAL DISTRIBUTION OF ASSETS FOR SMALL AND LARGE CORPORATIONS

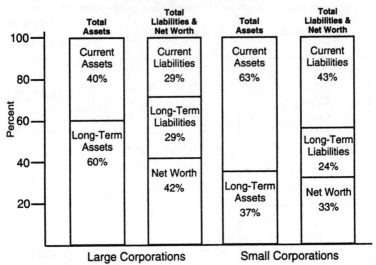

	Large Corporations		Small Corporations

RAISING CASH FROM THE BALANCE SHEET

Most traditional lenders will base their loans on the cash flow of the borrower. Depending on the stability of the business and the risk tolerance of the bank, your banker will expect debt coverage between 1.2 to 1.8 times. The following is an example of an acquirer's pro forma analysis of the EBIT debt coverage.

Operating income	$ 600,000	
Add back interest	$ 200,000	
Add back taxes	$ 200,000	
	$1,000,000	
Reorganization add-backs		
Excess compensation	$ 100,000	
Vehicles, travel, etc.	$ 100,000	
		$1,200,000
Less: Bank interest	$ 300,000	
Shareholder return	$ 200,000	
Noncompete agreement	$ 100,000	
Bank repayment	$ 200,000	
		$ 800,000

Debt coverage ($1.2 million divided by $800,000) = 1.5

In spite of the above analysis, your banker will ultimately look to the balance sheet for collateral. You might expect to raise the cash as follows:

		Allowable Amount
Accounts receivable	$1,000,000 × 75 %=	$750,000
Inventory	$2,000,000 × 25% =	500,000
Fixed assets	$3,000,000 × 75% =	2,250,000
	Loan Availability	$3,500,000

The preceding analysis was principally based on cash flow and debt coverage; the following analysis is an asset-based analysis.

Developing a Financing Package Based on Company Assets

The following example is printed with permission by Price Waterhouse from its book *The Buying and Selling a Company Handbook*.

Background

A target company has had a history of strong, steady cash flow with the current year at $2.5 million. A $25 million purchase price has been agreed upon by the buyer and seller. Appraisals indicate that the land and buildings have a market value of $4 million and the liquidation value of machinery and equipment is $3 million. Standard ratios by senior lenders are applied herewith.

1. Balance Sheet (000s)

Assets		Liabilities & Equity	
Accounts Receivable	$ 6,000	Accounts Payable	$ 3,000
Inventory	$ 8,000		
Land and Buildings	$ 2,000		
Machinery and Equipment	$ 4,000	Equity	$17,000
	$20,000		$20,000

2. Senior Debt Financing (000s)
   a. Revolving line of credit:

Accounts Receivable	$6,000 × 80% =	$ 4,800
Inventory	$8,000 × 40% =	$ 3,200
		$ 8,000

   b. Term debt: secured
   Land and Buildings (market)

	$4,000 × 80% =	$ 3,200
Machinery and Equipment (liquidation)		
	$3,000 × 60%	$ 1,800
		$ 5,000
c. Term Debt: cash flow		$ 7,500

3. Source of Acquisition Funds (000's)

Buyer's cash (equity investment)	$ 4,500
Senior debt:	
Revolving line of credit	$ 8,000
Term debt: secured	$ 5,000
Term debt: cash flow loan	$ 7,500
	$25,000

Summary

Price Waterhouse advises clients on how to structure acquisitions. In this case Price Waterhouse reminds us that a lender will not necessarily lend funds based on the result of applying standard percentages to recorded values. Lenders will also evaluate your ability to service the debt through an analysis of proper debt coverage.

CHAPTER 13

Picking Apart the Financials

In analyzing a company to acquire, one scrutinizes the financials for a number of different reasons. First, the current balance sheet and income statement give you a quick snapshot of how well the company is performing. Second, taking a minimum of three years' statements, and ideally five years', will show you how well management has run the business. Third, the recent financials will indicate to what extent you can leverage the balance sheet in order to finance the potential acquisition.

In this chapter, we will be analyzing the financials principally to assess management's ability, which is different from analyzing the numbers for the purposes of a valuation. For example, it is very possible to have a second- or third-generation family business with a well-known branded product that the company has manufactured for 100 years, a strong balance sheet, and an income statement that shows healthy gross margins but minimal profits. In this situation, you might determine that the target company is mismanaged and could indeed be very profitable. There are three basic conclusions, as follows:

1. As a buyer, you should not pay a full price for what the company could earn if properly managed.

2. If you buy the company, you probably should be reluctant to keep management in place based on the company's underperformance.

3. All things considered—the economy, the industry of the target company, its products, its reputation, its facilities, and its gener-

al financial condition—this could be a good acquisition at the right price, notwithstanding its current undermanagement.

It is therefore important to pick apart the financials to understand if and how the operations of the company can be improved. The following techniques are recommended.

DISCLOSE TRENDS

Using three years of past financials or two years plus the projected current year, arrange each item in vertical columns by percentages of the total.

Item	Balance Sheet Year 1	Year 2	Year 3
	Assets		
Cash	8%	6%	4%
Accounts receivable	37%	40%	45%
Notes receivable	3%	2%	0%
Inventory	20%	25%	30%
Prepaid expenses	2%	2%	1%
Total Current Assets	70%	75%	80%
Land and buildings	20%	17%	15%
Machinery and equipment	10%	8%	7%
Less depreciation	(2)	(2)	(2)
Goodwill	2%	2%	2%
Total Assets	100%	100%	100%
	Liabilities		
Notes payable	5%	3%	1%
Accounts payable	20%	28%	35%
Taxes payable	4%	3%	2%
Accruals	1%	2%	2%
Total Current Liabilities	30%	34%	40%
	Capital		
Long-term debt	10%	12%	13%
Stock	40%	36%	32%
Paid-in surplus	20%	18%	15%
Total Capital	70%	66%	60%
Total Liabilities and Capital	100%	100%	100%

Profit and Loss Statement

	Year 1	Year 2	Year 3
Gross sales	100%	100%	100%
Less: Returns/allowances	2%	3%	4%
Net sales	98%	97%	96%
Cost of goods sold			
Materials	(40%)	(41%)	(42%)
Labor	(20%)	(21%)	(22%)
Gross profit	38%	35%	32%
General and administrative expense	(20%)	(20%)	(20%)
Selling expenses	(10%)	(10%)	(10%)
Total Expenses	(30%)	(30%)	(30%)
Operating profit	8%	5%	2%
Interest	(2%)	(3%)	(4%)
Taxes	(3%)	(2%)	(1%)
Net profit after tax	3%	0%	(3%)

Analysis

In this case the sales were rising. However, in a period of three years the company went from making money to losing money. By looking first at the profit and loss statement and then at the balance sheet, we can determine what happened.

Returns and allowances. Any number over 2 percent should be of real concern. Either the quality of the product is poor or the company has a far too liberal return policy, or both.

Gross profit. This is the second most important item, other than net after tax. One can afford to operate at a reduced gross margin if sales increase dramatically and SG&A expenses do not materially increase. In this case, management should have been able to either increase prices to offset the higher material and labor costs or find alternative ways to keep these costs from increasing.

Selling, general and administrative expense (SG&A). This is commonly known as overhead. Many companies faced with severe price competition, making it unwise to increase prices, have the alternative of cutting their overhead in order to remain profitable. In this case, management did not select this alternative.

Accounts receivable. Along with inventory, this requires careful scrutiny because it should be turned into cash in a relatively short period of time. Former I.T.T. CEO and business icon Harold Geneen once said, "The company can lose money indefinitely, but once it runs out of cash, the game is over."

Inventory. Managing inventory is one of the most important functions of modern-day management. Just-in-time delivery, inventory turnover, order completion, etc., are the benchmarks for success. A number of years ago it was common to build cars, computers, etc., for stock. Nowadays, customers' orders are specifically matched to production schedules, which reduces unnecessary inventory, thus allowing management to utilize its cash most effectively. The major problem with this hypothetical company is the rapid increase in both accounts receivable and inventory, which is a result of management's not properly managing its assets. In order to finance these two items, the company has increased its accounts payable and long-term debt.

Long-term debt. Usually long-term debt is incurred to finance plant and equipment. However, in this case one can see that it was used to finance working capital, or more specifically the increased accounts receivable and inventory. In other words, the company is using more permanent capital to finance short-term obligations. This method of financing is not considered sound.

In summary, by going through every item and converting the numbers to percentages, one can quickly understand how the company is performing and why. A well-managed company makes adjustments quickly, assuming there are accounting systems in place to flag the various indicators. If the selling price of the product must be cut to meet the competition, then the lower gross margin must be offset by cutting the overhead (SG&A). If sales are faltering, then perhaps management needs to increase its sales expense but offset this increase by reducing some other expense. The point of this analysis is to evaluate management's ability to manage the business and to determine whether there are systems in place that will give management timely information in order to make these decisions.

BENCHMARKING

Numerous books and various consulting firms concentrate on benchmarking, which is basically comparing a company against certain industry standards. For financial benchmarking, Robert Morris Associates has compiled the most comprehensive figures not only for every industry and/or type of business but for various business sizes within these groups.

Robert Morris Associates is located in the Philadelphia National Bank Building in Philadelphia, PA 19107.

The purpose of benchmarking is to compare the target company with its peers in its particular industry. If we look at the retail business, for example, there are basically four major variables:

Volume
Overhead as percentage of sales
Inventory turnover
Cost of capital

It would not make sense to compare the financial ratios of a small office products retailer with those of a large chain of office superstores such as Staples. The ratios would not be meaningful. However, you might want to think twice about buying a small office products retailer if there is any possibility that you might be competing with a Staples, an Office Max, or an Office Depot sometime in the near future, as they could drive you out of business.

Based on the four major variables mentioned above, let us observe the different gross margins on which the following types of retailers operate successfully.

Type of Retailer	Gross Margin
Warehouse clubs	10–12%
Superstores	25%
Small retailers	40–45%
Department stores, high-end retailers	50%+

RATIOS

There are basically three kinds of ratios:

Balance sheet ratios	Various balance sheet items compared.
Operating ratios	Expense account items compared to income.
Operating items	Compared to balance sheet items and vice versa.

There are an infinite number of ratios; some of the basic ones are as follows:

Current Ratio (arbitrary numbers)

$$\frac{\text{Current assets}}{\text{Current liabilities}} = \frac{\$125,000}{\$75,000} = 1.67$$

Short-term obligations ($75,000 in this case) should have a cushion of liquid assets such that the current ratio is a minimum of 1.5 to 2.0.

Average Collection Time for Accounts Receivable

$$\frac{\text{Sales per year}}{365 \text{ days}} = \frac{\$1,000,000}{365} = \$2,740 \text{ average sales per day}$$

For some businesses, the acceptable average is 45 days. If we multiply $2,740 × 45 days, the accounts receivable would be $123,300. If accounts receivable in this case are substantially larger than $123,300 for a nonseasonal business, corrective action should be implemented.

Inventory Turnover (Figures From Balance Sheet)

$$\frac{\text{Cost of goods sold}}{\text{Inventory}} = \frac{\$400,000}{\$100,000} = 4 \text{ turns}$$

While every business has different norms for turnover, one rule of thumb that I like to use is the following formula:

Gross Margin	Turnover	Norm
50%	2	100
25%	4	100
10%	10	100

Return on Investment (ROI)

$$\frac{\text{Net after tax}}{\text{Invested capital}} = \frac{\$100,000}{\$500,000} = 20\%$$

No single ratio is as important as ROI, and there is no one acceptable number for all investors. The principal variable is the amount of risk associated with the investment, known as the risk/reward factor. A venture capital investment usually requires a 30 percent + ROI. A very solid company should return 18 to 20 percent. These ROI numbers ultimately compare to the safest investment, Treasuries, with an approximately 8 percent return.

CONCLUSION

It is important to pick apart the financials to determine how well the company is managed. The decision about the strength of management will affect the ultimate valuation of the company. There are obviously many factors to consider in analyzing the financials. One company may have a higher profit as a percentage of sales, but upon closer observation it may appear that more capital is invested in the company than is actually required. Therefore, scrutinizing the financials in great detail is imperative before acquiring a company.

CHAPTER 14

Looking Beyond the Numbers

Let us assume that you have spent a year seeking a company to acquire; you have spent considerable time negotiating the deal and an equal amount of time securing the necessary financing, and now all you have to do is some due diligence. You have retained a prestigious accounting firm to verify the inventory, accounts receivable, accounts payable, etc. However, you have charged yourself with the responsibility of evaluating the status of the company to be sure there are no skeletons in the closet and that you won't buy a pig in a poke.

You have outlined the four most important areas of concern, i.e., finance, management, manufacturing, and marketing. Specifically, you have segmented these areas of concern as follows:

Finance
Cash. If the target company is not taking trade discounts or is not able to buy at the quantity price or is late in trade payments, you might assume that there is poor cash management.

Lack of profitability. One might consider that the company lacks controls, has too much overhead, or underprices in order to make the sale. A comparison of the gross margins from year to year is a quick indicator of whether the manufacturing efficiencies are slipping or whether there is a price erosion.

Bank problems. One might find that the company's financial ratios are out of compliance, that it is under particular scrutiny from the bank, that it has used its complete credit line, or that it has suspect relations with its bank.

Outdated financials. One might discover that the company does not have monthly financial statements or detailed cash flow projections. Furthermore, one might discover that the company's annual financial statements are three to four months after year end and that the statements are not audited, all of which mean that they lack credibility.

Management

Continual crisis. Every time you meet with the owner, he or she is constantly interrupted by emergency telephone calls and secretarial demands for immediate decisions.

Substantial changes in key personnel. A review of the last three years shows an unusual turnover in key management positions, including CFO, sales manager, and vice president of manufacturing.

No changes in senior management for many years. This may indicate a stagnant business, not up with the times, and dominated by the CEO.

Lack of pride. While pride is somewhat subjective, one can often sense the tempo and spirit of the personnel by the tone of their voice and the bounce in their stride.

Manufacturing

Dying market. The company is in a dying market and has no capability to shift gears.

Rejects. One should determine the rate, the reason, and what quality controls are in place. What do the records show, and how does management address this important issue?

Just in time (JIT). What the inventory turnover is and whether there are too many vendors would be part of the JIT analysis.

Sales per employee. Many industries are different, but a fully integrated manufacturer should have at least $70,000 sales per employee, and a distributor should have $200,000 sales per employee.

Marketing

Loss of market share. The key in evaluating market share is to be able to compare the increase or decrease in unit volume with that of the direct competition. Sometimes specific price increases will increase dollar sales, but the true measure is unit sales.

Trade shows. During due diligence, one should observe the interest and activity in the company's booth at trade shows compared to its competitors.

New products. The rate and success of new products is partially related to the extent of the company's R&D. Part of 3M's success is due to the fact that 30 percent of its products are introduced in every five-year cycle.

Many sellers have a "sixth sense" that tells them when their industry and/or business has peaked or turned south. It is up to the buyer to smoke out the symptoms of trouble and beware of why the company is for sale.

The above is a quick overview of items that you should look into beyond the analysis of the financial statements. Almost all companies have warts. Prospective buyers tend to focus on these problems. It is more important to focus on the company's strengths, and in particular, what the company is doing well. The following is an example of a company that can be analyzed both ways, analogous to the expression that the glass is half full or half empty.

A third-generation family business with $20 million in sales has a management team of four. Three members of the team are from the family. The business is growing at 15 to 20 percent annually, has an operating income equivalent to 10 percent of sales, and has no long-term debt. Its products are office partitions of excellent quality. Manufacturing is low-tech but very efficient in a favorable labor market. Sales are somewhat seasonal, and the workforce fluctuates between 150 and 200. The sales breakdown is as follows:

Home Depot	50%
Distributors	40%
Government	10%
	100%

The company depends on Home Depot for half its business; however, this manufacturer won the supplier of the year award from Home Depot based on service, quality, merchandising, customer support, etc.

Based on this limited information, would you buy this business and would you heavily discount the value because of the dependence on one customer? There is no clear-cut answer. If you have a tolerance for a certain amount of risk, you might buy the company with the full intention of broadening the sales base. Bear in mind that the new wave in business is for the customer-vendor relationship to be equivalent to a partnership. Many companies in the automotive parts business are heavily dependent on a major customer or two.

Ideally, your target company will have very few warts. In addition to the obvious problem of heavy dependence on a single large customer, other risk factors include the following:

INDUSTRY

Many times we have heard people talk about a company's being in the proverbial "buggy whip" industry, implying that the industry has passed its prime. Many issues concerning the target company involve external forces that are beyond your control. In the book *How to Buy a Business* by Joseph, Nekoranec, and Steffens, the authors state:

> By thinking about these competitive and industry issues, you may be able to expose the strengths or weaknesses of the business and its competitors. If a weakness is discovered, try to determine if it is temporary or a permanent part of doing business. External forces are often the most difficult to manage, so caution should be exercised in planning the ongoing business on the assumption that these forces can be modified or mitigated.

One industry with which I am familiar is the plastic grocery and produce bag business. BPI Packaging Technologies of Dighton, Massachusetts, with only $18 million in sales, is competing in an industry of giants such as Mobil and Sonoco, for which the plastic bag is a derivative of oil. Aside from this vertical integration, the small player faces other nearly insurmountable obstacles. The capital equipment requirements are enormous. BPI has six plastic film extruders, each costing approximately $1 million, plus another line of machines to print customer logos and a third set to convert the film into bags.

In addition, plastic bag manufacturers sell mostly to supermarket chains. In most cases these bags are considered a commodity item, and the buyers will switch vendors at the slightest price differential. Furthermore, the supermarkets are working on a very tight just-in-time inventory delivery system, so that plastic bag manufacturers are expected to deliver to a central warehouse on a specific day within a two-hour time frame. In many cases, the manufacturers buy their raw product, oil, on the spot market. Spot prices vary from day to day, but the manufacturer must quote firm bag prices to its customers. The result is that the plastic bag manufacturer can get whip-sawed on the pricing differential. Even though BPI is a well-financed company, it faces enormous challenges, due mostly to the inherent nature of the industry.

The converse of the above example is companies in an industry that is past its prime or is too small to expect significant volume growth.

There are other industry considerations, such as possible product obsolescence in the high-tech industry or fad changes in the fashion industry. In order to have meaningful growth in the food industry, manufacturers must pay "slotting fees" to get their products on supermarket shelves. Almost every industry has its peculiarities, and it is up to you, the buyer, to thoroughly familiarize yourself with them.

PRODUCTS AND SERVICES

Back in the 1960s a friend of mine, Leif Nashe, decided to sell the Dovre Ski Binding Company. Although under $1 million in sales, it was one of the premier companies in its industry. A number of entities wanted to buy Dovre, including United Shoe Machinery, a well-known New England manufacturing company. Leif turned down United Shoe's generous offer because he insisted that the buyer be willing to keep the business in West Concord, Massachusetts, for the sake of his employees.

Leif was born in Norway and naturally grew up on the ski slopes, particularly the jumping hills. He started the company in the 1930s, just as downhill skiing caught on in the United States. His cable bindings were well-known and at one time had the highest industry rating worldwide for quality, price, service, reliability, etc. During World War II, Dovre received a windfall of orders from the U.S. Army. After the war, recreational skiing really started to catch on, and Leif capitalized on the industry's growth. Dovre rarely advertised and had no sales force. Marketing consisted of Leif calling on his ski dealers once a year, buying them a drink, and giving each dealer a special box of custom-made chocolates.

In the mid-1960s, Leif sold the business to two smart young Harvard MBAs on condition that they not move the company. By then, the ski industry was changing rapidly: The wooden ski was replaced by the Head metal ski and cable bindings by the modern "pop-out" safety bindings. Dovre had just started to produce the new bindings and was undaunted by the invasion of new high-tech German bindings.

The two buyers were aware that Dovre was no longer on the leading edge of product innovation, but what they didn't realize was how much money it would take to rebuild the company. No longer could they sell capable bindings, and no longer could they successfully solicit orders by handing out a box of chocolates to their dealers once a year.

Giant companies from Europe, like Salomon, had overnight invaded the U.S. ski industry; they were able to offer huge quantity discounts and "off-season" deals that allowed the dealer to withhold payment for six to eight months.

Without going into further details, the new owners used everything they had learned from their business school training. They vastly expanded their product lines, including ski and boat racks, imported cross country ski equipment, and finally, opened a factory outlet operation. By the early 1980s, the business was bankrupt.

Clearly a multitude of mistakes were made in the example above. Not only should the two young entrepreneurs have turned down the opportunity to buy the business, but having bought the company, they wandered too far away from their core business. If Peter F. Drucker had been the key adviser for the two buyers when they were considering the acquisition, he probably would have asked them three of his stock analytical questions.

- Is the company's market standing going up or down, and is its industry being negatively affected by alternative products or services?

- Is the company's achievement as a successful innovator in its market equal to its market standing, or does it lag behind it?

- Is the company concentrating on improving its productivity in order to gain a competitive advantage?

CUSTOMERS

Early in this chapter, I discussed the risks of being dependent on a few key customers, so I will not repeat that aspect. In addition to the mix of customers, it is important to understand the quality of customers, their financial stability, and their likelihood to grow. Naturally, if your customer base grows rapidly, it will increase your chances of growing also.

Back in the 1960s, I owned a fiberglass boat manufacturing company. Most of our dealers struggled to make a living. Inevitably we would extend thirty-day billing terms, which in turn led to shipping product to them in the fall with spring payment terms, commonly known as "dating", i.e., ship now and collect later (hopefully).

Our manufacturing company was not financially strong itself. Luckily we operated without too many losses, but we were fortunate that there was no industry downturn or recession.

Look at the target company's customer list. Ideally, many of the customers are from the *Fortune* 1000. Also track each customer's volume of business over the past three years. And finally, understand the characteristics of the industry payment terms. For example, some segments of the retail business, especially discount chains, continually dispute manufacturers' invoices. They may continually return so-called faulty merchandise, claim shortages in shipments, take 2 percent discounts beyond the specified ten-day period, and so forth.

Analyze the customers. Are they the type of companies and the type of people to whom you want to sell? If not, think twice about pursuing the target company.

Suppliers

Obviously, vendor relationships are important and should be transferable to the new owner(s). This should be of particular concern in the purchase of a distributor. Many relationships between the distributor and its suppliers are personal, and those that are contractual are for a very limited time period. If you are contemplating the acquisition of a distributor, be sure the retention of key suppliers is linked to the payout period for the purchase of the business.

Management

In looking beyond the numbers, it is imperative that you assess the management team early in the process. In the book *How to Buy a Business*, Joseph, Nekoranec and Steffens write: "Understanding the strengths and weaknesses of current management will help determine what changes are possible. The most important issue you need to consider is whether the owner is the reason for the success of the business. If so, the company is extremely vulnerable to management changes. If he or she leaves, can you fill this role?"

Most companies with sales under $5 to $10 million are heavily dependent on the chief executive officer. In many cases, a full management team is not in place. I know of one public company with sales just under $20 million that has no chief operating officer and only a part-time chief financial officer. A company's strength is often its management team.

LOOKING FOR THE COMPETITIVE ADVANTAGE

In looking beyond the numbers, you should be seeking characteristics that make the company special, separate it from its competitors, and in essence give the company a competitive advantage. The well-known Harvard Business School professor Michael Porter popularized the theory of competitive advantage in his best-selling book on that subject.

To determine the competitive advantage, I like to ask the president of a selling company three basic questions:

What differentiates your company?
How do you grow the company?
What would you do if the company received a sizable windfall in cash?

Surprisingly, many company presidents will not have a definitive answer to these simple questions, which merely dampens my interest in their business. Specific examples of competitive advantage would include:

Investment in capital equipment. A $7 million distribution company sells coffee and citrus juices to institutions, e.g., universities, hospitals, hotels, etc. It charges a higher price than its competitors, but it has loaned (not leased) over $1 million of dispensing machines to its customers, guaranteeing twenty-four-hour service. Unless this distributor's competitor is willing to invest sizable amounts of money in capital equipment, there is little chance that the distributor will lose its competitive edge.

Price elasticity. An adhesive company with sales of $3 million was showing operating profit and owner's compensation of $500,000 because it was able to raise prices considerably without loss of business. Since adhesives are often custom produced, the adhesive company is able to retain the formula as proprietary information. The actual cost of the adhesive in a customer's product, e.g., boat, camper, etc., is such a small component of the total cost that the risks of the customer's switching to another vendor are slight.

Low-cost producer/response time. A $15 million manufacturer in the office supply business is located in a modern plant in a rural area where occupancy and labor costs are relatively low compared to those faced by other industry players. Because the company services only a few, but large, accounts, orders are shipped in truckload quantities. The direct sales results in a very low selling expense, and the general and administrative staff is kept to a minimum. This company's competitive advantage is that it executes the basics very well, commonly known as blocking and tackling in football. The company's response time is quick, whether it is developing a new product for a customer or shipping within two days of receipt of order. If a customer has a surge of orders as a result of the seasonal factor of "back to school" business, this company will ramp up production by going to three shifts.

Uniqueness. Most of us know that location is one of the critical elements in the retail business. For most major retailers, it is desirable to be located in the primary malls as opposed to the secondary malls. Most malls have a restriction of one of each type of store per mall, e.g., one bookstore, one men's shoe store, etc. Therefore, if you own a chain of bookstores or men's shoe stores, you could be prohibited from renting space in the primary malls. When The Nature Company developed an exclusive product line of merchandise, there was virtually no retail competition. As a result, the company had almost no barriers to entry when it applied for space in a primary mall, except of course, if there was no vacancy.

Other examples of competitive advantage include patent protection, like that of the exercise machines of Nordic Track, license agreements, franchises, brand recognition, etc.

THE ROLE OF A DEVIL'S ADVOCATE

When looking at companies, it is important to look at the downside as well as the upside. The seller has the advantage over the buyer in that he or she will know more about the industry and the company than the buyer. The stated reason for selling the company may not be the real reason. Undisclosed reasons might include such things as the following: the industry may be quickly changing, the competition might be increasing, customers might be having financial difficulties, and capital spending requirements might be escalating.

Maybe the owner realizes that middle management is weak and there is no strong successor, or that there are no new products in the pipeline. Perhaps his or her gut feeling is that now is the time to sell. Many consumer product companies, whether they be sailboat or wood stove manufacturers, have gone from boom to bust in a short period of time. The consumer market can be fickle, while the industrial market is more stable.

There is an old story that I heard many years ago. I cannot remember if it was true or a myth. There was a somewhat distressed southern textile company that the board of directors was anxious to sell. A prospective buyer from the north came to visit the company. The board had the bright idea of dressing the janitor in a suit, seating him behind the president's desk, and giving him the role of CEO—for an hour. After the interview, the prospective buyer concluded that if the selling company's CEO knew so little about the business, just imagine what a smart fellow could do with it! Of course, the moral of the story is "buyer beware!"

On this last note, if you have some apprehension about buying the company, particularly as it applies to items beyond the numbers, then I suggest that you take the following advice of Andre Laus, principal of Bristol Group, a Providence, Rhode Island, business consulting firm.

It is unusual that a founder's, temporarily remaining in place is not desirable. Additionally, the best deal for buyers is one in which seller paper can be used as subordinated debt. Consequently, as long as former owners are owed money, then they have a right to view themselves as quasi-partners, and I would suggest that the insightful buyer consider structuring a share of future earnings improvement to the former owner's benefit—as long as he's in place. Of course, it is desirable for the seller to have some sort of security on the notes, and there should be a reasonable risk rate on the coupon. The fact that the seller continues for a short time as a quasi-partner, albeit as a debt holder, certainly creates value in the deal. The seller as your quasi-partner in the transaction has a vested interest in helping you foresee problems and keeping you out of trouble.

CHAPTER 15

Negotiating

Negotiating the purchase of a business is the most dramatic segment of the transaction. Just as Act III of a Shakespeare play is the climax, the negotiation is the climax of an acquisition. Inevitably, the buyer ends up paying more for the company than he or she originally planned and the seller ends up receiving less than he or she expected.

Throughout the book I have mentioned this axiom: The seller sets the price and the buyer sets the terms. With an individual buyer, the seller will probably be reluctant to accept unsecured notes and/or significant consulting and noncompete agreements which are also unsecured, because of the perceived risk of selling to an individual rather than to an established business.

Usually a seller will receive the best deal from a synergistic buyer who will gain additional complementary products/services and/or distribution with marginal increase in overall overhead. In other words, the modus operandi for the synergistic buyer is to make an acquisition whose result is 1 + 1 = 3. Therefore, a synergistic buyer can afford to slightly overpay for an acquisition because he or she can make up the difference by increased efficiencies and sales when the two entities are combined. On the other hand, an individual buyer is acquiring the company as a stand-alone and is usually fairly disciplined on return on investment (ROI). I have a friend who is a very successful businessman and who has several million dollars to put toward buying a company. After four years he still has not bought a company. My characterization of this fellow is that he always offers 5 times earnings before interest and taxes (EBIT).

For good companies, that formula is certainly realistic; however, very anxious corporate buyers will simply pay more.

There are basically three ways to negotiate.

Take it or leave it. Regardless of the seller's price and terms, you make an offer, perhaps your only and best offer, and let the chips fall where they may. This is obviously a disciplined approach. I call it the Margaret Thatcher method, as she demonstrated success by being stern and forceful during her tenure as prime minister of England. Unlike corporate buyers, you do not have to buy the company to prevent your competitors from acquiring it. In other words, nothing is forcing you to buy the company, and so you can easily walk away from the deal. The problem with the "take it or leave it" approach is that it is apt to sever the communication with the seller in case you want to get the discussions back on track. Furthermore, if your offer is made before other offers, your price will be used as a stalking horse to extract a higher price from others.

Split the difference. Assuming that you purposely underbid, leaving yourself some latitude to increase your offer, an oversimplified approach to negotiation is to split the difference between your price and the seller's price. For example, if you offer $3 million for the business and the seller wants $4 million, then $3.5 million is a reasonable compromise.

This for that. It is really important, if not imperative, that the buyer find out what the seller *really* wants as well as what are the seller's "hot buttons." It is very helpful if you take the time to break bread with the seller in order to determine his or her psyche. One should find out the nonmonetary items that are important to the seller such as the following:

- The seller would like to stay involved with the business in some small way and/or would like to maintain an office there.

- The seller would like to have one of his or her children remain in the business.

- The seller would like to see employment contracts for key personnel.

- The seller does not want the factory to be closed down and the business moved.

- The seller may have spent a lifetime building up a dealer network of small retailers and does not want the new owner to change the distribution system to mass discount chains.

- The seller may have subcontracted much of the piecework to various handicapped associations and does not want the new owner to terminate those relationships.

Knowing the nonmonetary issues will help you understand what concessions you can give up to achieve your monetary goal. You also have to assess how close or far apart you are in the negotiation. Let us assume that you have determined that the seller's price is based on a fixation on receiving the magical figure of $1 million after tax. In other words, the seller has dreamed and worked all his life to become a millionaire. Any other approach to valuing the business is not meaningful to him. There are ways to structure the transaction to mitigate some of the taxes. For example, if a C corporation sells its company stock instead of selling its assets, the company will avoid the double taxation, i.e., one tax to the corporation and another tax to distribute the money out of the corporation into the owner's personal account. One of the buyer's concessions could be to buy the stock of the corporation, even though this has the disadvantage for the buyer that assets cannot be written up to provide a higher basis for depreciation, and the buyer must assume contingent liabilities from the previous management. It may be worth it for the buyer to get the deal done.

It is not unusual for a verbal offer to be discussed as soon as the third meeting. It is better to get some cards on the table fairly early on. My experience is that many owners do not want to name a price before and until the potential buyer goes first. If a seller has retained an intermediary, there is often a better chance that the seller will discuss a price range or a methodology of pricing the company. Assuming that this is not the case, then it is up to the buyer to initiate the conversation regarding the pricing and terms of the deal.

In this conversation, the buyer should be cordial, polite, businesslike, firm, patient, candid, and open. While the buyer should show some humility, he or she should be confident and self-assured, and take the lead in the meeting. As an introduction to the conversation, the buyer should be complimentary about the seller's business, emphasize the buyer's capabilities to finance the acquisition, and continually remind the seller of the need to treat this matter as totally confidential.

The next facet of the conversation should be a general description of how you determine valuations of companies in general and how that relates to the seller's industry, followed with a brief analysis of how you went about valuing the seller's business. Having gotten this far, I would then say: "After considerable analysis, I am willing to pay you $2.5 million for your business." Watch very carefully to sense any and all reactions from the seller. It is highly unlikely that the seller will immediately accept your offer. It is more probable that he or she will respond by saying, "No way." At this point, the seller should reveal his or her price and how he or she arrived at that number. Let's assume the seller responds with a price of $3.5 million. Then you should respond by saying that maybe we should figure out how we can structure the deal so that you might get closer to the seller's price. You should ask if the seller is willing to help you finance the transaction, which of course means seller's notes (secured or unsecured). At this point, you should not discuss the financial aspects any further at this meeting. However, you should find out, if you haven't already, about all the nonfinancial issues discussed earlier in this chapter. It is better to wait until the next meeting to discuss the details of the structure of the transaction unless you feel that you and the seller are fairly close on the pricing.

As a buyer, it is important that you assess your advantages and disadvantages before you begin to negotiate. For example, if the owner has decided to sell the company, he or she usually has made the mental decision to complete the transaction even if the buyer's offering price is lower than what was originally expected. Your advantage is that the seller is somewhat committed to sell, but you are not necessarily committed to buy. On the other hand, if you really want to buy this business, there will undoubtedly be other buyers whom you have to compete against. Having numerous potential buyers gives the seller some leverage over you.

As a buyer, if you approach a company that is *not* on the market, you have little leverage because the owner is probably not motivated to sell. In this case, the owner would not have a need for a well-documented selling memorandum. Additionally, the owner always has better information on the company and probably has better knowledge of the industry than you do. The power of information should not be underestimated. It is believed that one-third of all acquisitions are failures and another one-third fail to live up to their buyers' expectations. Part of the reason is that buyers do not have sufficient information to properly evaluate the situation. Many buyers look for information to confirm or corroborate their hunches. Therefore, the first order of business in negotiating is to be well prepared with careful analysis—not just number crunching, but an alertness to the business and its industry.

Going forward, you should assess what are the real issues and how important each is to you and the seller, which items are negotiable and which are not negotiable. It is best to start with the negotiable items and see if a compromise can be reached. You should think of the possible tradeoffs and possible alternatives before you begin the negotiation. For example, if the seller wants the buyer's note secured, then the buyer can negotiate a lower interest rate on the note. You should predetermine your best price, only to be used in the last hour, and you should assess your bargaining zone ahead of time. And of course you should anticipate the reaction of the recipient of your offer.

TEN TIPS IN NEGOTIATING FROM A BUYER'S PERSPECTIVE

"Negotiation is a basic means of getting what you want from others," according to the authors of *Getting to Yes—Negotiating Agreement without Giving In*. Of course, one has to negotiate with substance, knowledge, and skill, but negotiating to buy a business requires a greater understanding of the dynamics of the deal than, let's say, buying an automobile. With that statement in mind, let us proceed with ten tips for buyers.

Style
Often we have heard the expression that a lawyer who represents himself has a fool for a client. This statement is not limited to lawyers and courtrooms. In the book *Smart Negotiating*, James Freund states:

> Anyone approaching a significant negotiation should consider whether to go it alone or use an agent. There are many good reasons to conduct negotiations through an agent:
> The agent's technical expertise or negotiation skills.
> The principal's emotional involvement in a high-stakes deal, which hampers his ability to negotiate effectively.
> The principal's desire to avoid having to answer certain questions or to react to a new proposal on the spot.
> The agent's ability to float a trial balloon without implicating his principal.
> The principal's reluctance to cross swords directly with a counterpart who will be working closely with the principal once the relationship is established.
> The possible advantages obtainable through limiting the agent's authority.
> The use of an agent isn't an unmixed blessing, however. It can involve such potential risks as:

- Faulty communication between principal and agent that harms the principal's cause.

- An agent with his own agenda or bias who doesn't faithfully represent his principal.

- A principal who won't level with his agent and thus impairs their dealings with the other side.

- A nitpicking agent who misses the big picture and thereby undermines the deal.

- The inability, due to interposed agents, of one principal to reach the other agent's principal directly in order to be able to persuade, to pressure, or to extract a decision.

The obvious answer to the above two scenarios is for the principal and the intermediary to work as a team. Of course, the first decision to be made is who should be the lead spokesman. If the intermediary is to be the spokesman, then the principal can play the "good guy" and the former can be the "bad guy." The good guy/bad guy routine is a form of psychological manipulation. In other words, the intermediary takes the forceful position and, when necessary, the principal can step in with statements such as, "In the interest of moving the deal ahead, we will concede that issue." On the other hand, if the principal is the spokesman, one approach is for him to be a little bit like Lieutenant Columbo. As we know, Columbo asks blunt and naive questions that result in candid answers by the other party.

Information

A buyer can never obtain enough information on the industry, the company, the owner/employees, the products/services, etc. Unless you have reason to trust someone, don't. When an owner tells you why he or she is selling the company, be sure that the reason can be confirmed and that the sale is not due to some hidden fact. The seller has the advantage of knowing more about the situation than you do. Perhaps a casual visit with the owner away from the company will enable you to understand more of the key issues.

Leverage

This works both ways. As a buyer, you should be able to sense under what constraints, if any, the owner has to sell, i.e., financial, time, emotional, etc. The seller has leverage over the buyer if there are numerous other buyers negotiating or about to negotiate with him or her.

Brainstorming

Before entering into negotiations, spend several hours with a corporate valuation expert to determine a rational price range and deal structure. If possible, bring a group of your peers together to obtain various opinions and ideas as to how you might present your position.

Anticipate

One of the most important skills a negotiator can possess is the ability to see the situation from the other side. A buyer should go into the meeting with several options and with an open mind. If you cannot agree on a substantive issue such as the price of the business, then agree on a procedure in an attempt to bridge the gap. One buyer suggested that both the buyer and the seller retain a mutually agreed-upon valuation firm to arrive at a price. If the firm determined a price that was mutually acceptable, then the buyer would pay for the valuation. If the seller refused to accept the firm's valuation, then both buyer and seller would split the cost of the report.

Presentation

It is very important for the buyer to present a plausible case for how and why the price was determined. The buyer should express interest in the company as well as giving the reasoning behind the proposal and then the proposal. The offer should be supported by objective criteria and relevant precedent.

Control the Price Issue

Traditionally most buyers prefer that the seller initially state a desired price. The first figure that is mentioned is considered the anchor price, the price that is the basis for further discussion. In the book *Smart Negotiating*, James Freund states:

> Too many negotiators wait for the other party to make the first proposal, only to have him trot out an exorbitant figure and then dig himself into a real hole supporting it. If you think there's a chance of this happening, take control of the negotiations with your own carefully considered first proposal. The major omission is the failure to back up initial positions with credible and convincing rationale.

As a buyer, you want to take control of the price. You want the seller negotiating off your opening number, not off his or her number. However, under no circumstances should you mention the price until you have made a plausible case for your opening bid and gone through an objective process. Part of the reasoning behind this is that once the seller hears your proposed price, his or her attention level wanes.

Nonprice Issues

You will hear over and over again the expression, "The seller sets the price; the buyer sets the terms." Or you might hear the statement, "Terms are more important than price." When we think of terms, naturally our initial focus is on the payment structure of the deal. Actually there are many other nonprice issues, such as key employment contracts, a commitment not to move the factory, an obligation for the company to maintain a commitment to the town, the retention of the owner's son in the business, etc. Many deals that were about to crater have been resuscitated by such issues. Inventing an idea, any idea, that can be decided on later shows your initiative to break the logjam.

Bluffing and Concessions

Before you start bluffing and conceding, you should have full knowledge of your "reserve" price—the limit at which you will do the deal. Again, I draw on the concise advice from the author of *Smart Negotiating*:

> Save your bluff for a significant issue.
> Bluff at the end of the process.
> Make your offer appear consistent with something you have been saying all along.
> Try to come up with a plausible explanation for why there's no give in your position.
> If possible, couple your bluff with a show of flexibility on some other issue.
> If you're forced to back down, have a "changed circumstances" ready to go in order to mitigate any harm to your credibility.

Regarding concessions, keep them small and infrequent. Also, express your sacrifice even if the concession is relatively painless. Don't concede something until you ask your counterpart to justify his request, and do not be too quick to make the concession. Also, be careful not to become swept up by equal-dollar concessions. If the seller reduces the asking price from $4 million to $3.6 million and you go from $3 million to $3.4 million, the seller has come down 10 percent and you have gone up 13 percent.

As a buyer, you should use two other negotiating tools. One is deadly silence, which you purposely let pervade a room when you are at an impasse. Invariably, your counterpart will become so uncomfortable that he or she may retract the previous statement. Another negotiating tool is the use of time, e.g., "We have to resolve this deal by tomorrow because I am flying to Europe on Wednesday."

Drafting the Deal

It is customary for the buyer to draft the purchase and sale agreement. While legal fees tend to be higher for the lawyer drafting the deal, you have better control over the document and the process by doing so.

NEGOTIATING GUIDELINES

Preparation

Assemble your documentation and go through the sequence of events of your presentation.

Presentation

Face to face, deliver your proposal backed with your reasoning. Realize that the seller may need time to digest the information from this initial meeting concerning the deal.

Demeanor

If your counterpart becomes very excitable and disagrees vehemently with your offer, remain absolutely calm and unflappable. Find out where you agree and where you disagree, and start resolving the easy issues first, leaving the most difficult issues until the end.

Options

Think of alternative ways to resolve your differences so that there is a win-win situation; however, always get something in return for a concession. Focus on the needs of both parties.

Preserve the Relationship

Keep the mutual respect intact and remain cordial and professional at all times. If you are at an impasse, break off and reconvene some other day in the near future.

Remember, perseverance is the key to successful negotiation. In order to prevail, you must persevere. Also, never commit yourself to a material point unless everything is on the table. If it is a substantial issue, you need to know what else is to be discussed and settled.

ADDITIONAL OBSERVATIONS

In Bob Woolf's book *Friendly Persuasion—My Life as a Negotiator*, he emphasizes that fair play is always the winning strategy. Woolf appropriately quotes Edward R. Murrow:

> To be persuasive, we must be believable.
> To be believable, we must be credible.
> To be credible, we must be truthful.

Bob Woolf is not known for negotiating M & A deals, and I doubt if he ever negotiated one. He is known for negotiating over 2000 contracts for some of the biggest names in sports and entertainment. Often we can learn from others who are in a similar but slightly different profession.

In reading *Friendly Persuasion*, it becomes apparent that Woolf's style can be summarized by his own words: "I never think of negotiating against anyone. I work with people to come to an agreement! Deals are put together."

Of the 101 proven tactics, techniques, and strategies that Woolf cites, the following ten particularly caught my attention:

1. As basic as it sounds, your first mission in negotiating is to present your views as reasonable expectations and to secure the other side's full understanding of exactly what you want.

2. It doesn't hurt to ask. Salespeople are often reminded to ask for the order. In negotiating, you must ask for everything you want.

3. Your style should not be demanding or filled with ultimatums, and never let a counterpart's ultimatum intimidate you.

4. Silence is one of the most important tools. Either it is the things you *don't* say or it is a deliberate method of not committing yourself at that time.

5. You should assess both your leverage and your counterpart's leverage. You should convey that you want to do a deal, but you do not have to do the deal. It is "do or don't, but not do or die."

6. Be prepared with alternatives. Since there are a number of components to the deal (price, terms, collateral, intangibles), there are a variety of alternatives.

7. Take notes on everything relevant to the price, terms, and conditions during the meeting so that there is less chance of misunderstanding. Upon agreement on the deal, send your memorandum of understanding to your counterpart.

8. Come up or go down slowly on your concessions; otherwise you will imply that your previous position was probably out of line. Also, try to make minor concessions in return for your counterpart's major concession.

9. Do not give tit for tat. Just because your counterpart comes down $100,000, you do not have to go up the same amount. Also a drawn-out negotiation makes your counterpart feel that he or she "earned" the deal even if it was less than originally planned. If you pounce on an offer, you reveal your position too easily.

10. Perhaps the best advice from Bob Woolf is that "some of the best moves are the ones you don't make"—i.e., know when to hold and know when to fold.

In the book *Deal-Breakers and Break Through*, John Illich cites Napoleon's flexibility of never presetting his battle strategy as a lesson for negotiators. "Napoleon simply prepared thoroughly for a battle he knew was coming and conceived his battle strategy right on the spot after carefully determining what his opponent would do." John Illich goes on to say, "Negotiation is a freewheeling activity in which anything can and often does happen."

Other negotiating points emphasized in the above book include:

- Try to deal directly, face to face, with the person who has final authority to bind the agreement.

- Deadlines, even self-imposed deadlines, provide an important source of negotiating power.

- Repetition is a potent force. Reiterate the key supporting facts at every opportunity, blending them into the presentation until they are indelibly etched in the opponent's mind.

- Beware ... experienced negotiators might deliberately skip from one issue to another and back again to confuse or muddle their opponents thinking. Many negotiators fail to attain equalization quickly and effectively. The necessity of equalizing an opponent's position is a vivid illustration that negotiation is, in the final analysis, mind versus mind.

- Controlling the negotiation becomes paramount because lack of control means lack of power.

- Avoid polarization ... declaring "This is my final offer; take it or leave it" makes it almost impossible for your counterpart to offer an alternative proposal.

- When you make an offer or counteroffer that contains a deadline for acceptance, you cut down your opponent's options significantly. How significantly depends upon the nearness of the deadline.

- Timing is the most critical element in closing. The assumption technique should be practiced with care and tact, such as: "Do you want our office to prepare the closing agreements?"

CHAPTER 16

Letter of Intent

The letter of intent (LOI) is a precontractual written instrument from the buyer to the seller that usually covers the preliminary understanding of both parties. Other names used for the LOI are memorandum of understanding and agreement in principle. The LOI precedes the acquisition agreement, better known as the purchase and sale agreement. In order for the LOI to be nonbinding, it must state that this is the case.

Letters of intent are written after the two parties have had a serious discussion concerning the price, terms, conditions, and time period of the proposed transaction. Commonly, in my experience, buyers submit an LOI after they think they understand the parameters of what the seller will accept. In many cases, the buyer uses the LOI as the initial basis of negotiating. If there is reason to believe that the two parties are fairly close to agreement, the buyer will draft a second LOI. If the buyer is experienced or is working with an experienced intermediary, it may not be necessary to involve a lawyer at this time. However, it should be noted that lawyers resent being pulled into the deal after the LOI, and if it is necessary to make a material change in the future, it becomes very difficult to do so.

The LOI is the centerpiece of the transaction. It both eliminates the less serious buyers and/or sellers and uncovers key issues early on in the process.

As you prepare the letter of intent, the more knowledge you have about the company and its financials, the stronger the case you will be able to build. I urge you to solicit a second or third opinion from a competent intermediary and corporate appraiser. A few hours spent with these professionals at approximately $200 per hour would be well worth the expense. However, although you should take their advice seriously, ultimately you have to make the decisions.

The elements of the letter of intent are as follows:

1. The price.

2. The form of purchase: Stock or asset sale (assumption of what assets and liabilities, and exactly what is being purchased and what is not).

3. The structure: Cash, notes, stock, noncompete and/or consulting agreements, contingencies.

4. Management contracts: For whom, duration, and incentives.

5. Closing costs and responsibilities of buyer and seller, e.g., environmental due diligence, title searches.

6. Representations and warranties: Boilerplate legal statements.

7. Brokerage fees: Who pays and how much.

8. Timing for completion: Drop-dead date for due diligence and financing; how long before the exchange of money and final closing.

9. Insurance: Proof of insurability and/or what happens with policies.

10. Disposition of earnings before closing and viability of nonordinary expenditures before closing (conduct of business).

11. Access to books and records, key customers, and key employees prior to closing.

12. Disclosure of any outstanding noncompete agreements or obligations with third parties.

13. Statement that this is a nonbinding agreement subject to the buyer's obtaining satisfactory financing and subject to satisfactory due diligence by both parties.

14. Strict adherence to confidentiality by buyer (a breach could cause the seller to sue the buyer). Buyer promises not to disclose information of seller to outsiders and not to disclose that negotiations are underway.

15. Statement that the seller will take the company off the market for a designated period of time of forty-five to sixty days (a breach could cause the buyer to sue the seller).

The next step is to deliver the letter of intent in person to the seller and explain each item point by point. As trite as it may sound, body language is very important—eye contact, sincere smile, etc. As you discuss your offer, remember that there are a number of issues:

- Price
- Terms
- You, the buyer, and the chemistry with the seller
- Nonfinancial issues
- How fast you can close

Usually, once the seller strikes a deal, the more quickly you can secure the financing, complete the due diligence, and draft the purchase and sale agreement, the less chance there is that the seller will change his or her mind. After the letter of intent is signed, an expeditious closing will take between sixty and ninety days, assuming that there are no major glitches such as environmental issues. Bringing the deal to a successful close will be a full-time job.

When you deliver the letter of intent, you absolutely do not want to lose momentum by having the seller say, "Thank you, I'll think it over." Ask the seller to bring advisers or other stockholders to the meeting. Allow plenty of time for the discussion, but make it clear that you expect to come to an agreement on the nonbinding letter of intent at least by the second meeting.

You should predetermine your negotiation strategy:

Determine your top price (although you may not pay it).
Identify key issues for both you and the seller.
Anticipate responses by seller.

You should also determine before the meeting whether you or your adviser will be the major spokesman. Perhaps if there are some negatives about the company to divulge tactfully, it should be mentioned by your adviser (bad guy), not by you (good guy). Such negatives could include outdated machinery and equipment that is uncompetitive for the future. A few comments like the latter will show the seller that you have a good understanding of the business and that you will have to invest more money in the company after the sale is completed. Furthermore, you can tell the seller that you cannot pay more for the business because you have others with a vested interest to satisfy, such as partners, investors, and bankers.

One of my worst experiences as an intermediary happened when I represented a very successful distributor of fruit juices, coffee, tea, and hot chocolate. One of the distributor's suppliers manufactured juice-dispensing machines. The manufacturer's sales were $9 million, and its operating income was $1 million. My client and four other investors were to buy the company for $5 million, all cash at closing! If successful, my accomplishment fee as an intermediary would have been $150,000.

My client and I went to the seller's office. I was in a mood to lock ourselves in the room and throw the keys away until the deal was signed. However, while the five partners had agreed to a $5 million purchase price, the other partners did not show up at the meeting. Even though the letter of intent was nonbinding, my client would not sign it by himself. We left the office with a verbal offer, but there was no psychological commitment by the seller. The golden opportunity slipped out of our hands, because soon after the seller received a higher bid, although with significantly less cash at closing.

While the following figures seem a little severe, Geneva Business Services, a nationwide intermediary, reports that 50 percent of all deals fail at the letter of intent stage. Another 25 percent of the deals fail at the due diligence stage, and 15 percent fail at the documentation stage. *Only 10 percent of all deals make it all the way to closing!*

As aptly defined by Stanley Foster Reed, author of *The Art of M & A*, a letter of intent is a precontractual written instrument which defines the respective preliminary understandings of the parties about to engage in contractual negotiations. In most cases, such a letter is not intended to have a binding effect except for certain limited provisions. The letter of intent crystallizes in writing what have, up to that point, been oral negotiations between the parties about the basic terms of the transaction.

While the letter of intent is usually nonbinding, it does create a moral commitment and allows the buyer to proceed with the extensive due diligence process with a feeling of confidence. However, the buyer should insist that the seller withdraw the company from the marketplace and not discuss the potential sale with anyone else.

The signing of the letter of intent triggers the buyer's commencement of the due diligence process and securing the necessary financing. However, it isn't only the seller who should be scrutinized. The seller will want to check you, the prospective buyer, out to be sure that you are creditworthy and that you are committed to completing the deal. As an individual, your credentials might be examined more closely than if you were a corporation.

Anticipating the seller's due diligence, verify your financial strength by presenting detailed financial statements, and emphasize your liquid assets. If asked, you should be prepared to submit a list of potential lenders or investors for this proposed acquisition. I hope you have done your homework by contacting potential lenders prior to the letter of intent.

Along with your financial position, the seller will want to know about your personal characteristics, so take time to meet with the seller socially. You want to maximize the likelihood of a successful sale.

The critical ingredients in the letter of intent are the following:

The proposed sale price
The down payment
The size, length, and interest rate of a note and, if it is secured, how is it secured
Other considerations affecting the price, such as partial earnout based on a predetermined formula
A list of contingencies

The contingencies would include the arrangement with the seller if he or she stays on. If the seller leaves, the agreement would specify the length and terms of any training period and include a noncompete agreement. Other contingencies would include

Review of the company's financial records
Examination of insurance policies
Availability of vendor and customer contracts
Assignment of lease
Asset or stock transaction

It is customary for agents who broker companies with sales of less than $1 million to ask the buyer for a good faith deposit of $5000 to $10,000, but it is not common for middle-market transactions. The cost for due diligence is the burden of the buyer. Depending on its complexity, due diligence can cost the buyer of a middle-market company between $10,000 and $100,000. If the seller backs out of the deal for any of a number of reasons, including seller's remorse, the buyer has no recourse unless he or she has a break-up fee written into the LOI. While the latter is desirable for the buyer, it is very hard to persuade the seller to agree. The success or failure of completing the transaction hinges on the LOI. Upon signing the agreement, both parties are morally but not legally committed to do their utmost to complete the transaction. The outcome depends on the results of the due diligence, the ability to get the deal back on track if it is temporarily derailed, and the sense of alacrity without loss of momentum.

The buyer may be apprehensive about submitted LOIs. This lack of action is often caused by a confidence problem. From my viewpoint, buyers without M & A experience should align themselves with professional intermediaries who will encourage them to move forward. Cautious buyers should remind themselves of football quarterbacks. Even the best quarterbacks average only 50 to 55 percent completion rate, but they may throw forty passes a game. As in football, buyers have to be willing to write numerous LOIs in order to score.

The important issue is not submitting the LOI, it is signing the purchase and sale agreement after the due diligence has been completed. Of course, the buyer's greatest fear is not knowing everything about the target company—that he might be buying a pig in a poke, that due diligence did not uncover everything. At the same time, the seller is afraid that information will leak out; that his employees, customers, and suppliers will hear about the deal prematurely; or that the buyer really doesn't have enough money after all.

As the buyer, you have the right to control the drafting of the LOI and the purchase and sale agreement. While it will cost you more in legal fees, it is critical that you exercise this option in order to write your own language into the agreement.

DATA NEEDED BEFORE REACHING A LETTER OF INTENT

Let us assume that you have visited the owner and CEO of a company two or three times, you have received three years of financials, you understand the owner's compensation and add-backs, and you are now ready to make an offer. The owner has not given you any idea of the acceptable price range, and before you analyze this situation any further, you want to get the seller's reaction, so you decide to use a trial balloon. Based on the information you have and using your best judgment, you tell the owner that you are prepared to draft a letter of intent with a purchase price of, say, $5 million, of which $3 million would be paid at closing. Additionally, you should state your intention of an asset purchase or stock purchase. Assuming that the seller indicates that you are close enough to draft a letter of intent, then the following items should be obtained:

1. Annual financial statements with footnotes for the last five years

2. A list of shareholders and key managers showing name, age, shares owned, current position, years of service, annual salary, fringe benefits, last raise, and breakdown of bonuses between discretionary and formula basis

3. A list of all contractual obligations

4. A list of the top twenty customers, substituting A, B, C, etc. for actual names, followed by annual sales for the last three years

5. A description of bonus or incentive systems

6. A list of aged accounts receivable

7. Add-backs or any earning adjustments that probably would not be incurred under new ownership

8. Real estate, machinery, and equipment appraisals (if any)

9. A breakdown of inventory among raw, finished, and work in process, (banks do not lend against the last).

10. Amount and description of capital expenditures for the last five years and an estimate of future needs

11. If a stock purchase, a copy of loan documents

12. If a stock purchase, a list of life insurance policies showing insured, face value, any cash surrender value, and annual premium

CHECKLIST OF ITEMS IN LETTER OF INTENT

1. Description of the buying organization: place of business, owners, etc.

2. Statement of price, structure, contingencies, and exactly what is being purchased

3. Description of any notes—interest rate, term, amortization provision, secured or unsecured, negotiable or nonnegotiable, and whether the buyer will have the right to offset part of the note if the seller does not meet certain conditions in the purchase and sale agreement.

4. Management contracts—for whom, duration, and incentives

5. Explanation of closing costs, including intermediaries' fees and who pays what

6. A statement that representations and warranties will be a part of the purchase and sale agreement

7. Description of profit-sharing arrangements

8. A list of contingencies that have to be resolved in order for the transaction to be completed, e.g., environmental problems, title transfers, etc.

9. Planned changes to be made, such as management, and continuity items, such as not relocating the plant

10. Estimated date of closing

11. Transferability of insurance

12. Reconciliation of debts or collections with shareholders

13. The same continuity of business until closing date

14. Access to books and records

15. Description of consulting and noncompete agreements

16. The adherence to confidentiality by both parties and the understanding that the letter of intent is nonbinding and that the seller will take the company off the market for a specified period of time

17. Whether the parent company (if there is one) should also sign the letter of intent and/or if the guarantors of the selling company's obligations (if there are any) should also sign the document

18. Whether to create an escrow account to handle postclosing adjustments to the purchase price to reflect changes in inventory, final audited financials, collections of accounts receivable, etc., to offset seller's contractual claims

OBSERVATIONS

Writing an LOI is time-consuming. Although it is a fairly short document, it requires some serious thought. Because it is a nonbinding agreement, if so stated, you have the comfort level of knowing that you can back out. However, the chances are slight that you can materially change the price and terms of the deal after you have entered into the LOI.

One of the biggest concerns of the seller is whether the buyer has the financial resources to complete the transaction and to have sufficient reserves thereafter in case the business needs another infusion of capital. As a buyer, be prepared to share your financial information with the seller.

As stated by David Broadwin, transaction attorney for Foley, Hoag & Eliot in Boston: "You should devote careful attention to LOI, not only because they memorialize the terms of a proposed transaction and give the principals a feeling that they have reached an understanding, but also because they exert a profound influence on the definitive documentation of the transaction."

CHAPTER 17

Putting the Deal Together

STRUCTURING THE DEAL

Most sellers start out wanting all cash for the deal. However, a figure that appears to be fairly accurate is that only 36 percent of deals are all cash at closing. There is an old axiom that the seller sets the price and the buyer sets the terms. What is evident is that if the seller demands all cash in the transaction, he or she probably will receive a lower price for the company.

Buyers are often capable of paying all cash at closing, but are afraid they will lose all their leverage if the business does not turn out to be what was represented. The new owner often wants some hand-holding during the transition period and therefore will structure a consulting agreement over a year or two with the former owner. Terms are perhaps more important for small companies that do not have audited financial statements, particularly if the sale is a stock transaction in which the buyer assumes all the assets and liabilities on the balance sheet. Even though an asset purchase is a safer method of acquisition for the buyer, the use of terms in the structure is a safeguard against any improprieties and/or oversights by the seller.

A normal structure for a deal might be the following:

Buyer's cash	30%
Bank's cash	30%
Note	20%
Noncompete/consulting agreements	10%
Earnout	10%
Total	100%

The cash from the bank is obviously what you borrow against inventory and accounts receivables. Typically a bank will loan you 50 percent on your inventory (excluding work in process) and 75 percent on current accounts receivables. The seller will want you to personally guarantee the note, asking for a second mortgage on your house, for example. Undoubtedly you will not want to do that (nor will your spouse), and you might offer to secure the note by subordinating it to the bank's note. These differences can often make or break a deal. On the other hand, noncompete and consulting agreements are traditionally non-interest-bearing instruments and nonsecured. The partial earnout is usually a way for the buyer to stretch to meet the seller's price. It is particularly helpful when the buyer values the company based on today's financial statements, and the seller is valuing the company on the future earnings potential. One method for a partial earnout is to structure it with 2 to 4 percent of the gross profit for a set time period, with a cap on the total dollar amount.

From a seller's perspective, accepting terms as part of the transaction allows him or her the benefit of the installment sales tax provision, i.e., taxes are paid over a number of years. In times of a credit crunch, economic conditions often preclude deals getting done for all cash.

During the 1992–93 recession in Canada, Doug Robbins of Robbinex Business Brokerage in Hamilton, Ontario, said,

> Closings are elusive partly because bank financing is nearly impossible. Of the last eight deals, none had bank financing and three had financings provided by angels with 15 percent guaranteed coupon backed by 25 to 40 percent of the owner's stock. Without bank financing, these angels are in first position on the debt, and even with equity kickers, the angels are at high risk. Deals are getting done mostly if the buyer has 50 percent of the purchase price with his own cash, and the seller will finance the balance.

Example of a Deal Structure

A niche specialty chemical manufacturer decided to sell. It was a family-owned business, and the founder had died. While the son was successfully running the company, the heirs wished to have liquidity, since all their assets were tied up in their nonliquid stock. The basic figures were as follows:

Sales	$20 million
Operating income	2 million
Long-term debt	0
Book value (net worth)	3 million

The buyer used a 4.5 earnings multiple on the $2 million operating income, which placed a value of $9 million on the company. The deal was structured as follows:

Buyer's own cash at closing	$3 million
Bank debt—cash at closing	4 million
Note to seller—secured by chemical co.	2 million
Total	$9 million

The above structure is very basic, but two items are noteworthy. The buyer was a buyout group with $25 million available to do deals. The group used only $3 million of its own money, and the note was secured not by the buyout group, but by the chemical company itself. The other noteworthy feature of this transaction was that the buyout group wanted the founder's son and present CEO to remain with the company in the same capacity. Therefore, the buyout group persuaded the son to buy back 10 percent of the company for $300,000 (10 percent of the $3 million equity), and as an incentive the son had the option to buy up to 20 percent of the company in the next five years.

Example of Another Deal Structure

The following example was provided by Joseph Myss of Wayzata, Minnesota, in his book *Divestiture Strategies for Owners of Private Businesses*. This case involves the use of an earnout portion to reconcile the $1 million difference in value between the buyer and seller.

The two parties agreed to use EBIT as the financial benchmark, and they negotiated a minimum EBIT that must be earned each year before the earnout takes effect. Additionally, the two parties agreed upon a percentage, in this case 75 percent of the amount above the base EBIT hurdle to be paid to the seller.

Illustration	In Millions		
	1995	1996	1997
	Actual	Projected	Projected
EBIT	$1,625	$1,780	$2,000
Base EBIT (negotiated)		(1,200)	(1,300)
Excess over base		580	700
75 percent of excess to sellers		435	525
Cumulative earnout payment		435	960

Conditions

Interest expense and miscellaneous other nonoperating income are excluded from the earnout formula. Unusual items are also excluded, such as sale of nonoperating assets, sale and leaseback of plant assets, and insurance recoveries postacquisition. The seller should have reasonable control over decisions that can affect the results that will be used to measure the earnout payments.

EARNOUT

Structuring the transaction in order to complete the deal to your satisfaction will be one of the most challenging aspects of buying a business. In many cases, when you and the seller seem deadlocked or unable to overcome your differences, an imaginative method of structuring the deal will often overcome the obstacles. Professional brainstorming by your advisers may provide the breakthrough.

Usually the most prevalent reason that transactions are not completed is the price gap between what the buyer is willing to pay and what the seller is willing to accept. Commonly the buyer values the target company on a multiple of past earnings and the seller values the company on discounted cash flow from future earnings. A possible solution is the use of an earnout to bridge the gap.

An earnout is a portion of the purchase price that is contingent on future performance over a certain time period, such as three to five years, and may have a maximum limit.

Earnouts are used not only when there is a significant price differential, but also in the following circumstances.

When there is a major customer concentration
When the company is about to introduce new products

When the company is expecting a very significant contract
When service companies are transferring relationships
When the buyer has limited equity
When the seller has been losing money

The benefits of an earnout are numerous:

The seller shares in the growth of the company
It reduces the buyer's risk of overpaying
It reduces the buyer's cash at closing
It reduces the purchase price payment at closing
It quantifies uncertainty
It protects the purchaser who was shy on due diligence

Sellers are often reluctant to accept earnouts because it is difficult to determine the true earnings. The seller has to have complete trust in the buyer.

ASSETS VS. STOCK TRANSACTION

Very early in the discussion of acquiring a particular business, it is imperative that the buyer and seller discuss whether the transaction will be an asset or stock sale.

The buyer almost always wants to buy the assets, because he or she can avoid most potential lawsuits from inherent corporate liabilities and can write up the assets, allowing greater depreciation to shelter future earnings.

On the other hand, the seller usually wants to sell stock, because for a C corporation there will be only one tax (compared to a double tax for an asset sale). Furthermore, if the seller has used accelerated depreciation for the machinery and equipment, he or she may face a possible depreciation recapture tax for selling the machinery at a higher value than that shown on the books. An asset sale is more time-consuming because of the Bulk Sales Law, more costly because there is a legal transfer of each asset, and more difficult because of the need for third-party consents on leases, loans, etc.

If the transaction is an asset sale, then the purchase price is assigned to specific assets at their fair market value (not the depreciated value on the books). The difference between the purchase price and the allocation of the purchase price is goodwill. Under the new tax laws, goodwill can be amortized over fifteen years, along with other intangibles such as non-compete and consulting agreements.

Because it is so important to understand the pros and cons of asset and stock purchase, I have received permission to replicate the following analysis prepared by Price Waterhouse in their book *Buying and Selling a Business*.

Assets Purchase
Buyer's Position

Advantages

Step-up basis of assets acquired to purchase price, allows higher depreciation/amortization deductions.

Recapture tax on presale depreciation and investment tax credit paid by seller.

Buyer can pick and choose assets to buy and liabilities to assume.

Buyer is generally free of any undisclosed or contingent liabilities.

Normally results in termination of labor union collective bargaining contracts.

Employee benefit plans may be maintained or terminated.

Buyer permitted to change state of incorporation.

Disadvantages

No carryover of seller corporation's tax attributes (i.e., tax basis of assets, earnings and profits, operating and capital loss carry-forwards, accounting methods, accounting periods, installment reporting, or previous sales and employee benefit plan contributions).

Nontransferable rights or assets (i.e., license, franchise, patent, etc.) cannot be transferred to buyer.

Transaction more complex and costly in terms of transferring specific assets/liabilities (i.e., title to each asset transferred, and new title recorded; state sales tax may apply).

Lender's consent may be required to assume liabilities.

May lose right to use corporation's name.

Loss of corporation's liability, unemployment, or workers' compensation insurance ratings.

Assets Purchase
Seller's Position

Advantages

Seller maintains corporate existence.

Maintains ownership of non-transferable assets or rights (i.e., license, franchise, patent, etc.).

Maintains corporate name.

Disadvantages

Taxation occurs at the corporate level upon liquidation.

Generates various kinds of gains or losses to the seller based on the classification of each asset as capital or ordinary.

Transaction may be more complex and costly in terms of transferring specific assets/liabilities (i.e., title to each asset transferred and new title records; sales tax may apply).

Lender's consent required to assume liabilities.

Stock Purchase
Buyer's Position

Advantages

Tax attributes carry over to buyer (i.e., tax basis of assets, earnings and profits, operating and capital loss carryforwards, accounting methods, accounting periods, installment reporting on previous sales, and employee benefit plan contributions).

Transaction is less complex (i.e., endorsement of stock certificates).

Avoids restrictions imposed on sales of assets in loan agreements and potential sales tax.

Preserves the right of the buyer to use corporation's name.

No changes in corporation's liability, unemployment, or workers' compensation insurance ratings.

Nontransferable rights or assets (i.e., license, franchise, patent, etc.) can be retained by the buyer.

Disadvantages

No step-up in basis (i.e., seller's historical tax basis is carried over to buyer) unless buyer elects and incurs additional tax cost.

All assets and obligations (i.e., disclosed, not disclosed, unknown, and contingent) are transferred to the buyer.

Recapture tax on presale depreciation and investment tax credits falls on buyer.

Normally does not terminate existing labor union collective bargaining contracts.

Generally results in the continuation of employee benefit plans.

State of incorporation remains the same.

Dissenting shareholders' right of appraisal of the value of their shares with the right to be paid appraised value or remain a minority shareholder.

Stock Purchase
Seller's Position

Advantages

Avoids taxation at the corporate and shareholder level.

All obligations (i.e., disclosed, not disclosed, unknown, and contingent) and nontransferable rights can be transferred to the buyer.

Generally provides capital gain or loss so that there is no need to calculate gain or loss by asset type.

Generally avoids ordinary gain.

Disadvantages

Seller cannot pick and choose assets to be retained.

Ownership of nontransferable rights or assets is lost.

Requires selling corporation's shareholder approval.

CHAPTER 18

Due Diligence

To my knowledge, no one has done a documented study of why many mergers and acquisitions do not live up to expectations. Without discussing all the various possibilities, it is reasonable to say that many acquisitions fail principally because due diligence was inept.

A comprehensive due diligence study is time-consuming, expensive, and very broad. The majority of the work takes place after the letter of intent is signed and goes far beyond such items as environmental disclosures and whether the owner has the legal authority to sell the business. For the purposes of this chapter, I have used the term "due diligence" to refer to investigating the company after the letter of intent has been signed, as opposed to the assessment of the business prior to this period. The purpose of the due diligence is to help you determine whether you want to go forward with the transaction or whether you want to renegotiate the price and terms of the deal based on your findings. If you are going forward with the deal, you want to be sure that you will be receiving the assets you expect, and that there will not be any unexpected liabilities or unexpected expenses postacquisition. One resource is the publication by Coopers and Lybrand, *Checking Into an Acquisition Candidate*.

The following suggestions are merely ten items that I have highlighted to give you a flavor of the enormous variety of due diligence matters.

1. In buying the assets of the business, as opposed to the owner's stock, supplier and customer contracts will have to be reassigned to the buyer in order to maintain a valuable right.

2. Review the *customer list* and corresponding annual sales volume. Numerous middle-market companies have one or two major customers, which places the company in a very vulnerable position if such an account is lost. It is not uncommon to have 80 percent of the sales produced by 20 percent of the customers. Obviously a more balanced distribution of sales is desirable.

3. Some businesses have subtle and unorthodox ways of conducting business that may be foreign to the buyer's comfort level. It may be necessary to give favors to key people in order to procure the sales. Try to understand the intricacies of each particular business.

4. Knowledge of personnel issues is a key factor to prevent surprises after the company has changed ownership. Obtain an organizational employee chart. If the company is a family business, are there nonworking members on the payroll, and/or are there members working without pay? Find out what each employee earns in the way of salary and fringe benefits, and how and when raises, benefits, and stock options have been exercised. What employment contracts and other deferred compensation agreements exist?

5. Obtain a complete list of all machinery and equipment to appraise its approximate value and to ascertain whether it is outdated. Sometimes buyers assume that they are acquiring all the machinery on the factory floor, only to find out later that certain pieces have been leased.

6. It is prudent to find out early on in the company buyout whether there is any litigation. Obviously, the extent of the litigation may affect whether you want to proceed with the acquisition; if you do, you would certainly be more inclined to buy the assets of the business than the stock.

7. Carefully assess the financials. Audited statements are vastly more credible than unaudited statements. With audited statements, accounting firms verify such items as accounts receivable, inventory, promissory notes, etc. As a buyer, you should be receiving timely statements as you evaluate the company, if not on a monthly basis, at least on a quarterly basis. Be sure you analyze the aging of the accounts receivable to determine the nature of the customers' paying habits. Your banker will be particularly interested in this aging list, as it represents collateral

for your borrowing. Analyze the inventory breakdown among raw materials, work in process (WIP), and finished goods. Most banks do not lend money on WIP inventory. The inventory turnover rate varies with different industries, but it is an important number to measure. The last-in, first-out (LIFO) method of inventory calculation understates earnings because it reports inventory costs at the older prices (which are usually lower, given the inflationary trend in our economy). Therefore, companies using LIFO instead of FIFO report more conservatively.

8. It is important to understand the company's return policy and guarantees. Some companies have an open-ended arrangement on returns, which can be costly. One distributor that imports in-line skates from the Orient and sells to discount chains let its return policy get out of control. The distributor's total sales were $20 million. Gross margins were a very tight 20 percent and returns amounted to 2 percent, or $400,000! The discount chains were taking advantage of the distributor and returning merchandise for reasons that were unwarranted. As a buyer of a new company, you want to be sure that sales are not generated in part by very liberal return policies and/or by overly generous payment terms (net ninety days) or consignment sales.

9. Pay attention to the expense item *Professional Services*, to be cognizant of what and why the services were provided. For example, if the accounting fees showed an unusual increase for the last year, perhaps it was a result of an IRS audit. If so, the buyer will want to know the details. If the legal fees were considerably higher, perhaps this was for defense of a lawsuit. Other professional services like environmental consultants might reveal the tip of the iceberg.

10. If the company has a pension plan for the employees, be sure that it is not underfunded.

According to Stanley Reed, author of *The Art of M & A*, "The basic function of due diligence is to assess the benefits and liabilities of a proposed acquisition by inquiring into all relevant aspects of the past, present, and predictable future of the business to be purchased." Due diligence is a process that starts as soon as you are introduced to the target company and is ongoing even after the final purchase and sale agreement has been signed. Because some transactions are rushed in order to minimize the disruption for the selling company, a buyer should then try to incorporate more extensive representations and warranties into the selling document.

Only 10 to 15 percent of small to medium-size companies have audited financial statements. Audited statements, while costing a company 50 to 100 percent more, are significantly more comprehensive than an accountant's review or compilation. As a buyer, you should rely less on the accuracy of reviews and compilations, as such items as accounts receivable and inventory have not been verified by the accounting firm. The name of the game in due diligence is, do not assume anything. For example, if you walk onto the factory floor and see a lot of machines, do not assume that the company owns them all. Some may be leased. If you are looking at plastic injection-molding machines, do not assume that the company owns the molds, tools, and dies. They may be consigned from the customer of the parts. If the selling company does not have noncompete agreements with key employees, do not assume that the top engineer or sales manager will not leave the company and go to a competitor as soon as the acquisition is completed. The entire process of due diligence boils down to whether you should buy or not buy the target company based on certain price and terms. My analogy is passing the Wasserman test in order to receive a marriage license. If the target company does not pass the due diligence process, you should not buy the company.

There is a significant difference in the degree of due diligence depending on whether the purchase is an assets or a stock transaction. Obviously, if you buy the stock of the company, you are assuming all the assets and liabilities, with all the inherent ramifications, subject to the modifications of the representations and warranties. On the other hand, if there is an environmental problem on the real estate, just because you lease the property does not allow you to escape the penalties of the regulatory authorities.

Due diligence is more difficult when you are acquiring a division or a subsidiary of a larger company, particularly when the financials have been consolidated. The four areas of concern are as follows:

1. That all costs are properly reflected, whether they involve products or services being bought or sold between the two entities.

2. That business between the two entities is on an arm's-length basis, and items are not bought and sold because of the intercompany relationship.

3. That the division or subsidiary has the quality and depth of management to successfully operate independent of the parent company.

4. To what extent the parent company's access to services at favorable rates, e.g., accounting, tax, legal, insurance, benefits, information services, etc., substantially reduces the cost to the division or subsidiary.

PROCEDURE

Let us swing into action! Both parties have signed the letter of intent, in which the ground rules for conducting the due diligence have been outlined. At this point, another, more comprehensive confidentiality agreement should be executed which among other items states that the buyer will return all information if the deal crumbles. You will need to put together a team of due diligence experts, one of which should be an experienced accounting firm. Usually the seller will want to keep this investigation stage to between thirty and sixty days. The team of experts would include

Appraisers	For real estate and machinery/equipment
Engineer	Plant and equipment
Accountants	Financial
Lawyer	Legal
Environmentalist	For ground/water/asbestos etc.
Intelligence	Management audit

What you should expect to receive is the following:

1. Documents—Corporate by laws, minutes, financial statements, engineering assessments, tax certificates, patents

2. Statements—Liens (if any), encumbrances, Uniform Commercial Code (UCC)

3. Reviews—Litigation risk review

4. Audits—Environmental

5. Market studies

6. Contracts—With suppliers, customers, employees/employer, consultants; leases/mortgages; loan agreements; licenses; agreements with shareholders; pension plans/profit sharing plans/

fringe benefits; insurance policies; stock options; product warranties

7. Checklist

One way to organize the due diligence process is to set up a matrix of assets and liabilities with three categories to determine the real underlying values.

Items +	Amounts Recorded in Dollars			
	Undervalue –	Overvalue –	Unrecorded =	Difference
Plant/equipment	Depreciated			
Joint venture	Not recorded			
Lease	At favorable rate			
Inventory		FIFO		
Accounts receivable		Uncollectible		
Pension		Less than obligation		
Pending litigation			No reserve	
Pending severance			No reserve	
Product reserves			No reserve	
Etc.				_____
Total				_____

IN REVIEW

In reviewing the highlights of due diligence, it is important to keep three points in mind.

1. Verify the critical elements of the acquisition. Concentrate on the key issues of the target company and its industry. If you are buying a high-tech company, concentrate on transferring intellectual property without encumbrances. If you are buying a consumer product company, concentrate on possible product returns or recalls. And if you are buying a heavy manufacturer, concentrate on environmental issues.

2. Weigh the risk/reward factors of doing the deal. Small repercussions may be acceptable, but disasters must be avoided.

3. The net result of due diligence is not necessarily a go or no-go on the acquisition. You may still want to buy the company, but because of certain circumstances you may deem it necessary to renegotiate the deal by changing the price or structure.

There are four types of due diligence, financial, legal, business, and personal.

Financial Due Diligence

The acquisition audit should be conducted by an accounting firm that has a lot of experience and expertise in this extremely important type of investigation, particularly if the financials are unaudited. The objectives are twofold. One is to verify the figures in case there should be an adjustment to the purchase price. The second and more important is to determine whether the selling company is guilty of deceptive bookkeeping in order to spruce up the financials.

There are a number of items that will tip off the due diligence team that the books are being cooked, such as recording sales before the order has actually been shipped, recording consignment sales as actual sales, overvaluing the inventory, not posting all the accounts payable, etc. Your investigation should compare the company's income tax records with its financials, ascertain that withholding taxes have been paid, and check original documents to see if they have been altered, as well as conduct other audit procedures such as verifying payables and receivables.

A good due diligence team will red-flag rising selling expenses, inventory dead wood, extended terms on sales, slowdown on accounts receivable collections, or rising inventories, especially in finished goods.

Legal Due Diligence

From a legal standpoint, a thorough investigation would include the following items:

Authenticity of trademarks and patents
Adequacy of insurance coverage
Assumption of license rights
Environmental liabilities
Underfunded pension plan
Status of contracts

In the case of contracts, if there is a need to bring them all up to snuff, a portion of the purchase price might be adjusted downward. For example, there might be a plethora of contracts ranging from key employees, union, vendors, customers, leases, agents, etc., and so the legal expense to update the contractual arrangements could be sizable.

Business Due Diligence

The business due diligence includes the company's products, markets, competitors, employee relations, and industry regulations. In many cases, the buyer is searching for the real reason the company is being sold. The first order of business is to evaluate the company's key operating ratios over the past five years and compare them with the average for its particular industry as documented by Robert Morris and Associates. Key ratios would include

Gross profit/sales
Cash flow/sales
Selling, general, and administrative/sales
Selling expense/sales
Cost of goods sold/sales = inventory turnover

The three major items on which to focus are as follows:

The Industry

If an entire industry is growing, then all boats rise with an incoming tide. Nelson Gifford, former CEO of Dennison Manufacturing Company, reflecting on his three dozen transactions, said that you can often overcome paying too high a price for a business if it is in a fast-growing industry. On the other hand, you can underpay for a company in a declining industry and the outcome will be a poor acquisition in the final analysis. Also, it is important to understand the ramifications in a down market. If the proposed transaction is highly leveraged, then a target company selling heavily into the defense industry or a target company in a cyclical industry may not survive a down market.

Sales

To properly measure sales growth, it is important to divide the total number of employees into total sales to determine the sales per employee. The resulting figure is indicative of a company's efficiency. Most manufacturing companies should have sales of between $70,000 and $100,000 per employee. If sales costs are rising faster than actual sales, then perhaps the market is maturing and there will be a market slowdown. While this discovery may be of concern, it may not be a deal breaker. However, it does require further investigation to determine why noncustomers buy from the company's competition, what marketing is necessary to target noncustomers, and what other channels of distribution should be pursued.

Products

In evaluating a company, there are some items, like lack of profitability or perceived poor management, that can be rectified. However, if the industry is declining, the sales are declining, and the product is suspect, then it is safe to say that you should not have to do much more in the way of overall business due diligence.

There are agencies that will conduct an investigation of the CEO of the selling company to determine whether he has a criminal record, was dishonorably discharged from the military, has declared personal bankruptcy, has encountered IRS problems, etc. If you are investing millions of dollars and committing your energy to an enterprise, you would be remiss if you failed to determine whether the person representing that enterprise has a dubious background. Some firms like Cushing & Company in Boston (617-423-1144) provide comprehensive, insightful analysis of the strengths and weaknesses of management. Cushing & Company assesses the attributes, capabilities, and direction of a company's management. Its information comes not from the top but from the people in the labs doing the research or those on the factory floor. One must access lower management to fully understand top management, but the methodology and discretion is the key element in this regard.

CONCLUSION

There are a number of firms that specialize in M & A investigations above and beyond the normal due diligence process. Since 1982, Competitive Intelligence Inc. of Seattle, Washington (206-284-3480) has provided hard-to-get details on target companies. Due diligence is a critical component in a successful acquisition. The advice by Olivia Robinson of Competitive Intelligence is very appropriate: "You can never know too much about buying a business, but you can certainly know too little. If knowledge is power, the lack of it can only mean vulnerability."

CHAPTER 19

Representations and Warranties

The representations and warranties reflect the situation as of the date of signing the purchase and sale agreement. The representations are designed to uncover certain operations, such as business dealings that are not at arm's length, deferred compensation arrangements, unknown liens on assets, and penalties resulting from late tax filings. If a seller fudges on any representations or warranties, it is a breach of contract. According to the book *The Art of M & A—A Merger Acquisition Buyout Guide* by Stanley Foster Reed,

> These conditions are intended to disclose all material legal, and many material financial, aspects of the business to the buyer. The seller also gives assurances that the transaction itself will not have adverse effects upon the property to be conveyed. The buyer should be aware that lenders providing acquisition financing will require the buyer to make extensive representations and warranties about the target as a condition to funding.

Representations and warranties are very important in an acquisition, and according to Reed, cofounder of the Merger Week at Northwestern, "a buyer or seller will be able to back out of the agreement if it discovers that the representations or warranties of the other party are untrue to any material extent."

The purchase and sale agreement defines the parameters of both the purchaser's and the seller's representations and warranties. The heaviest negotiating near the closing date usually involves the representations and warranties and the indemnifications. Also, the seller's representations and warranties normally account for the largest part of the purchase and sale agreement. The investigation *follows* the execution of the purchase and sale agreement and obviously *precedes* the closing. If an adverse material fact surfaces after the closing, then the seller will have to compensate the purchaser based on a breach of representation. The following seller's representations and warranties are the most important:

1. *Financial Statements.* A closing audit is imperative to verify the authenticity of all the items, particularly inventory, receivables, and payables. Then a postclosing adjustment is factored into the final floating payoff at closing.

2. *Assets.* The buyer wants to be sure he or she is gaining full title to the assets, particularly to such items as intellectual property, patents, etc. Also, the buyer wants assurances that the machinery and equipment are in good working order.

3. *Taxes.* Not only is it critical to verify the seller's tax liability if it is a stock purchase, but if it is an asset purchase, you want to be sure that there are no liens on assets because of failure to pay taxes.

4. *Employee relations.* Employment contracts and employee benefits are very important even in an asset sale, because if a new owner knowingly or unknowingly takes away an employee's privilege, then he or she will walk into a hornet's nest.

5. *Environmental problems.* Many transactions today are being canceled because of environmental liabilities. Just because you lease the premises instead of buying the property does not mean that you will not be held responsible in part for the contamination caused before your arrival. Unfair? You bet!

6. *Pending and potential litigation.* This becomes a bigger issue with a consumer product company because of our litigious society. The seller will want to place a time period and/or cap on the total responsibility. Usually the buyer ends up sharing some of the risk for previously made products.

7. *Authorization.* The seller must have any necessary authorization to sell the company from stockholders, directors, and/or third parties like the bank.

The seller will in effect be expected to ensure to the buyer that

All liabilities are represented.
All contracts are disclosed.
All wages and taxes are current.
All insurance is current.
All bonus plans are disclosed.

THE BASKET PROVISION

About ten years ago, I sold a sporting goods store that I personally owned. Not knowing whether the pending sale was to be consummated, I ran the business in a normal manner. To promote our new line of Fuji bicycles, I placed a discount coupon advertisement in a certain publication. Over the next few weeks I either forgot about the impending advertisement and/or it seemed irrelevant as my attention focused on the sale of the business. The day after the sporting goods store was sold, customers started to redeem their discount coupons with the purchase of bicycles. As this undisclosed liability amounted to only a few thousand dollars, this example could be considered a frivolous claim and hardly a material amount. However, other such incidents and amounts could add up, becoming a significant aggregate loss for the buyer, even if there is no single breach that has a material adverse effect on the business. According to Reed, "the precise effect of the basket amount on all of this is uncertain. It might be argued that the basket amount is a numerical definition of the word material."

The basket provision is also used to protect the seller by indemnifying him or her for damages only up to a certain amount. Furthermore, there is usually a cutoff date for the buyer to make claims against the seller, e.g., three years is the outside limit. One way to facilitate the buyer's claims is to allow him or her to offset these amounts against the note due to the seller. Another method is to set up an escrow account equivalent to 5 to 10 percent of the purchase price. The phrase "no material adverse change" or "not material to the transaction" is the key. In fact, the seller may insist on inserting the word *material* when referring to liabilities, litigation, etc. While the word *material* can be construed as ambiguous, the parties can set a dollar threshold, the basket amount, that defines materiality in particular circumstances.

While most of the burden for representations and warranties lies with the seller, the buyer may be required to warrant that the acquisition does not violate its loan agreements or, if stock is to be used, that it is properly authorized.

Obviously, if the transaction is a stock sale in which the buyer assumes all the assets and all the liabilities, the representations and warranties are more lengthy and complex. Often the buyer's willingness to undertake a stock transaction depends on the tightness and thoroughness of the representations and warranties. For the seller, the important issue is which representations and warranties survive the closing and which ones cease. Those that customarily cease at closing include warranties on equipment and guarantees on licenses. Those that often survive the closing includes matters of litigation.

In summary, the following advice of Nelson Gifford is noteworthy. As former CEO of the Dennison Manufacturing Company, he was involved in approximately three dozen transactions. He said that from the buyer's point of view,

> The critical aspect of negotiations is what is stated in the representations and warranties such that the document reflects the following:
> Everything you know, you told us.
> Everything you told us is true.
> Everything you didn't know, you should have known.

CHAPTER 20

The Closing

The closing is the formal transfer of the business. There are four key elements that must take place prior to closing:

1. Both parties have agreed to the price and terms, and the seller has shown evidence that he or she has legal authority to sell the business.

2. Due diligence has been completed by the buyer, and the seller's representations and claims have been substantiated.

3. The financing is secured and the proper liens are in place so that the lender can release the funds for the acquisition financing.

4. Remedies are available to the buyer if the seller breaches the representations and warranties.

Clearly the closing is no time to cut corners financially. You need expert legal advice, as a foolish mistake at this juncture could cost you ten times the amount in the future. As the buyer, it is your prerogative to have your lawyer draft the purchase and sale agreement. Doing so will put you in the best position to control the process, from drafting the contract to writing the checklist used at the closing. It is customary for the buyer's attorney to draft the original agreement, then the seller's lawyer handles the revision, and finally the buyer's attorney completes the final agreement.

Emotions can run high at the closing. Hopefully, mutual trust has developed between the buyer and seller during the many months of courting and negotiating. The buyer will have spent thousands of dollars on inspections, due diligence, and obtaining the proper financing. Not only will the seller have spent money for appraisals and consulting fees, but the emotional experience of selling a business is often very taxing. It is important for both sides to maintain a positive attitude, approach problems reasonably, and not hold out for the last dollar.

There are two major elements of the closing that happen simultaneously:

Corporate closing. Transfer of stock or assets pursuant to the acquisition agreement. Representations and warranties should be true in all material respect. All covenants and required agreements have been performed. All stockholders' approvals have been obtained. Litigation has been settled, noncompete agreements have been signed, and, where appropriate, resignations of officers and directors have been obtained. Also, all third-party consents such as those of insurers, landlords, intermediaries, etc., have also been obtained.

Financial closing. Unless all the conditions of the deal that affect the lending institution are met, all the liens are in place, and there is an enforceable sales contract with all terms and conditions spelled out, the lending institution will not release the funds. Alternatively, the funds will be held in escrow by the title company or an escrow attorney until all the contractual conditions are met. Once these conditions are met, escrow can be closed (transfer possession), and titles and assets are passed from seller to buyer.

The purchase and sale agreements usually have four sections.

Description of the transaction, such as a stock or an asset sale.

Terms of agreement, such as price and method of payment (cash, notes, stock, etc.). This section also includes the agreed-upon role of the remaining management team, such as corporate position and remuneration.

Representations and warranties are usually the most heavily negotiated items after the letter of intent is signed. Each party wants protection against any misrepresentations. A warranty is a guarantee or assurance that the property or item is or shall be as represented.

Conditions and covenants include noncompete agreements, identifications, and promises to do or keep from doing a specific act.

It is advisable to have a preclosing one week in advance in which all the documents have been distributed, all conditions have been satisfied or waived, and any open matters have been negotiated to conclusion. If not all the conditions have been met or if a vital signature or an important document is missing, then an escrow closing takes place. Instead of the euphoric high of a successful closure, the closing becomes conditional.

The closing usually takes place at one of the attorney's offices or at the buyer's bank. Along with the principals, there are attorneys for the buyer and seller, the attorney for seller's bank, intermediaries, and perhaps a real estate broker. There could be six to a dozen people, and the ordeal can take from one to five hours. There are numerous documents to sign, such as loan agreements, leases, personal guarantees, etc.

A stock transaction is much easier than an asset deal because buying the company is like getting onto a moving train. You buy the company "lock, stock, and barrel," including all assets and all liabilities. With an asset purchase, you have the following items to contend with:

Purchase price adjustments
Utility and tax prorations
Vacation accruals
Deposits
Lease and insurance transfers
Bulk sales law compliance
Transfer of telephone numbers
Patent assignments
Bills of sale and/or deeds
Licenses to be transferred
Etc.

The best way to ensure a smooth closing is to set up a checklist to avoid any last-minute mishaps. The following model checklist was developed particularly for asset purchases by C. D. Peterson, author of *How to Sell Your Business.*

Time and place of closing
Who needs to attend
Documents required
Amount of funds to be disbursed in specified form

Corporate tax and employer identification numbers
Licenses transferred or obtained, e.g., liquor license
Prorating calculations for taxes, wages, utility bills, etc.

Adjustments for landlord, supplier, or utility deposits
Transfer of banking arrangements
Transfer of keys, alarm, and computer codes
Transfer of telephone number
Customer lists

Clearance of outstanding liens or encumbrances
Compliance with bulk sales law
Assumption or discharge of leases or mortgages
Definition of seller's obligations in business transition
Provision for continuity of insurance
Adjustments for inventory and receivables at closing
Provisions for uncollectible receivables
Disposition of outstanding claims

The real estate lease or purchase agreement
Consulting and noncompete agreements
Allocation of the purchase price to assets, goodwill, etc.
Provision for intermediaries' fees
Representations and warranties
Buyer's security for seller's notes

A preacquisition contingency is an unresolved situation that exists at the closing and is resolved later. Obviously such contingencies should be kept to a minimum, but we live in an imperfect world and sometimes closings are not perfect, and so it is better to resolve minor issues in the fashion described herewith than to abort the entire closing.

It is important that both parties to the transaction be represented by the principals of their respective companies so that changes, material or otherwise, are not challenged for lack of authority. Closings should not take place on a Friday or the day before a holiday in case the closing continues into the following nonbusiness day without the ability to transfer or invest funds. It is important to have adequate support staff to make last-minute revisions in documents. I heard of a transaction that did not close because of improper instructions for wiring funds from one bank to another. The next day the seller changed his mind about selling. A wire transfer of funds is payment through a series of debits and credits transmitted via computers. The bank deadline for wire transfers is usually 3 p.m. The types of risk-free checks are bank certified and cashier's check.

For the buyer, the closing represents the apex of the acquisition search and perhaps the largest single personal monetary transaction in his or her business career. Upon completion of the closing, the buyer will embark on an adventure full of opportunities, rewards, and risks. It probably will begin with corks popping and bubbles flowing, followed by statements of confidence but feelings of apprehension. For private company acquisitions, the usual clandestine process has been particularly taxing for the seller. For intermediaries, there is an enormous satisfaction from orchestrating the deal, usually from beginning to end. For the moment, optimism prevails.

CHAPTER 21

Postclosing—How to Make the Acquisition Work

One of the great tennis stars, Rod Laver from Australia, is known for his statement "you are most vulnerable when you are ahead."

The acquirer of a business is susceptible to making mistakes during the delicate period of ownership transition. The buyer is apt to experience an emotional and physical letdown following the lengthy and intense process of negotiating and finalizing the acquisition. The purchase of private companies is usually conducted without the knowledge of the employees; therefore, the new owner's initial concern should be gaining the confidence of all the employees. Introduction of the new owner by the former owner should take place the day after the closing to create as much harmony and confidence as possible.

The employees will naturally be apprehensive because a major change in the company represents uncertainty and the unknown. The old owner should assemble all the employees so that he or she can introduce them to the new owner. The latter should deliver a straightforward, sincere speech to gain the employees' confidence and calm their fears. If asked, the new owner should not guarantee that there will be no job losses, as honesty is paramount. The best response is to explain that it will be necessary to fully understand the company before making any decisions. However, the first order of business is to prevent employee defections or a slowdown in productivity due to lack of employee enthusiasm.

Obviously there is so much to do postclosing that the real challenge for the new owner is to be sufficiently organized and patient that he or she does not make many mistakes. Successful acquisitions often start with a comprehensive postacquisition plan that evaluates the company's strengths and weaknesses as well as an initial overview of:

Customers	Manufacturing
Suppliers	Research
Employees	Organization structure
Products	Reporting methods
Markets	Financial controls

According to George Berbeco, CEO of the Devon Group in Waltham, Massachusetts, which has acquired four middle-market companies, he initially spends several hours with the key employees. For example, Berbeco may try to help the production manager improve the back-order situation and thereafter spend less time to monitoring his or her progress. Berbeco goes on to say that as soon as possible, he personally visits the company's top ten customers to solidify their ongoing relationship. Finally, Berbeco says that if he does make employee cuts, he does it as a one-time event instead of letting employees go individually.

In making major decisions, it is important to go slowly enough initially to understand the company's strengths and where it is most profitable. If the company is not too large to interview every employee, individually or in groups, their input on how to improve the business is usually most insightful. The key to success is to listen carefully and communicate, communicate, communicate. If you do have to discharge employees, either subsidize part of their outplacement or pay them a severance package. Not only is it morally correct, but the remaining employees will respect you accordingly.

Aside from the operational segments of the business, it is also important to put the succession plan together without delay. For example, if one buys a business with a 50 percent partner, then a buy/sell agreement should be signed so that if one of the partners either wants to leave or dies, there is a predetermined buyout arrangement or formula that will leave the remaining principal a free rein to run the business.

Second, the owner(s) should have life insurance payable to the company in order to buy out the stock of the deceased partner or to subsidize the company's operations going forward.

Third, if real estate is part of the business acquisition, then it could be wise to separate the two parts because it facilitates analyzing the company's operations and makes it easier to sell the company in the future. To go one step further, the machinery and equipment can also be separated and leased to the company.

One of the ways to demonstrate continuity after the acquisition is to retain the name of the business. The ego of many new owners compels them to use their own name. If one does plan to change the name, it is better to phase in the name change over several years by incorporating both names during the transition. The goodwill from a well-recognized name is often worth keeping.

In January 1994, Tom Tremblay acquired Guard Air Corporation of South Hadley, Massachusetts, an industrial power tool manufacturer. A year later Tom reflected about his postclosing experience, and in order of importance listed:

1. Without hesitation and immediately, buy your wife a huge bouquet of flowers and take her out to the finest restaurant in the area. Not only is the acquisition stressful for you the buyer, but the repercussions of this intense process will affect your spouse and tax the marital relationship. It is quite possible that one's spouse has provided encouragement when necessary and counseled one during the darkest moments in the acquisition process. Recognition and appreciation of your marital partner is the first priority.

2. The deal is done, and there are people to thank, business associates to inform, and community members to acknowledge. When you buy a middle-market company, there are bankers, lawyers, intermediaries, consultants, accountants, advisers who helped you. A letter to the president of the bank praising the particular loan officer or an announcement to your corporate neighbor in the industrial park will help you build important business relationships and solidify your support group for the next time you reach out for their cooperation. You may want to buy another company in a few years, so don't forget all those who helped you, even if they were not involved in this particular transaction.

3. There is so much to do upon buying a business that you scarcely know where to begin. Start with the life blood of most organizations: the employees—in the office, on the factory floor, at their

sales representative's office. Let them see that you are interested in their work and their input. In Tremblay's case, he felt that it was imperative to visit all the sales representatives of Guard Air to better communicate with them and to better assess their contribution to the company.

4. After interfacing with the sales side of the business, it is logical to visit the major vendors. Each year vendors become more critical to the success of middle-market companies because there is more reliance on just-in-time deliveries and a trend toward relying on fewer vendors. Using fewer vendors can improve quality and price, but it also results in higher risks regarding on-time deliveries. Visiting major vendors and assessing their financial status is one of the top priorities.

5. Within a month, you should be ready to visit your major customers. In Tremblay's case, Guard Air uses sales representatives to sell to 800 distributors, and so obviously he initially had time to visit only the major accounts. The objective is not only to keep the business under the new ownership but to increase the volume. This effort of calling on major customers is akin to marketing intelligence in which one elicits criticism of the product, the service, and/or the organization of the newly acquired company. Feedback may include recommendations for product improvement, discount schedules, data sheets, etc.

Based on the above information, the acquirer of the new business can proceed to make the necessary changes in the company and hopefully will be on the way to making the acquisition work.

CHAPTER 22

Why Deals Fail

BEFORE CLOSING

My definition of a deal, before closing, is that the two parties appear to have a verbal agreement sufficient for the buyer to draft a letter of intent. For a variety of reasons, which will be discussed shortly, about 50 percent of the deals that reach the letter of intent stage fail to result in actual transactions. It is important to differentiate this from a buyer who merely submits a letter of intent without discussing the proposal on the supposition that the seller might either accept it or at least counter with an alternative proposal. The following items are "deal breakers" after a verbal understanding has been reached.

Deal Breakers

- The seller realizes that after paying taxes and reinvesting the money, his or her income will be vastly reduced from what he or she is currently taking out of the business.
  Response: Most buyers sell out for reasons other than financial, i.e., burnout, no successor, lack of funds to grow the business, competitive pressures.

- The seller or buyer is negotiating with another party, and the other arrangement is more attractive than this letter of intent.
  Response: The highest price is not necessarily the winning offer. Other factors such as personal chemistry between buyer and seller can be more important. Buyers who move quickly and professionally increase their chances of success.

- Due diligence on either side brings to the surface undesirable factors that cause a withdrawal from the letter of intent.
  Response: A more up-front detailed analysis of the other party will help obviate aborted letters of intent.

- The buyer is unable to secure the acquisition financing and/or the seller wants more up-front payment than the buyer is willing to provide.
  Response: Buyers often underestimate the amount of cash required to do a deal. Aside from the cash at closing, there are sizable expenses for the intermediary, lawyers, accountants, appraisers, etc., and more money may need to be invested in the company for working capital. Financing is often left as a final detail in structuring an acquisition. Many failed acquisitions are attributable to inappropriate capitalization.

- The buyer and seller cannot agree on particular aspects of the transaction, especially when their respective advisers become involved.
  Response: While letters of intent are usually brief, ranging from one to ten pages, basic issues should be predetermined, such as whether it is a stock or an asset transaction, key management compensation, security for the notes, severance package for employees if the business is to be moved, rent on the real estate, etc.

- The stockholders of the selling company do not agree with the proposal or do not want to sell the company under any conditions. Often a buyer will be negotiating with the CEO of the selling company who has a minority ownership position. The power lies with the outside inactive majority owner. This situation frequently happens in family businesses.
  Response: More experienced buyers realize that they should be communicating with the real decision makers as early as the second or third visit.

- Seller's remorse results in the owner's backing out of the transaction because so much of his or her life is tied up in the company that he or she cannot bear to part with it. Sellers may realize that they would not know what to do with themselves if the business were sold.
  Response: It is very important to understand the real reason the

owner is willing to sell the business, not necessarily the stated reason. Sometimes a business that is for sale because it is losing money will show a dramatic turnaround. The owner may regain confidence and take the company off the market. A buyer should appeal to this seller by allowing the seller to phase out gradually—making him or her the chairman, a director, or a consultant to the company.

• The buyer's sensitivity to earnings! If the company shows a bad earnings quarter after the letter of intent, the buyer often becomes apprehensive about the entire transaction.
Response: Aside from reasons beyond the CEO's control, some businesses suffer when the CEO spends full time on the sale of the company. The lower earnings may be a result of this distraction.

• Deterioration of trust between the principal buyer and the principal seller.
Response: The principals should make an effort to get to know each other in a social setting outside the business environment in order to build personal chemistry and rapport.

• Impatience—some deals take a lot of time to put together because of dissenting stockholders, environmental problems, buyer's financing, etc.
Response: There is a difference between lack of momentum when little is being done to move the project forward and hurdles that are complicated. In the latter case, patience is necessary.

• Reserves and escrow accounts: Some buyers get carried away with caution and legalese to the point that they do not want to assume any risk on such matters as accounts receivable, environmental matters, etc., and therefore try to set up full reserves and escrow accounts.
Response: There is a point in acquisitions at which the buyer has to decide the dividing line between a "businessman's risk" and a "prudent man's" decision.

• Inexperienced transaction lawyer: The jargon in the M & A business is that lawyers are either deal makers or deal breakers.
Response: Negotiating transactions usually requires compromise on both sides. Attorneys who try to win every point end up losing for their client.

AFTER CLOSING: REASONS FOR DEAL FAILURES

- Overpaying for a company, particularly when most of the money is up front, may leave you with no reserve to improve working capital or to overcome shortfalls.

  Response: Profitable, fast-growing companies can often compensate for the buyer's overpaying because they will grow their way out, but moderately profitable companies with slow growth will not redeem the buyer's mistake of overpaying.

- Overleveraged transactions in which operating income barely covers the debt service, leaving little for capital improvements. Business is so competitive that successful companies must constantly reinvest in their future.

  Response: Usually a transaction should have at least 30 to 40 percent equity in the deal, the balance being bank debt, seller's paper, and/or noncompete or consulting agreements.

- The buyer does not really understand the business. Perhaps the buyer has previously been successful in a low-tech business and then buys a high-tech business, or was successful in a white-collar business and buys a blue-collar business.

  Response: Some buyers do not see enough deal flow and buy one of the first businesses that is available, or they are overconfident and misjudge their capabilities.

- Placing too much faith in existing management and failing to bring in new blood.

  Response: Many middle-market companies succeed because the owner/CEO is extremely capable; however, the middle management is often subservient. When the owner/CEO leaves, the remaining management does not perform as well on its own.

- Some buyers assume that sales will remain stable after the acquisition, not realizing that competitors view a change of ownership as an opportunity to strike at the existing customer base.

  Response: Service businesses are most vulnerable, and so anything that accentuates the new ownership, like changing the company's name, is a mistake.

- Overestimating the company's growth potential, when in fact its market is mature. Gaining market share in a stable industry is more difficult than growing in an improving market.

Response: Many buyers should base their near-term profit projections as much on cutting costs and reducing overhead as on increasing sales.

Having acquired a company, how does one mitigate the chances of failure? The following suggestions are mentioned in the book: *The Buying and Selling a Company Handbook* by Price Waterhouse.

Formulate a Plan: Whatever the size of the business you are buying, developing a strategy for after the deal closes is extremely important to a smooth transition. Before closing, you should understand the business, including its strengths and weaknesses, and how you will run the business when it's yours. A detailed written plan will serve as your touchstone for monitoring performance of your new company, including the transition. Successful buyers always have a plan and monitor every action against it. Problems that arise during the transition period were probably foreseeable—and avoidable, had buyers adequately planned ahead.

Understanding: Until you fully understand the new business, its employees, its customers or markets, its products and its competition, it makes little sense to implement major changes.

Timing: Once you understand the business, then proceed with your post acquisition plan as quickly and efficiently as possible so that you can prevent further financial problems, unfavorable employee morale and/or shortcomings in productivity. Announce major changes (especially in personnel) as quickly as possible.

Employee Relations: New owners often overlook the importance of retaining existing personnel. These people know the business; overlooking their experience can be detrimental. Employees are intangible assets and successful acquisitions begin with the proper management of existing employees.

Customer Relations: Sellers know their customers well and are often in a position to transfer their customers' accumulated goodwill to new buyers. Negotiate an employment contract with the seller. Customer retention is vital for a successful acquisition.

Supplier Relations: Often buyers automatically keep the same suppliers used by prior owners and ignore all the other prospective suppliers knocking on the door. As a result, they may be unaware that they are not receiving the best prices or terms currently available. Present suppliers may have stopped offering competitive prices or terms years ago when they realized previous owners would never consider switching to new suppliers. It does not hurt to shop around.

Goodwill: Buyers often undervalue the acquired business' existing name. Many times names are changed simply because the new owners want to see their own names on neon lights. If you have purchased a successful business with a reputation for outstanding products or services, the last thing you should do is change the name and in so doing, signify a change in ownership and a perceived change in the quality of the business' products or services.

CHAPTER 23

Legal and Tax Issues

ASSET AND STOCK TRANSACTIONS

Inevitably the buyer and seller are confronted with the question of how the transaction should be structured. It is a tax issue. On the one hand, the buyer wants an asset purchase in order to step up the value of the inventory, plant, and equipment in order to increase future depreciation deductions, while the seller wants a stock sale to mitigate the capital gains tax and avoid the recapture tax. The latter results when the capital gain of the business exceeds the depreciation already taken. The end result is frequently a significant amount of income that the seller must recognize.

If the decision is to purchase the business in an asset deal, then the various components of the business should be broken down, e.g., land, buildings, equipment, inventory, patents, and goodwill. The buyer obviously wants the least amount of goodwill on the books because it is considered a soft asset. Also, the buyer will want a lower value placed on land than on buildings because it is not a depreciable item.

On the other hand, sellers of a C corporation are faced not only with a double tax if they sell the assets instead of the stock but with the possible recapture of some depreciation previously taken on the equipment of the corporation. With heavy capital equipment-based companies like plastic injection molders, the depreciation recapture may be substantial, will be taxable at the maximum rate of the corporation, and will ultimately erode the purchase price available to the seller.

COVENANTS: CONSULTING AND NONCOMPETE AGREEMENTS

Aside from the basic motive of employing key personnel part time and preventing them from competing, buyers have a tax reason for including these covenants in the purchase and sale agreement. Payments made by a buyer to a seller for these covenants are deductible by the buyer as a regular expense in the year in which payments are made. Conversely, payments received by the seller for these covenants are taxable as ordinary income instead of being taxed at the lower capital gains tax rate. Furthermore, a $1 million noncompete agreement in which $333,333 is paid at the end of each year for three years has a total present value of $828,951 using a 10 percent discount rate. One advantage for the seller is that the tax payments are spaced over a three-year period.

While the buyer in many cases wants the covenants for consulting and noncompete agreements for these genuine reasons, the buyer also intends to use the covenants to pay the seller over time and to allocate the purchase price to intangible assets, thus reducing the goodwill on the balance sheet of the new company. These covenants are, however, more advantageous to the buyer than to the seller because they will generate ordinary deductions to the buyer but ordinary income to the seller, and the tax on income is higher than the tax on capital gains.

To the extent that the overall purchase price can be reduced by allocating payments to covenants with the seller, there will be that much less residue of purchase price to be allocated to goodwill.

REAL ESTATE

Real estate is a very important issue in a transaction. The following are various possible situations:

- The selling company owns the real estate and wants the buyer to (1) move the business, (2) buy the building, (3) lease the building.

- A real estate trust associated with the selling company owns the building and currently (1) leases below market rents, (2) leases above market rents.

- The selling company rents from a third-party landlord and (1) can sublet, (2) cannot sublet.

Since the real estate is a major consideration, the buyer should address the potential problems early on, and if necessary have discussions with the third-party landlord, if there is one. Perhaps the seller will be held liable by the landlord if he or she subleases. Perhaps the buyer will have to show the bank and other lenders a definitive lease agreement before the acquisition financing is in place. From a buyer's perspective, if he or she foresees the need for additional space, zoning and compliance matters should be determined prior to the purchase.

SECURITY ON THE SELLER'S NOTES

Most transactions are structured so that there are three or four components.

Cash at closing
Seller's notes
Covenants: consulting and noncompete agreements
Perhaps a partial earnout

The issue of how the buyer will secure the notes always seems to be a negotiated item. Usually the buyer has pledged the key assets to the bank for the acquisition financing and normal credit lines. If the bank requires only accounts receivable and inventory as collateral, then the seller can take a first position on the machinery and equipment and a second position on the bank's collateral. On smaller transactions, it is common for the buyer to personally sign for the notes and perhaps offer a lien on a summer home or whatever. If there are two individuals buying a business, the seller's lawyer will probably want the buyers to personally sign a "joint and several" agreement, which means if one partner fails to live up to the commitment, the other partner is responsible for the short-fall. As a buyer, avoid joint and several agreements.

TAX-DEFERRED TRANSACTIONS

An installment sale, by definition, is when at least one payment is to be received after the close of the taxable year in which the sale occurs. In other words, the recognition of the capital gain is postponed. If such a sale is structured properly, both the seller and the buyer benefit. In the case of the seller, the taxes are deferred, and in the case of the buyer, the payments are also deferred.

From a seller's perspective, the deferred payment may be exchanged for a promissory note by a third party or a standby letter of credit; however, installment obligations secured by cash or certificates of deposit of U.S. Treasury instruments do not qualify.

CHAPTER 24

Letters, Memos, Forms, and Contracts

Earlier in the book I discussed the three elements required for a successful acquisition search, namely, process, professionalism, and persistence. The use of certain forms in the acquisition search not only is important in organizing the process, but ensures a higher degree of professionalism.

BROCHURE

The first order of business is to print a rather simple, straightforward brochure or investment proposal about yourself and your acquisition entity. In Chapter 7, "Assessing Your Acquisition Strategy" under the subheading "Business Entity," an outline of this document was presented. Whether your investment proposal runs for many pages or you decide to prepare a one-page three-fold brochure, you have conveyed a message that is not only informative but professional. Some individuals who are seeking credibility in the eyes of the potential seller may make a greater effort to gain this respect through association; for example, listed on the brochure might be the following:

Accountant	Coopers & Lybrand
Attorney	Ropes & Gray
Bank	Bank of Boston
Directors	Recognizable names

Many of the suggestions on how to present yourself in the brochure you may consider to be "smoke and mirrors" or purposely deceptive. I am not urging you to do anything dishonest or to say anything that is not true, but I am suggesting that you do everything legitimate that you can to overcome your perceived disadvantage as an individual buying a middle-market company.

Suggestion: Choose the name of your company so that it does not sound like a consulting firm, an investment company, or a sales business; otherwise, when you telephone or write the target company, the recipient's first impression will be to avoid the communication. I have a friend who has a background in the valve business and wanted to buy a valve company for himself. He printed a terrific brochure for his acquisition search, but he made one mistake. The name of his company was XYZ Management Company. It should have been XYZ Valve Company or just XYZ Company. A word such as *management, partners, group,* etc., is a tipoff to the recipient that you are not an operating company. Although you may not be an operating company, you do plan to become one upon an acquisition. Potential sellers by nature are apt to take more seriously an overture by an operating company than by an investment or holding company.

Suggestion: Just as I suggested earlier that you gain credibility through association, think twice about using your hometown street address on the brochure. Street names such as Sandy Pond Lane are a dead giveaway that you are operating out of your house. Using a post office box number is an alternative, and subleasing an office in the downtown area of a major city is worth considering.

Suggestion: When people are job hunting, they often have several sets of resumes that differ in the "objectives" section at the top of the page. Let us suppose that you are seeking both manufacturing and distribution companies or that you are seeking both office products and food manufacturers. It is more effective in your literature if you customize your presentation accordingly, just as people do with resumes. While some buyers feel that it is advantageous to present themselves to business friends and intermediaries as generalists or opportunists, it is usually less effective. Certainly the owner of a target company is more likely to discuss the sale of the business if your acquisition objectives have some relevance to the business.

SEARCH LETTER

In Chapter 9, "Finding the Deal," there is some mention of mass mailings and/or individual letters to the presidents of target companies to uncover interest on the part of possible sellers. While the response rate will be predictably low, the effectiveness will depend on a number of factors. Here are some suggestions:

- If you are obtaining the name from a directory and it is not a current edition, you should call the company to be sure the listing for the CEO is correct.

- Type "Personal & Confidential" on all envelopes. Use of an actual stamp instead of the postage meter will help personalize the letter.

- The more personal the letter, the better. Almost anything you can do in this regard will help, especially in the opening paragraph. Also, before writing the letter, send away for product literature in order to better understand the target company.

- The search letter is only the opening gambit. Using a copy of this letter as your guide, you should then be persistent by following up within ten days with a telephone call. If you are unable to reach the CEO by telephone, write another but different letter, then telephone again, followed by a very discrete fax, and finally, if you are still undaunted, send a Federal Express communication to emphasize your determination. Obviously, you should use the latter technique only with companies in which you have a very keen interest.

MEMORANDA ON COMPANY VISITS

As a way to stay organized, set up a three-ring binder to log in all company visits with ensuing information. I have found the following format for a one-page memo the most useful.

```
TO:               File Name
FROM:             Yourself
DATE:
RE:               ABC Company
                  Address and telephone number
1. Background:    When company was organized
                  Name and age of CEO
                  Ownership breakdown
```

```
2. Business:      Describe the basic operation
3. Distribution:  Sell through what channels?
                  Sell by own sales force, sales
                  reps, distributors, small dealers,
                  super stores?
4. Plant/employee: Own or lease?
                  Size of plant, number of employees
                  Union or nonunion?
5. Financial:     Sales
                  Gross profit
                  EBIT
                  Book value
                  Growth rate
6. Competition:   Who?
7. Conclusion:    Opinions of the company
```

CONFIDENTIALITY AGREEMENTS

It is customary for the owner or CEO of the prospective selling company to require you to sign a confidentiality statement. Unless the seller is actively selling the business, he or she will not have such a form in the file. Therefore, I recommend that you carry your own confidentiality agreement in your briefcase in order to expedite matters. This format is fairly standard:

Confidentiality Agreement

In connection with our interest in purchasing the assets and/or stock of _____ (the Company), we have requested that we be permitted to examine the financial and other business records of the Company. We understand and agree that the information contained in these records is of a confidential nature and that it will be used by us solely for the purpose of making an offer for the assets and/or stock of the Company. We will not disclose, nor will our agents, servants, employees, or attorneys disclose any of the information contained in these financial and other business records, including the identity of the company, to any other person except to such investors, bankers, attorneys, or other persons necessary to consummate the sale to the undersigned.

Signed: _____ Date: _____
         (Print)

       _____
         (Signature)

FEE AGREEMENT WITH INTERMEDIARIES

Intermediaries, of course, have their own fee agreements, but if they do not have a signed agreement with you and they do not have one with the seller, you will not hear about the deal from them. I urge you to be proactive and tell intermediaries that you will be pleased to pay intermediary's fees; in fact, go one step further and send the intermediary your own version of an agreement. If you have your own fee agreement, you can simply mail the signed form to every intermediary with whom you want to do business. It will show the intermediaries that you are aggressive, anxious, professional, and ready to review deals. Here is a form you might consider using.

```
                    Your Company Inc.
                         Address
TO: XYZ Intermediary
     1. WE ARE AGREEABLE to paying you and/or your
associates a fee based on the purchase price or other
consideration for any company, agency, distributor-
ship, or other business entity or organization,
whether expressed in cash or stock or any other remu-
neration; whether payable at closing of transaction or
on extended payout; and regardless of which party pays
the remuneration, when you are instrumental in helping
us purchase, sell, or acquire any substantial interest
in such company which we agree to accept. Of the pur-
chase price, the fee to you and/or your associates
would be:

     5 percent of the first        $1,000,000
     4 percent of the second       $1,000,000
     3 percent of the third        $1,000,000
     2 percent of the fourth       $1,000,000
     1 percent of the value thereafter

     The payment of this fee shall be due and payable
in cash at the time of closing.
     2. Your Company Inc. will confirm in writing any
introduction or referral.
     3. If any of the principals of the parties intro-
duced to Your Company Inc. become involved in a trans-
action as contemplated herein and such transaction is
consummated, an intermediary's commission will be due
XYZ Intermediary irrespective of who conducts the
negotiations.
```

4. This agreement shall be binding upon and inure to the benefit of the parties hereto, their administrators, executors, heirs, successors, or assigns, any corporation and other entities now existing or to be formed having substantially the same principals as either of the parties hereto.

If you accept this understanding, kindly countersign and return the enclosed copy of this agreement.

                                    Your Company, Inc.
                                    By: _____

Accepted:
XYZ Intermediary
Street Address
City, State, Zip
Telephone
By: _____ , _____
                                            Title
Date: _____

GENERAL PROPOSAL LETTER

While most buyers prefer to "talk out" their general proposal with either the CEO of the target company or their intermediary, an alternative is to send a letter that broadly describes the proposal. Here is an example of such a letter.

Dear Mr. Smith:
The following is a proposal to acquire the assets of Big Time Inc. (the "Company"). This letter is an outline of a proposed transaction and is not meant to be binding on any party at this time, and is subject to the signing of a mutually acceptable, definitive purchase and sale agreement. In addition, this offer is subject to the requisite due diligence effort normally attendant on a transaction of this magnitude. With the aforementioned kept in mind, our offer is as follows:

Transaction   A new corporation ("Newco")
                       will be formed by Your Company
                       Inc. to acquire the assets of
                       the Company.

Terms and Estimated Purchase Price	$4.0 million to $5.0 million cash at closing. We would be willing to purchase the Company without the real estate and enter into a lease at current market rates and terms. In this case, our offer would range between $3.5 million and $4.5 million.
Conditions of Transaction	A. We anticipate that a transaction could be consummated and closed within 120 days. B. This proposal is subject to financing commitments satisfactory to us. We are happy to provide you with references regarding our ability to finance the transaction. C. Representations and warranties of seller with respect to accounts receivable, inventory, fixed assets, disclosure of liabilities, litigation, labor matters, corporate existence, etc., will be required. D. We would anticipate completing our due diligence process within thirty to forty-five days, whereupon we would want to move immediately to the execution of a purchase and sale agreement. E. If in the due diligence process and prior to the closing, we, in our sole judgment, wish to excuse ourselves from this transaction, we may do so without any liability, fee, penalty, or cost. F. All fees and expenses of this transaction, including but not limited to legal, investment banking, accounting, broker, and due diligence, will be

paid for by each of the respective parties.

Should you have any questions regarding this proposal,
please do not hesitate to contact me at (000) 111-
2222.

Very truly yours,

TERM SHEET

If you and the potential seller have verbally agreed on the price and terms
of the transaction, then it would be helpful to put the basic financial
arrangements on one piece of paper before you go directly to the letter of
intent. Such an example would be as follows:

Term Sheet
Carlisle Corporation
Outline of Preliminary Proposal for an Asset Purchase

Gross purchase price	$5,000,000
Less debt assumed*	(500,000)
Net purchase price	$4,500,000

Form of consideration:

John Smith (50 percent owner):
Cash	$1,850,000
Four-year consulting and nonompete agreement ($100,000 annually)	400,000
John Smith's consideration	$2,250,000

Joe Doe (30 percent owner):
Cash	675,000
Carlisle stock	675,000
Joe Doe's consideration	$1,350,000

Employment contract for Joe Doe:
Three-year contract for $100,000
annually with additional annual
bonuses of $50,000 provided
company's annual operating
profit of $700,000 is maintained.

```
Mary Jones (20 percent owner):
     Cash                          450,000
     Carlisle stock                450,000
     Mary Jones's consideration  $ 900,000
     Employment contract for Mary Jones:
     Two-year contract for $70,000
     annually

Total Consideration Paid                   $4,500,000
```

*Interest-bearing debt (usually bank debt)

LETTER OF INTENT

The importance of the letter of intent is emphasized in Chapter 16. My experience is that it is best to draft an agreement of one or two pages that is *not* legalese. The simplicity of such a letter of intent makes it less threatening in the eyes of the potential seller than a document with legal jargon and lengthy qualifications.

The letter of intent has two contractual elements, i.e., that the seller will take the company off the market for a specified period of time and that both parties (particularly the buyer) will keep all confidential information confidential.

All letters of intent should specifically state that this is a nonbinding agreement and of course should state the price, terms, and whether the purchase is an asset or stock transaction. It is customary for the buyer to draft the letter of intent as well as the purchase and sale agreement. This is a sample of the letter of intent.

Letter of Intent

Esterbrook Corporation Incorporated proposes to purchase all the assets of Mercury Security Corporation (MSC) of Boston, Massachusetts, including goodwill, customer list, and all other intangible and balance sheet assets, to be substantially the same as those set forth on the balance sheet of MSC as of _____, 1995 (Exhibit A). The name Mercury Security Corporation or any derivation of the word Mercury is *not* transferable.

1. *Purchase Price:* The purchase price for the assets will be $_____ payable in cash at closing.

2. *Noncompetition Agreement:* The principals of MSC agree not to compete, directly or indirectly, with the business of Esterbrook as it pertains to MSC in any of its markets for a period of five years after closing. For such consideration, Esterbrook will pay $_____ per year for five years to John Smith.

3. *Lease of Building Space:* It is agreed that MSC will use its best efforts to transfer the lease to Esterbrook at current or market rental as permitted by lease.

4. *General and Specific Liabilities:* Esterbrook will assume the liabilities as shown on the balance sheet dated _____, but will not assume any other liabilities past, present, or future.

5. *Audit:* Esterbrook will cause an audit to be conducted by Esterbrook's auditors at Esterbrook's expense as of a date to be selected.

6. *Expenses:*
   a) The stockholders, Esterbrook, and MSC will each pay their own expenses, including legal expenses, up to the time of the closing.
   b) Esterbrook and MSC agree that no intermediary is involved in this transaction other than _____, of _____, whose compensation is the responsibility of MSC.

7. *Letter of Intent:* This letter of intent is nonbinding and may not be construed as an agreement on the part of any party. In the event that the parties are unable to agree on a mutually satisfactory definitive agreement providing for the transactions contemplated by this letter of intent, none of the parties shall be liable to any other party or to any other person. The conclusion of any definitive agreement will be subject to the following:
   a) Approval of all matters relating thereto by counsel for Esterbrook and MSC;
   b) Review of all business, legal, and auditing matters related to MSC, the results of which are acceptable to Esterbrook;
   c) Approval of all matters related thereto by the Board of Directors of Esterbrook and MSC and the voting shareholders of each company, if required;

      d) Completion of such financing as Esterbrook may require to effect a closing;

      e) Preparation and completion of all closing documents;

      f) The closing date to take place in or within 90 days of the execution of this agreement.

8. *Continuing Obligations:* Until termination of the letter of intent, MSC shall not, and all of MSC's officers, directors, employees, agents, or representatives (including, without limitation, brokers, advisers, investment bankers, attorneys, and accountants) shall not, directly or indirectly, without prior written consent of Esterbrook, entertain negotiations with or make disclosures to any corporation, partnership, person, or other entity or group in connection with any possible proposal regarding a merger, consolidation, or sale of capital stock of MSC, or of all or a substantial portion of the assets of MSC, or any similar transaction.

9. *Confidentiality:* Both Esterbrook and MSC agree to maintain complete confidentiality of all confidential material each company exchanges with each other as outlined in separate confidentiality agreements.

All documents in respect to this transaction will be prepared by an attorney or law firm selected by Esterbrook, subject to such documents being reviewed by and being acceptable to legal counsel for MSC.

Mercury Security Corporation	Esterbrook Corporation Incorporated
By_____	By_____
Title_____	Title_____
Date_____	Date_____

PURCHASE AND SALE AGREEMENT

In the book *The Art of M & A*, the author writes: "It is very important for the buyer to protect its customary right to control the drafting of the documents. It is the shortsighted buyer who tries to save legal fees by letting the 'other guys' do the drafting." Furthermore, the purchase and sale agreement, also known as the P & S agreement or acquisition agreement, has the following characteristics:

1. It is a legally binding agreement.

2. The buyer will seek to protect itself in such areas as pending litigation, undisclosed liabilities, and environmental problems.

3. The seller rarely sells for "all cash," leaving the buyer leverage to hold out on further payments if the transaction is not what the seller represented it to be.

4. The seller may opt for a lower price at closing for all cash rather than risk postclosing adversity.

5. The *Conditions* section lists issues that must be satisfied before the parties become obligated to close the transaction.

6. The *Indemnity* section relates to discoveries after the closing.

7. The *Representations and Warranties* section assures each party of the other's legal and financial ability to consummate the transaction.

8. The *Covenants* section of the agreement defines the obligations of the parties with respect to their conduct during the period between the signing and the closing, e.g., the seller conducts the business in the ordinary manner.

The following is a sample purchase and sale agreement (an asset purchase).

Date_____

Asset Purchase Agreement

This is an agreement among RST, Inc., formerly known as Carlisle Inc., a Massachusetts corporation with a place of business at _____
("Seller"); John Doe of _____
("Stockholder"); and Carlisle Inc., a Massachusetts corporation with a place of business at _____
_____ ("Buyer"). For consideration paid each other, the parties covenant and agree as follows:

1. Assets to be sold.
   Seller will sell, transfer, and deliver to Buyer free and clear of any liens or other encumbrances, Seller's business and the assets and properties of

Seller, tangible and intangible as listed herein.
Except as otherwise expressly provided in this
agreement, the Assets shall include only the following assets owned by Seller at the time of
closing.

A. Machinery and Equipment.
All machinery and equipment, furniture and
fixtures, and the like as set forth in Exhibit
B attached hereto.

B. Tools, Dies, and Fixtures.
All tools, dies, and fixtures owned by the
Seller.

C. Inventories.
All inventory, including raw materials, work-
in-process, finished goods, repair parts, and
supplies; all inventory records; and all outstanding purchase and sales orders.

D. Accounts Receivable.
The Buyer will use best efforts to collect all
accounts receivable and pay those receivables
as collected to the Seller within 90 days of
closing in accordance with an agreed-upon list
of such receivables as found on Exhibit E as
of the date of closing. Upon demand of Seller,
Buyer will reassign for collection of uncol-
lected receivables 90 days after the closing.

E. Corporate Name and Trade Names.
All processes, patents, patent applications,
trademarks, signs, advertisements, trade
names, copyrights, drawings, and logos,
including the name "Carlisle, Inc."

F. Customer Lists and Contracts.
All customer lists, files excepting accounting
records, licenses, permits, contract rights,
and sales backlog as found on Exhibit C, and
telephone and fax number _____. Seller
will provide buyer with access to Seller's
accounting records upon reasonable notice for
customary business purposes.

G. Goodwill.
The goodwill of the Seller.

Excluded from the sale shall be all cash, bank
accounts, utility security deposits, and prepaid
expenses and the land and buildings, which shall
be leased to Buyer by Seller in accordance with
the Lease attached hereto as Exhibit A.

2. **Liabilities.**
   Buyer agrees to assume up to $_____ of
   Accounts Payable in accordance with Exhibit J.
   Buyer is specifically not assuming any other liabilities whatsoever of Seller, including without
   limitation, all taxes of whatever kind or nature,
   accrued or payable by Seller to any taxing authority prior to and including the closing date, all
   of which the Seller agrees to pay.

3. **Closing Date.**
   The closing will take place no later than 1:00
   P.M. _____, at the offices of Seller or
   at such other time and place as the Buyer and
   Seller may hereafter agree upon. Adjustments and
   prorations shall be made effective the end of
   business _____.

4. **Purchase Price.**
   A. **Price.**
      The purchase price to be paid for the Assets
      is Five Hundred Thousand ($500,000) Dollars,
      which sum shall be paid as follows:

Certified or bank check at closing	$200,000
Buyer's promissory note	
per paragraph 6	200,000
Accounts Payable per paragraph 2	100,000
TOTAL	$500,000

   B. **Allocation.**
      The purchase price for the Assets shall be
      allocated as follows:

Inventories	$ 100,000
Machinery and Equipment	200,000
Goodwill	50,000
Accounts Receivable per paragraph 1(D)	150,000
TOTAL	$ 500,000

5. **Personnel Agreements.**
   A. **Noncompetition Agreement.**
      Stockholders will enter into a noncompetition
      agreement with the Buyer, in the form attached
      as Exhibit D.

6. **Buyer's Note at Closing Date.**
   In part payment of the purchase price, Buyer shall
   make and deliver to Seller at the Closing Date a
   negotiable promissory note in the amount of Two

Hundred Thousand ($200,000) Dollars, bearing annual interest at eight (8.0%) percent, for sixty (60) months and requiring equal monthly installments of interest and principal beginning thirty (30) days after the closing contemplated herein. Such note shall be secured by a first security interest in Machinery and Equipment acquired and shall be personally guaranteed by Buyer in the form attached as Exhibit H. The form of said note and security agreement, and UCC financing statements are attached hereto as Exhibits F and G.

7. Seller's Use of Name.
   It is understood and agreed that Seller will not use the name "Carlisle Inc." to pursue any business interests nor will Seller sell, lease, or convey usage of its name to any entity or individual.

8. Seller's Representations and Warranties.
   A. Corporate Authority.
      Seller is a corporation duly organized, validly existing, and in good standing under the laws of the State of Massachusetts and has the right and authority to enter into this agreement and carry out the terms and conditions hereof applicable to it and the execution, delivery, and performance of this agreement will not violate or conflict with the provisions of the Articles of Organization or Bylaws of the Seller.

   B. Agreement Default.
      Seller as a result of the Closing will not be in default under any agreement or other commitment to which it is a party or by which it is bound.

   C. Financial Statements to Buyer.
      Seller has delivered to Buyer the Financial Statements through _____. Said Financial Statements are true and complete. Seller shall provide interim financial statements for the period ending _____ as soon as practicable after closing.

   D. No Material Change.
      Since _____, there has not been, to Seller's knowledge, any material change in financial condition, assets and liabilities, or business, other than changes in the ordinary course of business.

E. <u>Tax Returns, Audits, and Tax Payments.</u> Within the times and in a manner prescribed by law, Seller has, and shall have through the closing date, filed all federal, state, foreign, and/or local tax returns required by law and has paid all taxes (including without limitation, income, franchise, sales, use, meals, transfer, payroll, and ad valorem taxes), assessments, and penalties due and payable with respect to the Business of the Seller. The Seller is not delinquent in the payment of any other governmental tax, assessment, or other charge.

F. <u>Marketable Title.</u> Upon the transfer of the assets at closing, Buyer shall acquire title to such property free of all liens and encumbrances and free of all claims of third parties.

G. <u>Good Condition.</u> To Seller's knowledge and except to the extent disclosed to Buyer or known to Buyer, all Seller's equipment and similar tangible personal property are in good condition and repair, consistent with the age and remaining useful life thereof, and their use is in conformity with all applicable laws, ordinances, and regulations. The Assets are being sold in "as is" condition, and any and all warranties from manufacturers or dealers in existence at date of sale are included in the sales price. Buyer acknowledges that Buyer has been provided a full and complete opportunity to inspect the Seller's machinery and equipment and similar tangible personal property, is satisfied with the results of all such inspections, and that the Seller and Stockholders have made no warranties or representations with respect thereto.

H. <u>Customer Commitments.</u> Attached as Exhibit C is a list of all presently existing customer commitments to which Seller is a party or by which it is bound. To Seller's knowledge, all such commitments are valid and enforceable in accordance with their terms.

I. <u>Litigation.</u> To the Seller's knowledge, there is no pending or threatened action, arbitration, suit, notice, order, real estate tax contest, or legal, administrative, or other proceeding before any court or governmental agency, authority, or body, against, or affecting Seller, either directly or indirectly, with respect to the Assets pending or threatened that will survive the closing. There is no order, writ, injunction, or decree of any federal, state or local, or foreign court, department, agency, or instrumentality that directly or indirectly relates to the Assets. Seller has complied and is complying in all material respects with all law, ordinances, and government rules and regulations applicable to it and its properties, assets, and business.

J. No Untrue Representation.
To Seller's knowledge after inquiry, no representation or warranty by Seller in this Agreement, or certificate furnished or to be furnished to Buyer pursuant hereto or in connection with the transaction contemplated hereby, contains or will contain any untrue statement of a material fact.

K. Continuation of Truth.
The representations, warranties, and covenants set forth in this agreement will continue to be true in all respects as of the closing date and shall survive the Closing.

L. Licenses Obtained.
All government licenses, permits, and authorizations necessary for the ownership of Seller's properties and the conduct of its business as currently conducted are listed on Exhibit I, and Seller has all such licenses, permits, and authorizations.

M. Liabilities.
At the closing there will be no liabilities, commitments, or contingencies of Seller whether accrued, secured, or determinable that encumber the assets other than those expressly assumed by Buyer under the terms of this Agreement.

N. Continued Business.
Seller is not aware of any reason why its customers, subcontractors, or suppliers will not continue to do business with the Buyer after

the closing in the same manner in which they have done business with the Seller prior to the Closing. This does not assure or imply that the existing customer base will be retained after the closing.

O. Stock Ownership.
The Stockholder named herein owns One Hundred (100%) Percent of the outstanding stock of the Seller.

P. Absence of Certain Changes.
Since the date of this Agreement and as of the Closing, there shall not have been any:
(a) Transactions by Seller affecting the Assets except in the ordinary course of business.
(b) Material adverse physical change in the Assets.

Q. Profits Pending Closing.
Profits from the date of this Agreement up to and including _____, shall be the property of the Seller.

9. Buyer's Representations and Warranties.

A. Corporate Authority
Buyer is a corporation duly organized, validly existing, and in good standing under the laws of the State of Massachusetts and has the right and authority to enter into this agreement and carry out the terms and conditions hereof applicable to it and the execution, delivery, and performance of this agreement will not violate or conflict with the provisions of the Articles of Organization or Bylaws of the Corporation.

B. Agreement Conflict
This Agreement does not conflict with the Buyer's bylaws, corporate charter, or any other internal requirement of the Buyer. _____ individually and collectively, are subject to no agreement or other constraint that conflicts with their carrying out the terms of this agreement.

C. No Government Approvals
The transaction contemplated by this agreement does not require any state, local, or federal government approval.

D. Inspection of Assets
Buyer acknowledges that he had an opportunity to inspect and actually did inspect all of the

assets sold under this agreement and is satisfied with the results of such inspection.

E. No Untrue Representation

Buyer's warranties and representations contained in this agreement are true as of the
date of the agreement and shall continue to be
true in all material respects up to and
including the date of closing. This provision
shall survive the closing.

10. Indemnification

The Seller hereby agrees to indemnify, defend, and
hold the Buyer harmless of and from any and all
debts, liabilities, costs, and expenses of any and
every nature whatsoever resulting from the breach
or violation of any obligations. representations,
covenants, or warranties of the Seller contained
in this agreement and from any liability or obligation of the Seller arising out of the Seller's
ownership or sale of the Assets or the Seller's
operation of the business except for those
accounts payable assumed by the Buyer pursuant to
paragraph 2 of this agreement and as specifically
identified in Exhibit J. Except as specifically
set forth in said Exhibit J, the Buyer shall not
and does not assume any other of the liabilities
or obligations of the Seller.

The Seller, at its own expense, shall have the
opportunity to be represented by counsel of its
choosing, and control, at its expense, the defense
of any claim that may be brought against the Buyer
in respect of which the Buyer may be entitled to
indemnifications. The Buyer shall promptly give
written notice to the Seller of any such claim. In
the event that the Buyer does not receive written
notice from the Seller within fifteen (15) days of
such written notice, the Seller shall be deemed to
have waived the right to be represented by counsel.

In the event the Seller breaches or violates
any provision contained herein, the Buyer shall
have a right to set off against any payments due
Seller under this agreement, under a Note of even
date in the amount of $200,000, or against any
payment due _____ under a
noncompetition agreement between the Buyer and
_____, an amount equal to
the amount of any claim successfully brought
against the Buyer as a result of said breach or

violation if Seller elects to defend the claim or
the amount of damages suffered by the Buyer if the
Seller elects not to defend. Prior to such setoff
by the Buyer, the Buyer shall give fifteen (15)
days written notice to the Seller setting forth
therein the reason(s) for said setoff. The Buyer
shall exercise such right of setoff by applying
such damages against payments due the Seller as
they fall due pursuant to the promissory note
referred to in paragraph 6 of this agreement and
against payments due under the noncompetition
agreement referred to in paragraph 5 of this
agreement.

Any notice sent to the Seller should be
mailed, postage prepaid, registered or certified
mail, return receipt requested, or delivered by
overnight carrier and addressed to the parties at
their respective addresses as set forth in the
Agreement, with a copy in case of notice to the
Seller sent as follows:

> To Seller's attorney: Name
> Address
> City

11. Condition of the Closing.
    A. Conditions of Sellers' Obligations.
       (a) Payment.
       Buyer's delivery to Seller at the Closing Date
       of payment in the amount of Two Hundred
       Thousand ($200,000) Dollars payable by
       Certified or Bank check without intervening
       endorsements.
       (b) Buyer's Note.
       Buyer's delivery to Seller at the Closing Date
       as defined herein of a promissory note in the
       amount of Two Hundred Thousand ($200,000)
       Dollars.
    (c) Security Agreement and Financing Statements.
       Buyer's delivery to Seller of a security
       agreement and UCC financing statements as set
       forth in paragraph 6 and Exhibits F and G.
    (d) Buyer's Guarantee.
       Buyer's delivery to Seller of a Guarantee from
       _____ as included in
       Exhibit H.
    (e) Detail Accounts Receivable Listing.
       Buyer's and Seller's written agreement of the
       detail accounts receivable as of date of clos-

ing as set forth in Exhibit E is included
herein.

(f) <u>True and Complete.</u>
The representations and warranties of Buyer
shall be true and complete in all respects,
and Buyer shall have performed and complied
with all agreements and conditions required by
this agreement.

B. <u>Conditions of Buyer's Obligations.</u>
Buyer's obligations at the closing shall be
conditional upon the following:

(a) <u>True and complete.</u>
The representations and warranties of Seller
shall be true and complete in all respects,
and Seller shall have performed and complied
with all agreements and conditions required by
this Agreement.

(b) <u>Bill of Sale.</u>
Seller's delivery to Buyer of a bill of sale
and all other instruments necessary to convey
to Buyer good and marketable title to the
Assets.

(c) <u>Noncompetition.</u>
The signing of a Stockholders' noncompetition
agreement in the form of Exhibit D.

(d) <u>Lease.</u>
The signing of a Lease acceptable to Buyer and
Seller in the form of Exhibit A.

(e) <u>At the closing Seller will deliver to
Buyer:</u>

(1) <u>List of commitments and customers.</u>
An updated list of contracts relative to
Exhibit C, which list shall not vary significantly from its present form except in
the ordinary course of business.

(2) <u>Instruments.</u>
Appropriate instruments, including Bills
of Sale, and assignments transferring and
conveying to Buyer, good and marketable
title to the Assets.

(3) <u>Vote of stockholders.</u>
A certificate of Vote, duly executed by
the Clerk of Seller, as to the due adop-
tion by the Stockholders and the Board of
Directors of Seller of a resolution autho-
rizing the transactions contemplated of
Seller by this agreement.

12. <u>Seller's Conduct of its Business Prior to Closing.</u>
Seller agrees that it will make no changes in the
Assets and will incur no liabilities or obligations between the date of this agreement and the
closing date except changes, liabilities, and
obligations arising or occurring in the ordinary
course of business. Seller agrees that it will use
its best efforts prior to the closing to maintain
and preserve its business and to retain good working relationships with its suppliers, distributors, customers, and others with whom it deals.

13. <u>Bulk Sales Act.</u>
The Seller has provided Exhibit J setting forth
all creditors, claimants, or others that may have
claims or liens upon any of the assets to be
transferred herein. Notification will be given to
creditors of record. The parties agree to waive
compliance with all the provisions of Article 6 of
the Uniform Commercial Code dealing with bulk
transfers.

14. <u>Broker's or Finder's Fee.</u>
Buyer and Seller agree that no broker or finder is
involved in the sale of assets other than
_____ of _____ and
_____ of _____.
A broker's commission of $_____ to
_____ shall be paid at the
closing by Seller if the sale hereunder contemplated is consummated and the purchase price is
received by Seller.

15. <u>General.</u>
   A. <u>Written Notice.</u>
   All notices and other communications hereunder
   shall be in writing, and given by delivery or
   mail (by overnight carrier providing a receipt
   or facsimile followed by first-class mail,
   postage prepaid) to a party at its address set
   forth at the beginning of the Agreement or at
   such changed address as a party may have furnished to the other party in writing at least
   ten (10) days prior to the effective date
   thereof.

   B. <u>Severability.</u>
   If any provision in this Agreement shall be
   deemed unenforceable or void as a matter of
   law, such circumstance shall have no effect on
   the surviving portions of the Agreement, each

of which shall have full force and effect.
Buyer and Seller shall be required to use
their best efforts to agree upon and replace
any provision that has been declared legally
void or unenforceable.

16. <u>Miscellaneous.</u>

    A. <u>Binding effect.</u>
This agreement is binding not only upon
Seller, Stockholders, and Buyer,
_____ but also upon
Seller's, Stockholders', and Buyer's respective successors, heirs, executors, administrators, and assigns.

    B. <u>Governing law.</u>
The laws of Massachusetts as of the date
appearing below shall govern the interpreta-
tion and enforcement of this agreement.

    C. <u>Modifications.</u>
No modification of this agreement shall be
binding unless in writing and executed by all
parties with the same formality as this
Agreement.

    D. <u>Entire agreement.</u>
This agreement represents the entire and integrated agreement of the parties and supersedes
all prior oral and written negotiations and
agreements.

    E. <u>Liquidated Damages.</u>
Upon failure of the Buyer to fulfill Buyer's
obligations under this Agreement, the deposit
may be retained by the Seller as liquidated
damages for any such default. Such deposit
will be held by counsel for the Seller.

Effective as of _____

_____   _____

Witness   RST, Inc. FKA a Carlisle Inc.

                    _____

                            President

_____   _____

Witness   _____

                    Stockholder of RST

_____	_____
Witness	_____
	Buyer
_____	_____
Witness	_____
	Buyer
	_____
	President

Exhibits contained herein:
- A   Lease
- B   Machinery & Equipment
- C   Customer Lists & Contracts
- D   Noncompetition
- E   Listing of Accounts Receivable
- F   Buyer Note & Security Agreement
- G   UCC Financing Statements
- H   Guarantee
- I   Licenses & Permits
- J   List of Creditors

CHAPTER 25

M & A Organizations

When you venture forth to acquire a business, it is advisable to join a group whose members are active in mergers and acquisitions. The contacts at these meetings will help you network with professionals that might identify companies for sale or help you build your acquisition team.

Three prominent groups are listed below; two are regional and one is national.

Delaware Valley Buy-Out Group (DVBG)
1234 Market Street, Suite 1800
Philadelphia, PA 19107-3718
Telephone (215) 972-3989

DVBG was organized to facilitate responsible middle-market buyout activity in the Delaware Valley. It serves as the leading forum for buyers, sellers, and advisers to exchange ideas and keep abreast of the M & A market in the region. DVBG is a part of the Delaware Valley Venture Group, a professional association sponsored by the Greater Philadelphia Chamber of Commerce and its membership.

DVBG has corporate sponsors. Guests should call the above number for meeting reservations. The luncheons run from noon to 2 P.M. and are held at the Union League of Philadelphia. Topics of the speakers for the 1994–95 program included the following:

- Industry Consolidation Strategies

- What Sophisticated Investors Look For in Venture Capital and LBO Partnerships
- State of the Buyout Market
- Capital Market Update
- Milestones of a Successful Buyout

New York Venture Group (NYVG)
605 Madison Avenue, Suite 300
New York, NY 10022-1901
Telephone (212) 832-6984

NYVG was founded in 1984 as a monthly forum to stimulate inter-action among business founders and managers, equity investors and lenders, executives seeking new positions, professionals whose services are helpful to company managers and founders, and representatives of major corporations. During breakfast, attendees mingle and exchange information, and later, after hearing the speaker, they can use the micro-phone to introduce themselves and their businesses to the group (which usually numbers around 200).

Association for Corporate Growth (ACG)
4350 DiPaolo Center, Suite C
Dearlove Road
Glenview, IL 60025-5212
Telephone (708) 699-1331
Executive Director: Carl A. Wangman

ACG is an international business organization dedicated to fostering strategic corporate growth and development. There are over 3,000 mem-bers consisting of CEOs, COOs, CFOs, and other senior corporate exec-utives from large and small companies, as well as their professional advis-ers and leading international financiers. There are twenty-five chapters in the United States and Canada.

MISSION

The mission of the Association for Corporate Growth Inc., is to promote the professional interests of its members, who have leadership roles in strategic corporate growth, by offering a forum for quality programs and education to enhance each member's professional skills.

OBJECTIVES

The Association for Corporate Growth, Inc. is unique in its concept and objectives. It was founded in 1954 by a group of business executives interested in corporate growth through acquisitions and new product development. Its basic objectives are fourfold:

1. To assist its members in improving their management skills and techniques in the diverse areas of corporate growth, thereby making a contribution to their respective businesses

2. To enlarge the personal abilities of its members and further their professional development

3. To enhance the awareness and comprehension of its members of important issues having an impact upon growth potential

4. To benefit the business community

This non-profit organization helps fulfill these objectives by providing its members with the opportunity to share and exchange ideas, experiences, policies, and procedures on matters of common interest.

MEMBERSHIP

Membership includes representatives of firms manufacturing a wide range of consumer and industrial products, and firms supplying services closely related to the planning growth of such companies. As a professional society, the Association for Corporate Growth, Inc. grants membership on an individual basis only—there are no company memberships.

Chapter	Founded	Chapter	Founded
Arizona	1975	New York	1957
Atlanta	1974	Orange County	1984
Boston	1979	Philadelphia	1974
Carolinas	1990	Pittsburgh	1986
Chicago	1968	St. Louis	1985
Cleveland	1981	San Diego	1984
Dallas/Fort Worth	1974	San Francisco	1976
Detroit	1984	Santa Clara Valley	1985
Houston	1975	South Florida	1982
Los Angeles	1983	Southern Ohio	1993
Maryland	1983	Toronto	1971
Minnesota	1966	Wisconsin	1988
National Capital	1989		

SEMINARS

Every year ACG presents a very professional three-day seminar at a top resort in either Florida or Arizona during March or April. The seminar is attended by 350 deal makers with a celebrated group of speakers, round-table discussions, deal forums, and lots of networking.

CONCLUSION

Organizations of the type described above are important and often essential in enabling you to network, stimulating you, and educating you in the various aspects of mergers and acquisitions. There are, of course, other organizations across the country that are similar in scope, at least on a regional basis. The above organizations are merely representative of the type of resources available to the buyer in the middle market.

CHAPTER 26

Case Studies of Buyers

PERSISTENCE PAYS OFF

Phil Harris, age fifty-one, of QuadTech in Bolton, Massachusetts, bought this business in March 1991 from GenRad, an old-line electronics testing manufacturer. The company's base business is impedance bridges and standards as well as stroboscopes, with a total of $10 million in sales. A new series of precise testing equipment selling for approximately $8,000 to $12,000 each should add another $2 to $3 million of sales in Phil's fourth year of ownership.

Phil had a classic business background that included Wharton Business School, Xerox, and a position as a division manager of Wang during that company's growth years. Phil realized that he needed financial credibility to buy a middle-market manufacturer, and so he aligned himself with Hambro Venture International, a well-known worldwide venture capital organization. It was a win-win situation for both parties. Phil took an office at Hambro and used its support system as well as its name. Phil's mission was to find the company, negotiate, and close the deal. His arrangement was that he would be president of the acquired company and own a minority interest. Hambro would provide most of the equity and own a majority of the business.

Phil's second order of business was to establish a target mailing list, and so he went to Dun and Bradstreet with three specific criteria: geographically forty miles west of Boston, sales over $5 million, and business in a given range of Standard Industry Codes (SIC). Supplied with 1000 names of presidents and their companies, Phil realized he had to hit prospects' hot buttons. With the help of an executive from a large advertising agency, Phil carefully crafted a letter that stated that he was seeking a business exactly the same as theirs, that he had previously managed a business, that he had financing capability, and that further discussions would be held in high confidence. What was really different, however, was that Phil included a photograph of himself with his jacket off and his shirt sleeves rolled up, implying that he was a take-charge, man of action type. Each letter was personally signed, and each envelope had a postage stamp.

Normal response rate for this type of mailing would be 1 percent, but Phil received an unbelievable 9 percent response. As the telephone began ringing off the hook, Phil was left in the embarrassing position of talking to people who were responding to his personalized letter, yet he couldn't bring up the name and company on the computer screen fast enough to have an intelligent conversation. He therefore had his secretary take all his calls so that he had time to check the target company's profile before calling back.

At the same time Phil was sending out letters, he borrowed the huge Rolodex of the managing partner of Hambro's Boston office. He worked incredibly hard, prospecting and visiting four or five companies a day, but when his leads dissipated, he realized that he had to add an incentive. Phil offered people a $10,000 reward if they merely gave him a name of a company that might be for sale, provided, of course, that there was an ensuing purchase of the company. Additionally, Phil maintained a list of 300 people with whom he networked. Because the list was so large, he would send out letters periodically saying that he was still looking and please continue to remember him.

There were a number of reasons why Phil succeeded, but none compared to his persistence. He pursued one company for nine months and thought for sure that he had a deal, but it fell apart because the seller did not like the terms of the subordinated debt financing. He learned to quickly qualify the prospective sellers by "schmoozing" on the first visit, gathering financial information at the second meeting, and making an offer with a letter of intent at the third meeting. However, Phil still had not bought a company after all his effort. He was facing self-imposed pressure and was close to considering himself a failure. Instead of easing up, though, Phil increased his knowledge of M & A by reading numerous books on the subject, listening to tapes, and enrolling in accounting courses, even though he was a Wharton graduate.

After two years and two months, Phil and Hambro, with the introduction of an intermediary, bought the precision product line, with sales of $10 million, from GenRad. Phil had looked at 250 companies, and liked 20 of them. He made offers for ten companies and negotiated with four others before he hit the jackpot with GenRad. Asked what he would do differently if he could do it over again, without hesitation Phil said that he would have narrower criteria and would focus on corporate spinoffs by concentrating on contacting directors of corporate development of larger companies with small divisions.

As I left Phil's office, I noticed a plaque on the wall that his wife had given him.

> Nothing in the world can take the place of persistence.
> Talent will not; nothing is more common than unsuccessful
> men with talent. Genius will not; unrewarded genius is
> almost a proverb. Education will not; the world is full of
> educated derelicts. Persistence and determination alone
> are omnipotent. The slogan "Press on" has solved and
> always will solve the problems of the human race.
> — CALVIN COOLIDGE

Lessons to Be Learned

- Persistence pays off.

- Concentrate on corporate divestments, as there is a greater probability of doing a deal with a committed seller. Many owners of privately owned companies have "seller's remorse" and become overly emotional about transferring ownership.

- Communicate your focus on definite acquisition criteria, especially as they pertain to an industry. Just as job seekers might change the "objective" statement on their resume to suit a particular interview, impress your contacts with a narrow focus.

- Organize yourself for the acquisition search as if this were a sales and marketing assignment, for in fact you are seeking a customer and selling yourself.

NETWORKING IS A JOB

Stan Healy, age forty-nine, of Chemi-Cure Company in Brighton, Massachusetts, bought this tire service supplies and equipment distributor in October 1990. Chemi-Cure offers over 100 product lines, maintaining 5000 stock-keeping units (SKUs), from tire valves, patches, and hand tools, to tire balancers, tire changing equipment, and wheel alignment equipment. The company has sales of $5 million with approximately 1000 active accounts.

Stan had spent twenty years in management positions, including general manager of the Fastener Division of Dennison Manufacturing Company, North American vice president of Aritech, and president/COO of Arius Security, a $125 million distributor of products for the security industry (primarily burglar and fire alarm components and systems). An investment company had acquired Arius and within six months replaced the operating management group, including Stan, who was then forty-five.

With a ten-month salary severance from Stan's former employer, approximately $400,000 to invest in a business, and the support of his wife, Stan embarked on a business acquisition search. He had not ruled out the possibility of taking a senior management position in "corporate America," but when a position was offered to him, he turned down the opportunity to be a professional manager again, mainly because of his driving ambition to have complete control of his business life. From then on, Stan focused on buying a company.

Stan's strategy was to network with professional friends he had met in business, but he purposely stayed away from his social friends, not wanting to mix professional and personal business. Stan treated networking as a job similar to business development. Because of the respect of his business friends, Stan received bona fide leads from accountants, lawyers, bankers, and insurance agents. Surprisingly, the latter proved to be very prolific with good leads, partly because of their involvement with estate planning.

Stan's system was to use two 5" x 8" loose-leaf notebooks, which were more accessible than a computer. Every time he called or met someone, Stan logged in the date and the highlights of the conversation. This was the basis of his rudimentary follow-up system. His acquisition criteria were as follows:

- A distribution company: He had been involved in wholesale distribution activities for twenty years, and he wanted his assets to be primarily A/R and inventory; he was not interested in tying up capital in equipment, product development, etc.
- The company had to be profitable.

- The company had to be able to pay him a salary equal to what he had received as an executive in his former business.

- The company had to be within sixty minutes traveling time from his house.

Stan rented an office and used a secretarial/telephone service during the search. To every name he was given, Stan wrote a letter and made at least two telephone calls. If he did not receive any response after these three contacts, he dropped the lead. Stan felt that once he had entered into a dialogue with a referral, it was extremely important to inform the original source of the lead as to what had transpired. This effort was received very favorably by the sources and resulted in even more leads.

Six months into the search, Stan was introduced to Chemi-Cure Company through an accountant. The owner was sixty-two years old and had made a decision three years before to sell the business. While he had not retained an intermediary, the owner had anticipated the sale by hiring a large accounting firm to prepare financials that were consistent with generally accepted accounting principles.

The business had not previously been sold because the owner had placed an inflated value on it, particularly on the real estate which was part of the package. The negotiations stalled. A third element of the transaction surfaced, namely that the owner was in the middle of divorce proceedings and his wife's lawyer was holding out for a maximum price, since the wife had a vested interest.

At this point, Stan walked away from the deal for two weeks. He realized that perhaps he needed some help in the valuation and negotiation process, and so he interviewed numerous intermediaries. He selected Industrial Analytics of Wellesley, Massachusetts. These professionals were able to spend some time at Chemi-Cure to understand the operation, value the company, and help negotiate the deal. Fortunately for Stan, the property did not pass the environmental 21E test, and so the owner had to drop his insistence that the real estate be part of the transaction. (It is better for most buyers to rent rather than buy the building initially because renting ties up less money.)

The final result was that ten months into his search, Stan had bought a niche distribution business covering the East Coast, a company with only fifteen employees, including five salesmen, that generated $5 million in sales, or $333,000 sales per employee. The purchase was not without some surprises. The business was purchased at the top of the market in October 1990, just before the recession. One of the salesmen left before Stan could implement noncompete agreements, and joined a competing business, stealing $600,000 of sales. The company's bank was also taken over by the FDIC.

Stan Healy, who has exemplary credentials, was able to successfully buy a business. The salient points of the transaction are as follows:

1. He had a source of income that would last for ten months, and he had a sizable nest egg of money to invest.

2. He had the full support of his wife.

3. It was a full-time search in which he was able to systematize his networking.

4. He zeroed in on distribution companies, which is fairly specific. Most middle-market buyers target manufacturers.

5. Although he was an experienced businessman, he hired an adviser (intermediary) to bring the deal to a conclusion even after the company had been identified.

Compared to most individual buyers, Stan was able to consummate a transaction in a relatively short period of time. His systematic approach was effective, and he had a sharper focus than most individual "middle-market" buyers. His effervescent personality was an obvious plus in his quest to buy a business because of buyers' dependence on referrals.

Lessons to Be Learned

- Rely on your own instincts rather than someone else's advice. You are the one who has to live with the consequences. In other words, listen to your gut feelings.

- When considering the acquisition of a company, have a potential alternative acquisition, so that you do not become psychologically committed to the acquisition simply for the purpose of doing the deal.

- Be sensitive to any and all signals you receive during the acquisition process, whether they be objective or subjective.

- If the deal does not seem right, don't be afraid to walk away from it, regardless of the time, effort, and money you may have invested in pursuing that transaction.

SMALL COMPANY PURCHASE

John Ippolito, age thirty-seven, of Andover, Massachusetts, bought Fixtronix, Inc. in July 1990, after spending two years and two months searching for a suitable company. Fixtronix was a service business that repaired all types of consumer electronics. Ippolito and his investors saw the opportunity to create a brand identity for a commodity service in a highly fragmented industry. When the business was acquired, sales were only $200,000, but by 1993 they exceeded $1 million. In his presentation to the Harvard Business School Alumni Association in December, 1993, John outlined the process he undertook to find a business to buy.

John had pursued an entrepreneurial career path. He started a software company just prior to turning twenty-four, which he sold three years later to a larger software company. Two years later, when the parent company acquired a small turnaround company, they gave John the job of managing it. In January of 1988, John wanted to be on his own again and decided to look for another opportunity to manage his own business. He decided to search for a low-tech company to acquire as a number of his friends had done successfully.

The environment in which John undertook his search in 1988 was, in retrospect, a difficult one. John was only thirty-one and felt the need to establish himself as a credible buyer. There was a great deal of competition among potential buyers of "classic" low-tech manufacturing companies. John noted that, in Boston alone, there were virtually hundreds of qualified buyers, people that had successfully purchased companies before, people with far more capital to invest, and investment firms with portfolio companies trying to make complementary acquisitions. On top of this competition, there were not many good opportunities to choose from. And at the time, there was a large amount of capital available, which indirectly helped to drive prices up. Sellers were expecting to receive the same high multiples of earnings they were reading about every day in the *Wall Street Journal*.

John established a company named Merrimack Management Company from which to operate. He created affiliations with two potential investor groups. One was a group of well-to-do individuals that liked doing the type of transaction John envisioned, having perhaps done it before, and liked the idea of backing a young person who would work very hard for them in a highly leveraged situation. He also worked with an established investment firm. John had friends who were principals in the firm and were among the people who advised him that buying a company could be a smart and profitable thing to do. They were looking for the same type of situation as John, and represented a track record and a source of capital to finance an appropriate deal. The firm, Hammond Kennedy Whitney & Company, of New York, had a portfolio of companies with aggregate sales of over $200 million. John found that this affiliation and reference opened several doors and enabled him to secure appointments with business owners.

At first, John put most of his energy into networking among professional advisors and intermediaries. Ultimately, however, he came to believe that, although no potential source could be ignored, he would be best served by attempting to contact owners via direct mail. His reasoning was that most good lawyers and accountants have clients that are looking for acquisitions, and if they encountered an attractive situation, they would most likely refer it to a client. Intermediaries are motivated to get deals done as simply as possible, which means working with those parties who are most likely to be willing and able to complete a deal. In most cases, this means working with industry participants or others who will be willing to pay a premium for a good company.

John put together a written profile of the kind of company he was looking for. He was looking for companies with sales of $4 million to $50 million, with a minimum EBIT (earnings before interest and taxes) of $400,000, but preferably one of $1 million or more. John did not initially give serious consideration to turnarounds or service companies, because they did not meet either investment group's criteria. John's own experience included selling systems to industrial companies. In addition, his industrial engineering background made him feel he could add value to companies that manufactured products with engineering content. Over time, the industries he considered changed somewhat as he identified attractive industries through the process of researching the prospects of individual companies. He tried to be very flexible about whether or not existing management would stay with acquired companies, and found that the terms of every proposed deal were quite unique.

When he began his search, John put about thirty hours per week into it, spending the balance of his time consulting for income. When he was cautioned by one of the partners from Hammond Kennedy that the search might easily take two to three years, John thanked him for the advice, but didn't believe it. He thought that his drive, creativity and interpersonal skills would enable him to succeed in convincing a seller that he was the right buyer for their business.

After eighteen months, John had considered nearly two hundred businesses, making offers on three, but buying none. Promising situations seemed to fall apart for varying reasons. John became aware that he certainly would end up spending at least two years in his search, perhaps more. He decided to stop consulting in order to focus his full energies on closing one of the deals on his "short list" of six companies.

When John closed on the purchase of Fixtronix, he had been actively searching for two years and two months. At that time, he was still negotiating a purchase agreement for another, larger company, and thought Fixtronix would be a part-time endeavor that he could nurture into an income annuity. He fully expected to complete the other transaction with the larger company. Eventually, he decided to pursue Fixtronix full-time and pass on the other opportunity, because he believed that Fixtronix had more promise.

The numbers game. In preparation for his presentation, John reviewed his databases and found that he had sent out over 1,500 letters to prospects. From these inquiries and contacts with intermediaries and other professionals, he had looked at over 200 businesses. He had also received over 100 marketing documents from sellers or their intermediaries. From this pool of prospects, John sent fifteen "indications of interest" (general statements of interest in purchasing a business for a range of pricing, based on generalized terms and conditions). From these fifteen prospects, John made five offers, two of which were accepted. The offers and the time spent from initial contact until the letter of intent was executed or negotiating was terminated was as follows.

Company Revenues	Time Negotiated
$ 25 million	45 days
$ 16 million	6 months
$ 16 million	4 months
$ 4 million	18 months (accepted)
$200 thousand	60 days (accepted)

Based on his search experience and the experiences gained from four years of operating a low-tech business, John offered the following recommendations for a successful search.

- Seek a company in an industry compatible with your own background. You will be more credible, you will know the companies, you will have referral contacts, and you will understand the valuations. Generally, it will reduce your overall risks.

- Understand your own motivations for buying a business. If you come from a high-tech background and are now seeking a low-tech manufacturing company, recognize that there will be a vast cultural and intellectual difference between these environments.

- Write a business plan for the search with the expectation that it could take two to three years. There are probably 500 individuals and firms engaged in buying businesses in a large metropolitan area. Stress why you are different and what your advantage is.

- Consider the non-business and non-financial aspects of engaging in a full-time search. How will you and your family feel if you are still searching after two or three years? How will you feel after going that long without positive reinforcement?

LINING UP YOUR INVESTORS FIRST

Jeff Williams (alias), age forty-two, a former venture capitalist, established a buyout company named Jupiter. Jeff had an engineering and business school background. From his venture capital experience he was accustomed to valuing, structuring, and negotiating deals. In his quest to buy a company on his own, however, he lacked two important ingredients for success: capital and credibility in the eyes of potential sellers. As a relatively young man with a newly acquired house, a wife who had retired from her job, and three young children, Jeff was not able to go without income for the duration of the search and still provide sufficient equity to do a deal.

Jupiter was Jeff's vehicle for raising capital and gaining credibility. For the first few months, he contacted personal and business friends who he felt would be interested in being co-investors. The funding was set for two stages; first, to pay Jeff a base salary plus basic out-of-pocket expenses during the search, and second, to invest capital to acquire the company. Jeff obtained twelve investors to participate in the first phase of funding. These investors had the option to invest significantly more money in the second phase or pass on the deal.

Several of the investors served as a quasi board of directors, as Jeff called on them for their insight on various deals and would occasionally take one of them to a target company that was of particular interest. Asked what motivated the investors to put money in his project, Jeff responded, "A third believed in the enterprising concept of backing an energetic entrepreneur, a third felt it was a sound businessman's risk, and the final third were a combination of both." Perhaps the most insightful information I received from this interview was Jeff's comment that putting the investor group together was one of the more straightforward parts of the entire acquisition.

With the capital portion fulfilled, the next necessary ingredient to add was credibility. Knowing that there is a tight universe of corporate sellers within Jeff's target companies, he realized he needed to be able to deliver his message with credibility. Therefore, Jeff printed a Jupiter brochure that included

The company's mission
His background
Names of the directors and advisers
Names of law and accounting firms
Type of companies being sought

Additionally, Jeff did not make the mistake made by so many individual buyers. He established an office away from his home in a highly visible business community. In his case, it was in the center of the financial district of Boston. Once he had established it, he compiled his computer database of desired target companies. He sent as many as four separate mailings to each of these companies. Jeff also had a mailing list of 600 intermediaries such as lawyers, bankers, and accountants and a fax list of 300 intermediaries that could be "broadcast to" through a fax modem. Getting attention was the name of the game during the search process, and the Worcester *Telegram* and the Manchester, New Hampshire, *Union Leader* picked up his story and published it.

This story reaffirms what one hears so often: in buying a company, persistence is often the overriding reason for success. From the initial contact to the successful closing date, it took Jeff two years. Initially the company was introduced to Jeff by a marketing consultant who did public relations for the company. The profile of the company fit Jeff's criteria perfectly:

Manufacturer of a trademarked industrial product
Profitable sales of approximately $2 million
4000 customers total, including 2000 distributors
National accounts such as Frito Lay, Johnson & Johnson, Santa Fe
Growth even through the recession
Solid product reputation

The eighty-nine-year-old founder and owner had not begun to explore selling the business before Jeff arrived on the scene. Then the following series of events took place, which is worth noting.

1. Jeff stayed in touch with the owner, but the situation did not change from their original encounter until six months later. The owner's eldest son died, forcing the owner to devote full time to the business. The owner called Jeff, expressing his interest in selling.

2. Like those of the other potential buyers, Jeff's valuation was nowhere near the owner's price. But he kept in constant touch.

3. Jeff was close to a verbal agreement with the owner and a closing appeared imminent; however, the widow of the owner's deceased son fiercely objected, preventing Jeff (or any other buyer, for that matter) from getting clear title.

4. Nine months passed without any further headway, but then the two parties started to negotiate again. One month later, the founder had a stroke and the bookkeeper left.

5. A second son who had been filling in for his father took over the negotiating process. Although he was somewhat familiar with the business, he was unfamiliar with the process of selling a business. Therefore, Jeff had the arduous task of re-creating the negotiating process and convincing the seller that various adjustments were in order. In any event, the closing finally did take place, but not without enormous patience, persistence, and persuasion. Nine of Jeff's original investors ultimately became stockholders of the company.

The search and acquisition process took Jeff two years. He had reviewed 275 companies and made six offers during this time. Asked what sage advice he could impart to other buyers, Jeff commented that he thought it best to be objective and less ambiguous during the letter of intent stage. Often one is caught up with the spirit of getting the deal done, but one should precisely spell out price adjustments for old inventory or dubious accounts receivable.

The different perspectives on the company's value as translated into the perceived selling price and the perceived buying price are almost always a major stumbling block. As outlined in the chapter about negotiating, rational objective data shared by buyers with sellers is one of the most powerful arguments. In the years I have known Jeff, I have often heard him respond to an overpriced deal by asking, "How do you finance it?" I am sure he used this rationale in order to convince the owners that their family business had to be priced accordingly. In this case, as in most buyouts, the investors need a certain rate of return on their equity investment and the bank needs a certain debt coverage and payout level in order to go forward.

Let's hope that this acquisition lives up to its potential.

Lessons to Be Learned

● Get your database in order: targets, intermediaries, contacts, etc.

● Very few companies are really for sale. If you stumble onto one, full court press.

● Worry about finding a *good* deal. Financing dollars will follow good deals.

TURNING A FALTERING BUSINESS INTO A SUCCESS

In 1960 Franklin Wyman Jr., then age forty-one, was controller of a well-known old-line Boston retail chain, R.H. Stearns & Co. Frank had a penchant for sweets, and so he frequented Bailey's of Boston, an ice cream parlor, restaurant, and candy store. Bailey's manufactured its own candy and ice cream products.

While Bailey's had a superior reputation for quality and value, the store was faltering, and there were rumors that the business might be liquidated. Frank felt that Bailey's would be a fun business to own, and so he put together an investor group of three other business friends and approached Bailey's attorney. After two years the owner finally accepted Frank's "low-ball" offer. With only $7,500 of Frank's money plus his partners' investment, they bought a well-established food emporium with annual sales of $250,000.

Unlike most business buyers, Frank retained his other job. In fact, soon after he bought Bailey's, he was promoted to manager of R.H. Stearns' branch stores. Operating two businesses consumed ninety hours a week of his time, but was necessary to pay the educational costs for his four children at prep school and college.

Over the years, Frank bought out his three other partners and started to expand the restaurants, first opening one on Temple Place next to a busy area between the Provident Institution of Savings and the famous Locke-Ober five-star restaurant.

During the twenty-three years of growing the business, Bailey's had become a significant part of Frank's life. He increased the number of stores from one to nine and sales from only $250,000 to $4.6 million. All four of his children had worked in the business at one time or another, and Frank had become a minor local celebrity with his frequent radio and television advertisements.

In 1982, at age sixty-two, Frank realized that neither of his two sons was interested in taking over the business and that perhaps he should consider cutting back on his six-day work week. A mutual friend introduced Frank to an executive from Fanny Farmer, a national chocolate producer. Within nine months, Frank had become a seller of his own business, receiving over $1 million for the company, a handsome return on his very modest original investment. One-third of the purchase price was notes substantiated by a letter of credit from the Bank of New England. Instead of being elated with the transaction, Frank was depressed. He describes the loss of his life's most rewarding piece of work as similar to giving up a child for adoption. Perhaps it is hard to understand for someone who has not owned his own business. In fact, some owners withdraw from closing the deal because of their attachment to a business that has provided close personal relationships and a feeling of importance and accomplishment.

The saga of Bailey's continued, and like the cat that has nine lives, Bailey's got another owner in 1987 when Frank's successor was unable to run the business with the same attention to detail, promotional flair, and tight employee relationships. Ironically, Frank was chairman and part owner of a small investment banking firm when his successor at Bailey's decided to bail out of a business that had become more than he could handle. O'Conor Wright Wyman of Boston accepted the "for sale" assignment even though Bailey's was hemorrhaging badly, with declining sales, negative book value, $800,000 in long-term debt, and restaurant leases expiring. Faced with a rapidly declining business and mounting debt, the owner had to sell Bailey's quickly or face corporate and personal disaster.

O'Conor Wright Wyman valued the business and prepared a selling memorandum. For several decades the firm had successfully transacted M & A deals for clients both here and abroad, but this assignment looked to be one of the most difficult. Partly from a feeling of desperation and partly from instinct, the firm placed an advertisement in the *Wall Street Journal*. Serendipitously, a successful executive from another fast-food chain responded. Within six weeks from the beginning of the assignment, Bailey's was sold to this executive for the asking price, which was more money than the seller or O'Conor Wright Wyman expected.

While the buyer had been enormously successful with another restaurant chain, he tried to change the corporate culture of Bailey's, a Boston institution since 1873. Within two years of his purchase, the company was substantially out of business, no longer a Boston landmark. The following excerpt is taken from the O'Conor Wright Wyman brochure as a forewarning to those intending to acquire a business: "During the last two decades nearly one-half of all acquired or merged companies were less profitable after the acquisition or merger than before. Though the number of such transactions reached an all time high, nearly one-third were dissolved by the end of this dynamic period."

This is a story of both success and failure—the same business over a period of one hundred years encompassing five different owners.

Lessons to Be Learned

1. Success in buying a business will do no good if the owner is not able to run it.

2. Acquirers should go slowly when making changes in a newly acquired business. They should never assume that because they were successful in one business, they will have all the answers in another business.

3. A seller who has never sold a business should not be afraid to employ an intermediary. The cost is more than justified by the increased price the seller can generally obtain when the company is packaged and a systematic search for a synergistic buyer is conducted.

4. The seller should begin the planning for a transition in ownership many years before the event takes place.

FOCUSING ON CORPORATE DIVESTMENTS

Robert Metzger, age fifty-one, graduated from both the University of Notre Dame and Yale's MBA program in engineering. In his early business career, Bob was a manager of strategic development for a $300 million General Electric division, then controller for Disston, Inc, vice president of financial planning for M/A-Com, and later executive vice president of Cognex Corporation.

At age forty-one, Bob as executive vice president had helped raise $6.5 million in private placements for Cognex (the company now has a market value of about $250 million) and essentially managed the company's 100 employees. He was interested in running his own show by becoming president of a medium-tech manufacturing company. In early 1987, Bob started looking for a company to buy, and by April of that year, he resigned from Cognex to spend full time on the search. The following is how the story unfolded.

In the beginning, Bob contacted his business relationships, seeking companies for sale. Initially there was no deal flow, and so he obtained the Massachusetts Directory of Manufacturers and mailed a relatively short letter to about 175 CEOs. He received three direct responses, and seven others expressed interest when Bob followed up by telephone. Most of the respondents were companies that were either losing money, adding little value in their manufacturing process, or wildly overpriced by the owner. It was at this time that Bob changed his search course and approached larger companies that might have potential divestments. Most often corporate sellers are committed to completing a deal, have reasonable price expectations, and are willing to negotiate expeditiously.

With this new course of action, Bob contacted directors of corporate development. Since he had previously worked at General Electric, his inquiries to M & A departments were received favorably. During the 1980s GE, under the leadership of Jack Welch, sold off approximately 200 subsidiaries and divisions. GE offered Bob a robotics company. Then the director of corporate development said, "By the way, we have this rather old and tired wire and cable business in Lowell, Massachusetts, with $18 million in sales located in a 500,000-square-foot former cotton mill with a unionized labor force." GE had not hired an investment banker, but turned the project over to its internal marketing department. GE had contacted most of the industry players who would be the logical buyers, but there was no interest. Bob, however, was intrigued because this division had 100 patents, the purchase clearly could be financed with an asset-based loan, and the size of the company was desirable.

Bob's interest was quickly dampened when he started his due diligence on the industry by talking with Harry Shell, who ran the North American operations of BICC, one of the world's largest wire and cable manufacturers. Shell bemoaned the union and environmental problems, and with that Bob almost passed up the deal—until he ran into another CEO, Bill Binnie, who had been a contrarian acquirer of businesses, often buying heavy industrial companies at liquidation value. Binnie's advice was that one man's poison is another man's wine, and that convinced Bob to pursue the deal. Where there is adversity, there is opportunity. Bob recognized that he could withstand a high degree of difficulty if he could buy the GE division at a bargain price. The negotiated price was 70 percent of book value or 47 percent of market value of the assets, which included 100 GE patents. A letter of intent was signed the end of July, and then the fun began. Having spent the first six months of the acquisition search finding this company, Bob spent the next six months completing the deal. A key element for the buyer to discover early in the acquisition process is what items are nonnegotiable. In this case, as long as GE's business remained in Lowell, the successor employer was obligated to recognize the labor union and negotiate with it.

There were two environmental areas that had to be cleaned up by Clean Harbors. There was an asbestos abatement cleanup that added $1.1 million to the purchase price. Despite the hurdles, the deal closed one year after Bob began seeking a company to buy.

Many buyers have the luxury of sitting back and lighting up a cigar after the acquisition is complete. In Bob's case, his newly named company, Vulkor Incorporated, ran into difficulty one week after the new owner took charge. The union went on strike, probably because the employees were mad at GE for selling the company and because they wanted to intimidate Bob Metzger. The strike was settled in four weeks, and Bob succeeded in reducing the union job classifications from forty-nine to nine; he eliminated piecework bonuses, which reduced labor costs 6 percent, and froze wages for two years. As Massachusetts unemployment went from $2\frac{1}{2}$ to $13\frac{1}{2}$ percent in three years, he negotiated the contract renewal with an $8\frac{1}{2}$ percent labor rollback.

After five years, Bob sold Vulkor to Thermo-Link of Ohio in 1992. In the spring of 1994, he was at the point of buying his second acquisition, having signed a letter of intent. In both cases, the sellers were very motivated to sell and the companies had a high degree of leverageable assets. While many individual buyers may be concerned about their credibility in the face of potential sellers, the following paragraphs from Bob's letter to target companies went a long way to dispel the possible reservation of the company's owner.

Last year, I sold Vulkor, Incorporated, the wire and cable company that I owned and operated in Lowell, MA. Vulkor was formed to acquire the assets of General Electric's wire and cable business in 1987. I structured the transaction, obtained the necessary financing, built the organization and developed the sales strategy that grew the sales revenue by 50% in the second year of operation. This was done on my own with my own resources.

I am seeking a business that I can actively manage, as well as invest in and I have financial partners such as Metapoint Partners prepared to invest in the right situation.

Lessons to Be Learned

- You need to have a strong stomach.

- You have to be extremely tenacious.

- If you are buying a "union shop," do not negotiate with the union until after the acquisition. When you own the company, you are in a stronger position, as the union has to deal with you as much as you have to deal with it. Bob was able to reduce the union contract from 150 pages to 25 pages.

- For your acquisition, target corporate divestments that do not meet the strategic criteria of the parent company. You are almost always dealing with a committed seller, unlike the owners of many family businesses, who tend to waffle when selling.

- When the seller's expectations are overly optimistic, use an intermediary for negotiations to provide a third-party objectivity to a rational valuation.

- Upon the completion of the acquisition, make management changes early on in order to set a precedent. It is important to clean out the closet and impress your own culture on the company.

BUYING A HALF INTEREST IN A $2.5 MILLION COMPANY

At age thirty, Paul Nechipurenko became a principal in Noonmark Capital of Needham, Massachusetts, a private investment firm whose founding partner, Northrup Knox, Jr., owns a $6 million plumbing products manufacturer. Noonmark was actively seeking to acquire manufacturing and distribution companies in the Northeast with revenues between $5 million and $20 million.

While most of the stories of the acquisitions involve buyers aged forty-five to fifty-five, this episode is about a young man, aged twenty-five, who became 50 percent owner of a $2.5 million company and virtually ran the operation for two years, reversing the before-tax earnings from a $70,000 loss to an $81,000 profit. To properly set the stage, it is important to appreciate Paul's background, as it is relevant to the unfolding of the acquisition search.

Paul graduated from Harvard in 1987. He was then employed in a two-year program by the Corporate Finance Department of the Shawmut Bank in Boston. It was there that Paul, while valuing businesses, transacting private placements, and being involved as an investment banker in mergers and acquisitions, became fascinated with the M & A business. During the process of making deals for the bank's clients, Paul often sat across the table from principals with extensive operating experience who insinuated that nonoperating businessmen did not understand how to run companies. This suggestion struck a chord with Paul; instead of intimidating him, it motivated him to buy and run his own company.

After leaving Shawmut, Paul began a marketing campaign in 1989. His business contacts moved forward rapidly because he established a relationship with a venture capitalist who was willing to invest with him if he presented an attractive acquisition. Like most business buyers, Paul made the rounds by visiting bankers, CPAs, and attorneys. Every day he went out to sell himself as a young entrepreneur who was anxious to buy a company. He met hundreds of people, and despite his young age, everyone was enthusiastic about his mission.

Paul's statistics were not that different from those of other acquirers of businesses except that he achieved his goal in six months instead of two years. After being introduced to approximately 100 companies, he visited twenty-five, became serious with about five to ten, and made offers on three. Unlike most other buyers, Paul spent a fair amount of time interviewing with the various "alphabet" agencies in Massachusetts, such as the Massachusetts Business Development Corporation and the Industrial Services Program, but most particularly with the Boston Local Development Corporation, which helps finance underperforming companies.

The latter introduced Paul to AB&W Company of Dorchester, Massachusetts, an underperforming former division of United Carr Fastener held by two passive owners and one active owner aged fifty who was unable to give the business his full attention. The company was a metal stamping operation, producing clips and fasteners for electrical wiring for Ford, Chrysler, and General Motors. While Ford represented 45 percent of AB&W sales, this involved thirty SKUs with contracts spaced over three years. Paul was introduced to AB&W as a potential investor. When Paul first looked at the business in 1989, sales were $2.7

million and profits were negative. After allowance for debt, Paul valued the company at $200,000; he had $100,000 and negotiated to buy half the business for $50,000 down, the balance thereafter.

After acquiring 50 percent of the business in mid-1990, Paul took charge as the COO. His 50 percent partner for the most part turned the business over to Paul. Totally immersing himself in the company, Paul found that the product quality was acceptable but the manufacturing systems were inefficient; there were too many late deliveries and too many parts needed rework. Nevertheless, he struggled forward as the U.S. automotive industry entered its worst recession since World War II. Sales tanked, and Paul reduced his workforce from thirty to fifteen people. Operating the company very efficiently, Paul dramatically turned the company around, from numerous years of losses to a solid profit in his second year of management. Additionally, AB&W was cited as a Q-1 supplier by Ford, and received personal recognition from Alex Trotman (now CEO of Ford), and the *Wall Street Journal*. At that point, Paul was effectively the CEO, as his partner was spending less and less time in the operation.

In the summer of 1991, Paul exercised his option to "put" the stock back to the company at a predetermined multiple of EBIT minus bank debt—at a three year payout with an 11 percent interest rate. Filled with success and a feeling of accomplishment, Paul entered Harvard Business School that fall.

As difficult as it is to turn a business around, Paul admitted that finding a business to buy was more difficult than running it! In spite of that statement, Paul was able to acquire a company in only six months. However, he was willing to buy an underperforming company with four years of continuous losses, perhaps a more courageous move than most would undertake.

Lessons to Be Learned

- One has to have a total commitment in searching for a business to buy. You should take the attitude that whatever it takes to reach that goal, do it! It is important to have a passion for the project so that every day when you get out of bed, you know that you have a full day ahead of seeking opportunities and selling yourself to intermediaries, lawyers, accountants, financiers, business owners, etc. The process has very little immediate feedback in that you may have to look at several hundred companies in order to buy just one.

- Personal connections are very important. In Paul's case, he had a business friend who was well connected in the Boston area. This gentleman allowed Paul to use his contacts and his name in the introductory call. The fact that Paul was a Harvard graduate (later earning his MBA there also) opened numerous doors for him, as invariably the venture capital or buyout groups have many HBS graduates.

- Work with someone else on the project. In the search that led to the AB&W acquisition, Paul worked with a silent partner. In Noonmark Capital, his partner is Norty Knox, who has a different network of business friends, having graduated from the Yale School of Management and having acquired a Connecticut-based plumbing products manufacturer from Teledyne Industries. Paul has more of an operational background, while Norty has more financial expertise—a good balance because of their complementary skills.

THE TENACIOUS APPROACH

In May 1993, Jeffrey Chizmas, age thirty-six, bought Cider Mill Company of Acton, Massachusetts, a pet product manufacturer with sales of approximately $1,150,000.

Jeff's background is noteworthy, but throughout his former employment, he had always wanted to run his own company. At IBM, Jeff had been the manager of a branch sales office that was downsized out of existence. He then became vice president of sales of Wavetracer, a startup company that was venture funded by such esteemed investors as Advent, International Memorial Drive Trust, Ross Perot, and Sevin Rosen. Wavetracer was founded to provide superior engineered computer platforms; however, the company ultimately ran out of ongoing financing because it lacked the proper market focus for its products. Having had his last two jobs terminated, Jeff was more determined than ever to control his own destiny. Furthermore, Jeff's desire was to increase his income, and working for himself seemed the most logical approach in reaching his goal.

Out on his own in the fall of 1992, Jeff pursued his quest to buy a company with enormous vigor. He blitzed service providers such as accounting and law firms as well as M & A intermediaries, seeking referrals of companies for sale. He estimates that he was making 200 telephone calls a week! Having a strong sales background, Jeff realized that he had to sell himself and convince others that he had sufficient capital to do a deal, the fortitude to complete a transaction, and the ability to successfully run a company. In fact, Jeff had access to $500,000 of equity, which was very important because he knew it was imperative that he gain the business owner's respect both financially and operationally. Owners have so much of themselves invested in the business, both emotionally and psychologically, that they are always concerned to whom they sell their business.

Jeff realized that as an individual he lacked credibility in the eyes of many business owners in spite of his energy and tenacious approach to the search. Therefore, he retained not one but two intermediaries at the same time in order to identify target companies, and, more importantly, to represent him as a credible, serious, and qualified buyer. One of the intermediaries was New England Business Exchange of Wellesley, Massachusetts.

After considering perhaps a hundred companies over seven months of a very intense search, John Whorf introduced Jeff to Cider Mill Company, with sales of approximately $1.1 million. Cider Mill produced dog tie-outs and dog tree trolleys, which were sold to such outlets as Bradlees, Pet Super Stores, etc. After two months of negotiating in which the deal was called off more than once, Jeff convinced the owner of Cider Mill to sell to him. Price and terms were finally reached, but not without some creative negotiating in which Jeff bought 80 percent of the company, with the remaining 20 percent to be acquired later on at "fair market" value.

One year later, Cider Mill's sales had doubled, and the company had successfully paid down the acquisition debt. Jeff hopes to hire a manager to run Cider Mill, raise equity, and acquire another company.

Lessons to Be Learned

- Cover your bases by working with more than one intermediary, even if you have to put two on retainer at the same time. To the best of your ability, be sure that the intermediary shows you the entire inventory of companies for sale.

- You need an intermediary to work on your behalf because the good ones will add substance and qualify you by association as a legitimate buyer. In the end, the commission is well spent.

- Don't let a 5 or 10 percent price spread between you and the seller break a deal. If you buy the right company, you will make up the price difference in six months. Good companies cost good money.

BULL'S-EYE ON THE FIRST SHOT

In August 1986, Ray Cronin, age twenty-eight, along with Jim Grasso, age thirty-one, acquired a circuit board test company. Unlike most other buyers of small middle-market companies, the partners hit the jackpot on their first attempt to buy a company. Truly, the purchase of Circuitest Services Inc. is a Horatio Alger story, as the ordeal was full of challenges.

Cronin worked as a West Coast salesman for Megatest Company, a San Jose semiconductor test equipment manufacturer, between 1980 and 1983. Between 1983 and 1985, he added to his engineering degree by completing his MBA at Harvard Business School. Upon graduation, he became the eastern regional sales manager for Megatest. Jim Grasso also had worked at Megatest and other startups in the early eighties.

In January 1986, during a poker game, one of Cronin's card-playing friends mentioned that a small Nashua, New Hampshire, circuit board test equipment company with $350,000 in revenues was for sale. Cronin and Grasso visited Tony Ritchie, the owner of Circuitest, who was a classic entrepreneur, having started and sold four different companies. Ritchie's mission from the beginning was to run the company for maximum profit and then sell it for a maximum price. Cronin and Grasso had a different corporate vision, i.e., a commitment to being a leader in the advancement of bare board and interconnect substrate test technology. The partners felt that they would excel and become leaders in the circuit board test business, just as Megatest had done in semiconductor test equipment.

Ritchie, the owner of Circuitest, was a savvy negotiator, but in March, Cronin and Grasso agreed to buy the business for $250,000 (book value) plus a $100,000 note paid over two years. They hired Coopers & Lybrand to do the due diligence. Grasso also wrote an acquisition business plan. Then came the challenge—raising the $250,000! For five months Cronin and Grasso sought the necessary acquisition financing from both New Hampshire and Massachusetts banks. Although 1986 was a peak year for the New England economy, funding the acquisition became more and more of a problem. Finally, Cronin received a note from a Boston bank for $335,000 after convincing his parents to mortgage their house, collateralizing the balance of the note with the remaining equity in the house, and giving the bank 5 percent of

Circuitest's stock. Cronin and Grasso were not happy with this bank deal, and so as soon as the acquisition was completed in August, they found a new bank in New Hampshire that bought out the loan on less onerous terms. As Cronin said, "Dan Day, president of the Centerpoint Bank in Milford, New Hampshire, is a banker who tends to make decisions based on the person instead of the business, i.e., an old-fashioned approach that often works better."

Overall, the number of circuit board manufacturers (Circuitest's customer base) has decreased from 2200 nationwide in 1986 to 600 in 1994. It is a business that is fragmented, has low barriers to entry, and has inherent environmental problems because of the waste generated in the manufacturing process. Yet, over seven years, Circuitest has grown from $350,000 to $7.5 million in sales and is ranked second in the industry, with six different locations, including England. In 1989, Grasso and Cronin took on Duane Delfosse as an equal partner.

In retrospect, Cronin and partners had a vision of bringing bare-board testing to a high technological level and writing customized software programs for their testing. They established five different testing locations in this country and one in England, which indicates their emphasis on being close to their customers, both figuratively and literally. The fabulous success of Circuitest is not a result of the acquisition, but rather a result of what the owners did after the acquisition. Much of this book is based on the deal itself, i.e., identifying the target company, valuation, negotiation, and the close. Very few of these case studies have focused on the integration process, but in the Circuitest situation, the management team made sure that the previous owners introduced them to their key contacts so that there would be an orderly transition. Over time, Tony Ritchie phased out and the company flourished, but only after the three partners committed themselves to eighty-hour workweeks in order to reach their goal.

Lessons to Be Learned

- Buying a business is difficult and requires persistence, but it is nothing compared to the challenge of running and growing the business.

- Even in bootstrap situations such as this, it is critical to take the time to always hire the best possible people to grow the company. The founders/owners must be able to delegate.

- Everyone has weaknesses. They must be understood and discussed openly. In a growing business, it is critical that the weaknesses of the owners/founders be negated through delegation of responsibility to capable managers.

CHAPTER 27

Pearls of Wisdom

Throughout this book, different issues involved in buying a company are addressed in separate chapters. Cumulatively the text should be helpful to you in completing a transaction. In this chapter, however, I have brought together nuggets of information; hence the title of this chapter.

From an experienced deal maker's perspective, Andre Laus, cofounder of Bristol Group, a Providence, Rhode Island–based firm specializing in turnaround and corporate improvement, has the following comments for buyers:

> *Profits, profits, profits:* Like the analogy of the ingredients for successful real estate acquisitions, location, location, location, companies with consistent profits over a long time period are usually the best acquisitions. Reliability of earnings, year in and year out, is more important for most buyers than the total magnitude of earnings if the earnings are inconsistent. A very successful group with which I was previously associated acquired over a dozen midsize companies in less than ten years. Part of their success is attributed to the majority stockholder's criterion of acquiring only companies with ten years of unbroken profitable earnings. Such standards place a greater burden on the acquisition process, but the postacquisition results have been most rewarding.
>
> Additionally, the corporate culture that no cost is too small to address, cumulatively results in noteworthy profits. From a buyer's perspective, continuous cost management results in more profits, just as

increasing sales usually results in greater profits. Management should focus on both items with equal emphasis.

The quality of working capital: Working capital (current assets less current liabilities) should be viewed skeptically and beyond the immediate implication of the numbers. For example, if there is an excessive amount of receivables over ninety days, it may be indicative of the industry, the quality of the customers, or the company's own lack of financial discipline. Either way, the extent of this item may cause a buyer to reconsider the potential acquisition.

Also, inventory is an important component of working capital. Most businessmen analyze inventory with regard to annual turnover, but few people focus on the equally important issue of what percentage of the orders are shipped complete or if a system to measure customer order fill exists at all.

Strong customer orientation: Many of us have read Tom Peters' famous book *In Search of Excellence,* which keeps focusing on the importance of the customer in the eyes of "all" employees of the company. Some progressive companies have a customer council that meets quarterly. Buyers should be looking for companies that are customer-driven, as this is indicative of future success.

Strong employee orientation: Employee training programs, employee empowerment, and employee respect are all indications of a company that probably believes its most important asset is its people. Not a bad philosophy! An incidental tip is to look at the company bulletin board, which reflects how management feels about its employees. And, above all things, look at the men's washroom. If it isn't clean, reconsider buying the company. The employees probably do not take pride in their company, their products, or themselves—and the company accepts it.

No problems with the company: Within reason, buyers should try to avoid buying companies with serious problems. Of course, all companies have some problems, but before a new owner can start growing his new acquisition, he should heed the advice of Roy Little, the famous capitalist and owner of Narragansett Capital. Before seeking ways to grow a company, first concentrate on avoiding catastrophe, and second, be sure to keep the ship on a straight course. After those two points have been achieved, then one can focus on ways to grow the company.

In addition to Andre Laus's "pearls of wisdom," I have forty-four recommendations for deal makers:

1. A buyer should be talking with at least four or five potential sellers at any one time and actively negotiating with two or three.

2. Memoranda to oneself following each meeting, detailing the points discussed and minor or major matter agreed upon, are invaluable in keeping discussions on course.

3. You should avoid introducing a lawyer into discussions with principals before the elements of a business deal have been agreed upon. As soon as the buyer introduces such an expert into discussions, the seller does likewise. Since lawyers must protect the technical aspects of their clients' positions, more transactions have failed because of the premature introduction of such specialists than have been made.

4. Don't make a ridiculously low offer that will insult the owner.

5. Don't make complex deals.

6. Don't get hung up on assets; be a cash flow buyer. Lenders tend to look at fixed assets, while buyers concentrate on cash flow.

7. Keep the buying process moving as fast as possible. The buyer who is able to make rapid analyses and decisions will benefit from the momentum.

8. For any given deal, there is a limited window of opportunity. If you spend too much time raising equity after the target company is "in play," the window will close.

9. If you are having difficulty raising the necessary equity to complete the transaction, suggest that the seller keep the accounts receivables, the real estate, or even the machinery. Sellers can lease the equipment to the buyer.

10. If you plan to borrow money against machinery and equipment for your acquisition financing, your banker will need to have an official liquidation appraisal on the machinery and equipment. Anticipate this and have the appraisal done early instead of later so that the momentum of completing the deal is not lost.

11. Predetermine your acquisition borrowing power so that your financing will not come up short at the critical juncture of the transaction. For example, the following percentages are normal borrowing ranges:

Accounts receivable (90 days or less)	70–85%
Inventory (not work in process)	25–60%
Machinery & equipment (of forced liquidation)	50–80%
Land & buildings (of market price)	60–80%

12. The rule of one-third: After an equity investment of one-third of the purchase price, the cash flow must provide the CEO/owner's salary, a return on investment, and enough money to service the debt.

13. Besides profitability, some successful buyers often concentrate on the following ingredients:
    Strong and committed management
    Steady and predictable business in noncyclical industry
    Substantial market share
    Admirable corporate culture

14. Agree at the outset that the party that is acquiring the business will draft all the documents and the selling party will then review and make comments. Not only does this sequence provide order for the transaction, but it is to your advantage as the buyer to draft the documents based on your understanding and your language.

15. When buying a company, target an industry, product, or service that is on the upswing. Conversely, few acquisitions succeed if the industry, product, or service is on the downswing.

16. The announced reason for the sale of companies is rarely the real reason. Investigate, take your time, and listen carefully. If you are getting bad vibes about the deal, get out of the transaction quickly.

17. In order for your attorney to be a deal maker instead of a deal breaker, don't expect him or her to win every point in contention.

18. Sellers are often selling their legacy, and so the dynamics of the sale are often more important than the top bid. The preferred buyer, in the eyes of the seller, is not necessarily the high bidder, but rather the one who has the best intentions, the best chemistry, and/or the best credentials. Buying businesses goes beyond the numbers. Unfortunately, many buyers drop the ball in romancing the seller.

19. A buyer's insensitivity to the owner of the selling company can destroy a deal. Be sensitive to the seller's attachment to the company and its employees, customers, and vendors.

20. Most deals take time to complete, usually from two to five months after the letter of intent. While you have to exercise

some degree of patience, you must remember that 50 percent of all deals fail to close after reaching the letter of intent stage. It is very important to keep the momentum going, and it is imperative that you retain experienced counsel in closing deals. Most sellers, somewhere along the line, get cold feet, and so buyers must maintain the seller's interest.

21. Nonnegotiable items should be pointed out early in the negotiation, such as an asset versus a stock sale or that the seller's paper will be subordinated to the bank.

22. For companies without audited statements, make sure you substantiate their financials with their tax returns.

23. The older the business, the better established it is and the stronger its customer and supplier relationships.

24. The more industries in which the company sells its product, the more protection it has from cyclicality and/or an industry downturn.

25. The tax objectives of a buyer and seller are at opposite ends of the spectrum in an acquisition. The seller's goal in structuring a buyout is to maximize the after-tax cash in his or her pocket, while the buyer's goal is to maximize the seller's assets that can be depreciated or amortized.

26. The best growth companies, if a reasonable size (over $10 million in sales), usually "go public" if management wants to cash out. On the other hand, poorly performing companies are more apt to be acquired.

27. Buying companies is usually cheaper than trying to grow them from scratch.

28. From a buyer's standpoint, a business is worth less if it is a Subchapter S corporation because of the lower book value resulting from the earnings flowing through to the owners. A lower book value is also going to reduce the leverageability of the transaction.

29. Try to get very close to the other principal because there is a strong possibility that his or her advisers are not experts in mergers and acquisitions. Additionally, the potential seller is apt to receive some opinionated advice from "country club" friends that invariably increases the seller's insecurity about the deal.

Meeting alone with the other principal even during the final negotiation will frequently improve the chance of not having the deal derailed by advisers.

30. If the buyer is not receiving information that was requested from the seller, it is an indication of a possible coverup of facts. The buyer should consider other companies instead.

31. A critical issue in buying a business is access to capital.

32. Management: the most important issue you need to consider is whether the owner is the reason for the success of the business. If the owner leaves, can you fill this role?

33. Seller financing is a popular means of structuring the deal and is used in well over half of the transactions completed.

34. You should be sure that the CEO has the legal authority to sell the business. This may rest with the board of directors, a majority stockholder, a bank with a lien on the business, etc.

35. Knowing the strengths of a business is as important as, or perhaps more important than, understanding its weaknesses. Focus on the target company's competitive edge.

36. The art of the business acquisition process begins with techniques to find a large number of business deals and to find them before they come on the market.

37. Many people do themselves a disservice by looking at all deals that might be interesting. Targeting industries and types of businesses makes your search more efficient and more likely to succeed.

38. It is imperative that you follow up with anyone who gives you a referral. Report back to the person giving the referral, indicating what transpired. Not only is this professional courtesy, but it will lead to more referrals.

39. Make generous use of appraisers, i.e., corporate, real estate, equipment, etc. The appraisals will keep you from overpaying.

40. Price doesn't kill deals—terms do.

41. From a seller's perspective, if the deal falls through, a great deal of confidential information has been given to the wrong people.

42. Act with absolute clarity in all of your negotiations so that the potential deal breakers surface as early as possible and can be

dealt with for as long a period of time as possible rather than at the eleventh hour.

43. In any negotiations concerning a promissory note, the interest rate and payment schedule are key issues. Interest rates often will track rates of commercial lenders. Parties also should evaluate various amortization options, including interest-only periods and balloon payments, as alternatives to equal installments of principal and interest over a given term.

44. In negotiating, if the seller wants a stock sale instead of an asset sale for tax reasons, then the buyer should request a lower selling price. If the seller wants a fully collateralized note from the buyer, then the acquirer should negotiate a lower interest coupon.

CHAPTER 28

Conclusion

Finding a business to buy is a lengthy process. Ultimately, buying a business is the culmination of analyzing, negotiating, financing, and implementing your professional and personal skills and resources.

In the case studies of successful buyers in Chapter 26, the individuals were resourceful, committed, and tenacious in their quest to own their own company. For every successful acquirer of a company, there may be ten others who are unsuccessful. This latter group fail to buy a company for a myriad of reasons, but of equal concern are those who buy a company and then fail thereafter. This book is an attempt to bring some of my knowledge and the experience of others to those interested in buying a business.

Partly because large companies have recently restructured by laying off thousands of senior managers and partly because of the desire of many businesspeople to be entrepreneurial, the demand for middle-market companies far exceeds the supply. However, business schools do not teach people how to buy a company. Working for a manufacturing company does not necessarily properly prepare you to buy or run one. Being a corporate executive of a *Fortune* 500 company is far different from being a CEO of a middle-market company with a small support staff, long hours, tedious tasks, and tight finances. Owning your own business can be particularly taxing on your marriage.

This book, while comprehensive, does not make it less necessary for a buyer to surround himself or herself with excellent advisers—intermediary, transaction lawyer, accountant, corporate appraiser, tax consultant, etc. Because businesses are difficult to properly value, it is often prudent to have an independent valuation. The $2,000 to $10,000 you spend on this up-front expense could be just a drop in the bucket compared to what you might save in the final price. Such an appraisal helps buyers enormously in the negotiating process. In the final analysis, the business you acquire should be able to generate sufficient earnings to service the debt, pay you a competitive salary, and provide an annual return on investment of 20 percent or more.

In spite of all the books you may read on the subject of buying a business and all the expert advice you will receive, your gut instincts may ultimately be the most important factor determining what, if any, business you should acquire. While it is human nature for most people to be trusting of others, the stakes are high when it comes to buying a business, and so I urge you to be sure you know why a person is selling a company. The owner truly may be burned out or bored, but he or she also has the advantage of knowing more about the business and probably more about the company's industry than you do. Therefore, it is important to do the best you can to determine why the owner is selling. It is also important to spend enough time and effort on due diligence—not just number crunching, but product and market analyses. It may be better to spend more money for a healthy company than less money for a sick company. And finally, beware of the seller who insists on all cash at closing. If the seller agrees to help you finance the acquisition by having some of the purchase price paid in the form of a noncompete agreement, a consulting agreement, and/or notes, the seller is your quasi partner through the transition period, and you have retained a form of leverage in case there are any skeletons in the closet.

Throughout the book we have shown that acquisitions are difficult, but obviously doable if the potential buyer uses all his or her resources, relies on advisers, and is relentless in the search for a company to buy. Individual buyers usually have to meet the acid test when acquiring a company: pay themselves market-rate salaries, service the debt, and achieve a satisfactory return. Often the individual buyer is bidding on a business against a corporate buyer that can justify a higher price based on future synergism of the two companies, elimination of duplicate staff, economies of scale, and the benefits of selling new products through the same distribution channel.

The vicissitudes in doing a deal are enormous. For example, you must analyze the industry and the company in order to properly value the business, so that you can finance the transaction that will lead you to the negotiations, due diligence, and closing. You may be buying a company for the first time, but as Merrill Halpert of the Charterhouse warns, "Time works against you. The longer it takes to pull a deal together, the greater the possibility of the deal falling apart." When the momentum is lost, the deal is dead.

In many cases, it is more difficult to buy a small company, because the business probably does not have audited statements, and at first, you may not know exactly what you are buying. Surprisingly, most small businesses are not sold with all their assets and liabilities. If you insist on an asset sale rather than a stock sale, the seller's lawyer will probably advise the client to increase the price. Be prepared to find out what assets are to be withdrawn and what debt obligations are to be assumed. When the preceding items are resolved, will there be adequate working capital left to properly run the business?

I have offered numerous approaches and techniques for successfully doing a deal. While the case studies clearly show that most of the successful acquirers of companies were tenacious, two of the other attributes you need to successfully complete a deal are simply human qualities. One is to use your intuition as to what is right and what is wrong. The other is common sense. For example, if you buy a company in an industry with which you are not familiar, you are asking for trouble. Thoroughly understanding the industry in which your acquired company operates is not imperative, but it is a definite advantage.

Ideally you will want to acquire a business that has the following characteristics:

- Profitable, with a historical record of stable earnings
- Strong middle management that is willing to stay on
- Good market position in a niche business
- Strong growth rate with continued upside
- Affordable price

The above checklist is near utopian. Such a company may not be available for you to acquire. In fact, the problem most individual buyers have with acquiring middle-market companies is that they are almost paranoid about the "warts" on the businesses. Almost all companies have some warts. What the buyer should concentrate on is the core competency, the core skills, and the core business of the company.

If you have come this far in the book, I applaud you for your efforts. If executed correctly, buying a middle-market company can be one of the most exhilarating and challenging episodes of your life!

Glossary

Allocation of purchase price: In an asset sale, the purchase price must be allocated to certain assets; the balance is goodwill.

Angel: An individual high-risk investor who likes to make investments in promising acquisitions. Angels often have valuable business experience and can be helpful as members of the board of directors.

Asset-based lenders: Commercial lenders who are willing to take on more risk than commercial banks, lending against accounts receivable and inventory and being subordinate to commercial banks.

Asset sale: Purchase of certain assets and/or liabilities, leaving the seller the remainder as well as the corporate entity.

Auction: When the seller and/or its intermediary orchestrates the selling process by encouraging buyers to bid and rebid until the highest and best offer is received.

Audit: Examination of the financial records and accounting books in order to verify their accuracy.

Basket: A dollar amount set forth by the seller in the indemnification provision to cover any losses suffered by the buyer.

Book value: Also known as net worth, the figure derived by deducting all the liabilities from all the assets.

Bottom fishing: When a buyer will pay only a very low price for a business.

Bridge loan: A temporary loan to cover the financing shortfall of the acquisition until permanent funding is available.

C corporation: A type of corporation for which taxes are paid once at the corporate level and again when the earnings are distributed to the shareholders. These corporations are allowed to issue various classes of stock and to have corporate and alien shareholders.

Capitalization: A company's total ownership and borrowed capital. Ownership capital includes stock and paid-in surplus, and borrowed capital includes bank debt, bonds, etc.

Capitalization rate: The conversion of income into value as part of the valuation process by the application of a capitalization factor (any multiplier or divisor used to convert income to value).

Cash cow: A business that has a steady cash flow, but whose earnings have remained nearly the same for the past five years, showing little growth.

Cash flow: The amount of money left over after the cost of goods sold and general, selling, and administrative expenses, but before interest, depreciation, taxes, and amortization.

Collateral: Property pledged by a borrower to protect the interests of the lender. Bank loans are often collateralized or secured by the company's accounts receivables, inventory, and/or equipment.

Confidentiality: The provision of proprietary information by one party to another for that party's exclusive use, with a prohibition against passing it on to others.

Contingent: Dependent on or conditioned by something else. For example, the price established for the business may vary depending on some future event.

Contingent payments: Future financial obligations that are dependent on contractual events taking place.

Covenants: Binding agreements between the buyer and the seller that restrict each party from taking certain actions, particularly during the letter of intent period and closing.

Deal flow: A stream of potential business acquisitions moving across your desk in a quantity that allows you to select the few that meet your criteria.

Depreciation: The amount and rate at which tangible assets decrease in value over the normal life cycle as designated by the parameters of the GAAP and the IRS.

Discounted cash flow: A valuation technique that assigns a value in today's dollars to the cash flows that are expected to occur in the future.

Due diligence: The investigation of the other party's business practices in an attempt to uncover previously unknown information.

Earnout: A part of the purchase price that is dependent on a future performance variable, such as profits or sales.

Encumbrance: A lien against certain property that encumbers the company's assets, which could ultimately hold up or prevent the closing.

Entrepreneur: Taken from the French word *entreprendre,* a person who owns and runs a business.

Escrow: Money that is delivered to a third party and held on deposit until the party to receive it fulfills certain conditions.

Fair market value: What the assets would most likely sell for in the open market; this is often determined by a professional appraiser.

Finder's fee: A commission for merely identifying and introducing a buyer to the seller, not including other services such as valuing, structuring, or negotiating.

Floor price: The lowest price that a seller will accept.

GAAP: The acronym for generally accepted accounting principles, the Financial Accounting Standard Board's methodology of accounting.

Goodwill: The difference between the purchase price and the value shown on the corporate books at the time of closing.

Holdback provision: In the purchase and sale agreement, a provision stating that if a buyer winds up having to pay a debt that the seller did not disclose, it will be paid from an amount that was held back at closing and placed in an escrow account.

Indemnification: Exemption for the buyer from incurred penalties or liabilities after the closing as a result of incomplete representations and warranties of the seller.

Intangibles: Assets that are not physical, such as licenses, franchises, trademarks, customer lists, unpatented technology, etc.

Intermediary: An agent who is a mergers and acquisitions consultant to the buyer or seller and is expected to facilitate the transaction.

Investment banker: An intermediary who often provides additional services such as bridge loans or underwritings.

Lehman formula: The industry standard commission rate, which is a sliding scale, i.e., 5-4-3-2-1 percent on each successive million dollars of the purchase price.

Letter of intent: A preliminary offer to purchase a business, usually nonbinding, which if accepted by the seller leads to the drafting of a purchase and sale agreement.

Leveraged buyout: A transaction in which a company's capital stock or assets are purchased with borrowed money, causing the company's new capital structure to be primarily debt.

Lien: A charge or hold on assets, usually by a creditor until indebtedness is satisfied.

M & A: An acronym for mergers and acquisitions.

Mezzanine capital: Subordinated to senior debt, it is like a second mortgage, with higher interest rates and often including common stock purchase warrants.

Middle market: Companies with sales between $2 million and $150 million.

Multiples: An abbreviated terminology for capitalization rates.

Net present value: Money paid out in the future discounted at the opportunity cost of capital for a similar risk over the specified period of time.

Net worth: See *Book value.*

Networking: Maintaining contacts with a variety of people connected with buying and selling businesses.

Niche: Uniqueness in the marketplace; an area in which the company's product or service has a competitive advantage because there are few competitors.

Off-balance-sheet items: Unrecorded obligations such as repurchase agreements, pending lawsuits, and unfunded pensions.

OEM: Original equipment manufacturer, a company that produces products that are sold to other companies, which in turn make products for consumer purchases.

Perquisites (perks): Elements of compensation in addition to a regular salary, such as the use of a company automobile, country club membership, entertainment allowance, etc.

Pooling: An arrangement between stockholder groups to exchange equity securities (tax free).

Recast: Reconstruction of the financials to reflect what the income statement would be without excessive salaries and perks.

Representations and warranties: Indemnifications and covenants written into the purchase and sale agreement that provide factual information that is important to protect the buyer in the event of future problems.

ROI, ROE: Return on investment and return on equity; they must be greater than the cost of capital in order to create shareholder value.

S corporation: An unaffiliated corporation owned by thirty-five or fewer individuals in which the profits flow to the individuals without a corporate tax being imposed.

Seller financing: A situation in which the seller extends his or her own notes to the buyer in lieu of paying all cash at closing or obtaining other debt financing, such as bank loans.

Senior debt: The most secure bank debt and the first in line with primary collateral. Often senior debt is a short-term revolving loan that is paid down completely within a year.

SIC code: Abbreviation for Standard Industry Code, a numerical categorization of industries. Most business directories, manufacturing or service, are organized by geography and SIC code.

Skimming: The business owner's personally taking money "off the top" of the company revenue stream.

Stepped-up basis: In most asset transactions, the basis of the assets of the target corporation is stepped up in value to the purchaser's cost.

Stock sale: Purchase of the company's shares of stock; the buyer then assumes all the assets and all the debt, both tangible and intangible.

Subordinated debt: Nonbank debt, which is by definition less secure than bank (or senior) debt. To attract lenders, borrowers often give subordinated lenders rights to convert their debt to equity.

Tender offer: A publicized bid to buy shares of a publicly owned company at a price substantially above the current market price.

Tight money: A situation in which banks hold back on making loans, restricting acquisitions.

Walk-away price: The highest price that a buyer will offer.

Working capital: The difference between current assets and current liabilities; it represents the funds available to grow the business in the short term.

Supplemental References

Albo, Wayne P., and A. Randal Henderson. *Mergers & Acquisitions of Privately Held Businesses*. Canadian Institute of Chartered Accountants, 1987.

Bazerman, Max H., and Margaret A. Neale. *Negotiating Rationally*. New York: The Free Press, 1993.

Crouch, Holmes F. *Selling Your Business*. Saratoga, Calif.: Allyear Tax Guides, 1994.

Ernst & Young. *Mergers and Acquisitions*. New York: John Wiley & Sons, 1994.

Fifer, Bob. *Double Your Profits in 6 Months or Less*. New York: Harper Business, 1994.

Freund, James C. *Smart Negotiating*. New York: Fireside—Simon & Schuster, 1993.

Ilich, John. *Deal Breakers & Break Through*. New York: John Wiley & Sons, 1992.

Joseph, Richard A., Anna M. Nekoranec, and Carl H. Steffens. *How to Buy a Business*. Chicago: Enterprise Dearborn, 1993.

Klueger, Robert F. *Buying and Selling a Business, A Step by Step Guide*. New York: John Wiley & Sons, 1988.

Knight, Brian. *Buy the Right Business—At the Right Price*. Dover, N.H.: Upstart Publishing Company, 1990.

Mancuso, Joseph R. *How to Get a Business Loan*. New York: Fireside—Simon & Schuster, 1990.

Mancuso, Joseph R., and Douglas D. Germann, Sr. *Buying a Business (For Very Little Cash)*. New York: Fireside—Simon & Schuster, 1990.

Marren, Joseph H. *Mergers & Acquisitions—A Valuation Handbook*. Homewood, Ill.: Business One Irwin, 1993.

Myss, Joseph E. *Divestiture Strategies for Owners of Private Businesses*. Wayzata, Minn.: Joseph E. Myss and Associates, Inc., 1994.

Peterson, C. D. *How to Sell Your Business*. New York: McGraw-Hill Publishing Company, 1990.

Post, Alexandra M. *Anatomy of a Merger*. Englewood Cliffs, N.J.: Prentice-Hall, 1994.

Pratt, Shannon. *Valuing Small Businesses and Professional Practices*. Homewood, Ill.: Dow Jones Irwin, 1986.

Price Waterhouse. *The Buying and Selling a Company Handbook*. New York: Price Waterhouse.

Reed, Stanley Foster. *The Art of M & A—A Merger Acquisition Buyout Guide*. Homewood, Ill.: Business One Irwin, 1989.

Rock, Milton L. *The Mergers & Acquisitions Handbook*. New York: McGraw-Hill Book Co., 1987.

Silver, A. David. *The Middle Market Business Acquistion Directory and Source Book*. New York: Harper Business, 1990.

Snowden, Richard W. *The Complete Guide to Buying a Business*. New York: Amacom, 1993.

Woolf, Bob. *Friendly Persuasion*. New York: G. P. Putnam's Sons, 1990.

Index